IT Security Interviews Exposed

IT Security Interviews Exposed

Secrets to Landing Your Next Information Security Job

Chris Butler
Russ Rogers
Mason Ferratt
Greg Miles
Ed Fuller
Chris Hurley
Rob Cameron
Brian Kirouac

Wiley Publishing, Inc.

IT Security Interviews Exposed:

Secrets to Landing Your Next Information Security Job

Published by
Wiley Publishing, Inc.
10475 Crosspoint Boulevard
Indianapolis, IN 46256
www.wiley.com

Published by Wiley Publishing, Inc., Indianapolis, Indiana

Published simultaneously in Canada

ISBN: 978-0-471-77987-2

Manufactured in the United States of America

10 9 8 7 6 5 4 3 2 1

Library of Congress Cataloging-in-Publication Data

IT security interviews exposed : secrets to landing your next information security job / Christopher Butler ... [et al.].
    p. cm.
  ISBN 978-0-471-77987-2 (pbk.)
  1. Information technology — Vocational guidance. 2. Computer security. I. Butler, Christopher.
  T58.5.I836 2007
  005.8023 — dc22

2007018923

I dedicate this book to my two oldest children: Ariel and Erie.
Thanks for everything.
— Dad (Chris Butler)

About the Authors

Chris Butler (CISSP, JNCIS-FWV, JNCIA-SSL, CCSE, IAM/IEM) is a Senior Solutions Architect with Intellitactics. Chris has more than a dozen years of experience in the networking and security fields. He is a veteran of the United States Navy, where he worked in the cryptography field. Chris has designed, implemented, and supported some of the largest networks in the country for large insurance companies, investment firms, software companies, service providers, and pharmaceutical companies. He has also provided network and security consulting services for numerous U.S. government agencies, including the Department of State, Department of Defense, and the Department of Energy. He has worked extensively with the leading security and networking vendors throughout his career. He is also well versed in both commercial and open source network and security management software. Chris has also performed in-depth application analysis and network modeling using OPNET software for dozens of large companies. He is a member of the IEEE Computer Society and SANS.

Russ Rogers (CISSP, IAM/IEM) is a Senior Cyber Security Analyst and the former CEO and co-founder of Security Horizon, Inc. Russ is a United States Air Force veteran and has served in military and contract support for the National Security Agency, Defense Information Systems Agency, and the other federal agencies. He is also the editor-in-chief of *The Security Journal*. Additionally, he serves as the Professor of Network Security at the University of Advancing Technology (uat.edu) in Tempe, Arizona. Russ is the author, co-author, or technical editor for nearly a dozen books on information security. Russ has spoken and provided training to audiences around the world and is also a co-founder of the Security Tribe information security research Web site at www.securitytribe.com. His education includes a bachelor's and master's degree from the University of Maryland in Computer Science areas.

Mason Ferratt (JNCIS-FWV, JNCIA-M MSEE, BSME) is a Federal Systems Engineer with Juniper Networks in Charleston, South Carolina. He has performed large-scale network security engineering for numerous government clients. His most recent work involves the Department of Defense medical community, where his team is responsible for the security posture of all Navy and Army hospitals and clinics in the world. His specialty is in purpose-built intrusion detection/protection, VPN encryption, firewall, content filtering, and secure remote access devices. His prior jobs include network engineering design, modeling, and testing for the Department of State, and pre- and post-sales network engineering for several optical/WAN vendors (Corvis Corporation, Corrigent Systems, Lucent Technologies, Ascend Communications, and Network Equipment Technologies). He holds a Master of Science degree in Electrical Engineering from George Washington University, and a Bachelor of Science degree in Mechanical Engineering from the University of Virginia. He holds a Top Secret/SCI clearance and is an IEEE member.

Greg Miles (CISSP, CISM, IAM/IEM) is a co-founder, President, Chief Financial Officer, and Principal Security Consultant for Security Horizon, Inc., a Colorado-based professional security services and training provider and veteran-owned small business. He is a United States Air Force veteran and has served in military and contract support for the National Security Agency, Defense Information Systems Agency, Air Force Space Command, and NASA supporting worldwide security efforts. Greg has planned and managed Computer Incident Response Teams (CIRTs), Computer Forensics, and INFOSEC training capabilities. Greg has been published in multiple periodicals, including *The Security Journal* and *The International Journal on Cyber Crime*. He co-authored *Network Security Evaluation: Using the NSA IEM* (Syngress. ISBN: 978-1597490351) and *Security Assessment: Case Studies for Implementing the NSA IAM* (Syngress. ISBN: 978-1932266962). Greg is a network security instructor for the University of Advancing Technology (UAT) and an advisor with Colorado Technical University (CTU).

Ed Fuller (CISSP, IAM/IEM) is Senior Vice President, COO, and Principal Security Consultant for Security Horizon, Inc. He has more than 28 years of experience in operations, communications, computer information systems, and security. He is the primary lead for INFOSEC Assessments and Training for Security Horizon. Ed has served as team lead for INFOSEC assessments for more than nine years. He has served other companies as an INFOSEC Training Manager and Senior Security Consultant. Ed was integrally involved in establishing, implementing, and supporting the worldwide security program for the Defense Information Systems Agency (DISA), directly supporting Field Security Operations (FSO). He was a participant in the development of the Systems Security Engineering Capability Maturity Model (SSE-CMM) and has been a key individual in the development and maintenance of the Information Assurance Capability Maturity Model (IA-CMM). Ed also serves as a Lead Instructor for the National Security Agency (NSA) INFOSEC Assessment Methodology (IAM) and the INFOSEC Evaluation Methodology (IEM). Ed retired from the United States Navy with more than 23 years of distinguished service. Ed is a co-author for *Security Assessment: Case Studies for Implementing the NSA IAM* (Syngress. ISBN: 978-1932266962) and *Network Security Evaluation: Using the NSA IEM* (Syngress. ISBN: 978-1597490351) and a frequent contributer for the *The Security Journal*, a quarterly security periodical.

Chris Hurley (IAM/IEM) is a senior penetration tester working in the Washington, D.C. area. He is the founder of the WorldWide WarDrive and organized the DEF CON WarDriving Contest from its inception until last year. He has authored or co-authored several books on wireless security and penetration testing, including *WarDriving & Wireless Penetration Testing* (Syngress. ISBN: 978-1597491112), *The Penetration Tester's Open Source Toolkit* (Syngress. ISBN: 978-1597490214), *InfoSec Career Hacking* (Syngress. ISBN: 978-1597490115), and *Stealing the Network: How to Own an Identity* (Syngress. ISBN: 978-1597490061).

Rob Cameron (JNCIS-FWV, JNCIA-M, CCSP, CCSE+) is a Security Solutions Engineer for Juniper Networks. He currently works on designing security solutions for Juniper Networks that are considered best-practice designs. Rob specializes in network security architecture, firewall deployment, risk management, and high-availability designs. His background includes six years of security consulting for more than 325 customers. He is the lead author of *Configuring Netscreen and SSG Juniper Firewalls* (Syngress. ISBN: 978-1597491181) and *Configuring NetScreen Firewalls* (Syngress. ISBN: 978-1932266399).

Brian Kirouac (CISSP, IAM/IEM) is the Chief Technology Officer and Principal Security Consultant for Security Horizon, Inc. Brian has more than 15 years of experience as an IT professional. Before joining Security Horizon, he served in a wide range of information technology positions in both domestic and international environments. He was a network administrator for a major university, eventually migrating to system administrator specializing in UNIX and Windows integration. He was also the Lead Technical Security Specialist at a municipal four-service utility. In addition to his current position at Security Horizon, Brian serves as an instructor for the National Security Agency (NSA) INFOSEC Assessment (IAM) and INFOSEC Evaluation (IEM) Methodologies and team member of NSA IA-CMM Appraisals. Brian's publication history includes being a frequent contributor to *The Security Journal*, being both a refereed and invited speaker for SANS, and a refereed presenter for a NASA Conference on tethered satellites.

Credits

Executive Editor
Carol Long

Development Editor
Tom Dinse

Technical Editor
Russ Rogers

Copy Editor
Susan Christophersen

Editorial Manager
Mary Beth Wakefield

Production Manager
Tim Tate

Vice President and Executive Group Publisher
Richard Swadley

Vice President and Executive Publisher
Joseph B. Wikert

Compositor
Kate Kaminski, Happenstance Type-O-Rama

Proofreader
Kathryn Duggan

Indexer
Melanie Belkin

Anniversary Logo Design
Richard Pacifico

Contents

Contents

Contents

Contents

Contents

Acknowledgments

Eric Greenberg made this book possible for the guys and me. It is he who recommended me to Wiley. Thanks, Eric, I owe you.

I want to thank Carol Long for graciously accepting Eric's recommendation that I write this book. She was the driving force who concluded that such a book would prove beneficial to the job seeker. I tend to agree with her.

I want to thank Russ Rogers for instilling the NSA IAM/IEM methodology into my head, but, more important, I want to thank him for quickly pulling together a team of experts in their respective fields to contribute to the book. Russ was also the technical editor for this project. He had the very important job of keeping us honest. Thanks a bunch, Russ!

I want to thank Rob Cameron and Brian Kirouac for being so flexible in my time of need. I experienced a job change and a move across the United States. If it weren't for these two guys, the book (my portion) would have never been finished. Rob contributed the Firewall chapter, and Brian was kind enough to put together the Tools chapter. Thanks, guys!

I want to thank my buddy Mason Ferratt down in S.C. I went to Mason for his expert knowledge on IDP/IPS to contribute for that chapter. The Network Fundamentals chapter was a flip of the coin, and Mason won. Thanks, Mason!

I want to thank Ed Fuller for contributing the Security Posture chapter. Ed has many years of experience in assessing an organization's security posture, so this chapter had his name written all over it. Thanks, Ed!

I want to thank Greg Miles for contributing the Laws, Polices, and Guidelines chapter. Thanks, Greg!

I want to thank Chris Hurley for contributing the Wireless chapter. Chris has written numerous books on wireless, so he was more than perfect for the task. Thanks, Chris!

I want to thank Tom Dinse, development editor, for his extremely thoughtful review of and comments on each of the chapters. He is a breeze to work with, and I look forward to working with him again on future projects.

I want to thank my good friend Jim Feely for his deeply critical review of each of the chapters in the book. He provided me with countless items for revision to keep the book flowing smoothly within and across all the chapters.

I want to thank my friend Mara Cummings for her insightful and numerous reviews of Chapter 1.

Acknowledgments

I want to thank Susan Christophersen, copy editor, and I thank the publisher of this book, Joe Wikert.

Most important, I thank my wife, Tabatha, from now until the end of time for her extreme patience and flexibility. I also want to thank my very inquisitive children, Ariel, Erie, Eliea, Adrie, and Emerie, for their uncanny ability to consistently re-instill in me the will to write. I plan to return the favor someday to each of them.

Introduction

I am fully aware that almost everyone skips this section and heads straight for the Table of Contents. I am certainly guilty of the same offense. So, if you do happen to catch the first few sentences of this introduction, let me just say the following: This book is an attempt at summarizing what an individual needs to know in order to get a job in the information security field. We cover topics that we believe are most important for security professionals in 2007. Done! However, I invite you to read further because important information follows.

Overview of the Book

This book is a hitchhiker's guide to the information security field. It is short and sweet and gets right to the point regarding what you need to know to be successful in the job interview. This book can be read cover to cover or used as a reference. Regardless of how you choose to assimilate the material between the front and back cover, you are sure to learn something. We cover topics ranging from policy to salary and from hashes to the best wardriving chipsets. Each of the chapters in this book requires a dedicated book all to itself to properly represent the material. Therefore, we have pointed you to as many resources that we can. In addition, we specifically used short-form URLs (domain only) with search terms or gave you exact Google search strings. For example:

Google "Security Exposed site:wiley.com."

Click the first link you see, add it your cart, and check out. It really is that easy.

Who Should Read This Book

Anyone looking for a job in the field of security should consider a thorough review of this book. If we haven't written about a particular topic, we most likely direct you to another resource for you to use to brush up on your skills.

What We Did Not Cover

For those of you desperately looking for the section on certifications, STOP; there isn't one in this book. You need only look at the number of certifications offered by Microsoft, Novell, and Cisco to realize that the information security field has gotten out of control with the number of certifications that you can obtain. Therefore, I specifically chose not to discuss certifications in the book. With that said, you still need your answer, so I will give you one.

The answer is: "It's your choice!"

All I can say is, do your homework. Use the tools that are out there to determine what is best for you and your interests. We each have our own unique wants and desires relating to a job. If you are after more money, use the Salary Survey based on certifications to determine what is right for you (see Chapter 1). If you are looking for job-hopping opportunities, use the job boards as a gauge for the most sought-after certification by typing in a few acronyms.

My friend Jim Feely recommended that we cover VoIP security because there are numerous emerging threats. Jim was correct; we should have. However, we just did not have the real estate in this particular book. Perhaps we can discuss VoIP security in another book. If you need something now, check out the following references:

❏   Google "NIST 800-58."

❏   Google "VoIP Security."

❏   Check out the VoIP Security Alliance at www.voipsa.org.

Best of luck with the job search!

1

Finding, Interviewing for, and Getting the Job

So, you want a job in the field of Information Security. Do you have what it takes? Do you know what *you* want out of a job? How do you find the best job for you and your career? Later in the book, we review critical IT Security related topics, but in this chapter, we discuss what you want out of a job and how to find it.

Finding the perfect balance between your potential employer's needs and your own can be somewhat challenging. We discuss how to employ several different methods for locating a job. We also discuss how to compare two or more salary offers so that you can make the best decision with the information available to you. If you are lucky enough to have multiple offers to consider, you will want to review the entire compensation package when comparing opportunities.

Qualifications

A significant number of employers consider a Computer Science or Engineering degree the ideal qualification. However, a surprising number of employers will consider relevant past experience as a substitution for a degree. Just a few short years ago, you couldn't find a university that had developed an appropriate Information Security and Assurance curriculum from which one could obtain a degree. As a result, individuals with diverse academic backgrounds and the interest and ability to grasp technical information have become strong contenders in the field of Information Security. In my experience over the past 12 years, I've been surprised to see English majors working as Network Security Engineers and business majors working in Technology Manufacturing who have demonstrated incredible prowess in analytical thinking and problem-solving skills.

With that said, you will never see a job posting for an IT Security professional requiring a degree in art, history, or English. Are folks with these types of degrees capable of doing the job? Absolutely! Countless, highly skilled security practitioners are overlooked simply because they do not have the proverbial Computer Science or Engineering degree. Employers are beginning to catch on and, as a result, they are considering alternative ways of gauging aptitude and analytical thinking abilities. You may be asked to take a series of personality or aptitude tests (or both). If you're pursuing a government job or a contracting position with the government that requires high security clearance, you will most certainly be required to take such tests.

The most important traits required to succeed in the IT Security field are the desire and ability to learn new technologies, a good head on your shoulders, and, most important, a new way of thinking. For those of you not yet familiar with this new way of thinking, this book introduces it to you in both subtle and not-so-subtle ways. For example, your preeminent Computer Science (CS) or Engineering graduate probably did not learn the concepts of *least privilege*, *implicit deny/explicit permit*, and *defense in depth*. These core concepts are not included in a traditional CS or Engineering curriculum. Therefore, the erudite professional will assimilate these core values on the job and in training.

Pursuing a Degree

If you are just getting started on your undergraduate or graduate degree and you know that IT Security is the field for you, then one of the National Security Agency's (NSA) designated national Centers of Academic Excellence in Information Assurance Education (CAEIAE) may be worth considering. Out of the 3,500-plus higher-education institutions in the United States, only 75 (at last count) offer the Information Assurance curriculum adopted and evaluated by the NSA. These schools offer undergraduate and graduate-level programs in IA. For more information, Google "CAEIAE."

If you plan to pursue a job with the U.S. federal government, a degree from a regionally accredited college or university is almost certainly a requirement. The National Board of Education recognizes only six regional accrediting agencies. Regardless of whether you are pursuing a job with the federal government, having a degree from a regionally accredited college or university is the best investment for your money. Google "Regional Accreditation" and make sure that your school is accredited by one of the regional accrediting agencies, as shown in the following list:

- ❑ New England Association of Schools and Colleges (NEASC)
- ❑ North Central Association of Schools and Colleges (NCA)
- ❑ Middle States Association of Schools and Colleges (MSA)
- ❑ Southern Association of Schools and Colleges (SACS)
- ❑ Western Association of Schools and Colleges (WASC)
- ❑ Northwest Association of Schools and Colleges (NWCCU)

If your school is not listed for your respective region, you may want to consider transferring to an accredited school. Keep in mind that most, if not all, regionally accredited schools recognize transfer credits only from other regionally accredited schools, providing yet another reason that you should stay away from unaccredited schools.

The Perfect Job

What is the perfect job? Have you put serious thought into what you want? We hope that you are considering more than just the salary. Later in this chapter, we discuss an in-depth method of comparing two or more offers so that you can make the best decision.

As with any successfully implemented IT project, you must start with requirements. Consider finding your next job to be a small-scale, high-priority project. Employ a methodical and analytical approach during your search and you will be surprised at the results.

Grab a piece of paper or use your favorite spreadsheet program to start your analysis. Although doing so may be hard, ignore the money for now. Let's talk about the intangibles. Putting a quantitative value on a number of these benefits can be difficult, but they can make a drastic difference in your health and happiness at work.

The Intangible Benefits

Each of the following benefits has a qualitative value. These types of benefits will increase your work and life balance and make the job something to look forward to each day. Look for as many of these types of benefits as possible and be sure to keep in mind the following as you assess the importance of each one.

> If you are married with a family or are a single parent, your ideal benefits are drastically different from those of a single person with a cat and a parakeet at home. Even if you are currently single, your circumstances might change as you progress with the company.

❏ **Employee First:** In the past 12 years, we have interviewed with only one company that asserted its commitment to the employee's happiness and well-being as its number one core value. It is unfortunate that most organizations care only about the final product, service, or good. If employers simply understood that happy employees are productive employees, we might have some more exciting places to work. Ask your potential hiring manager about his or her commitment to the employee.

  ❏ **Employee-focused reputations:** Many companies achieve notable status for the employee-focused work environments they have fostered. Check out Google "Top Tech 50" for a list of top-rated technology companies and see whether your prospective new company is on the list. A great place to find a company is from the 100 Best Companies for working mothers. Check it out at www.workingmother.com. Both Forbes and Fortune maintain top companies lists also.

  ❏ **Work-life balance:** Many companies have evolved in their philosophies where work-life balance is concerned. Companies that used to drive their employees toward "burn-out" under the guise of increased productivity are abandoning those practices in favor of encouraging more balanced work habits from their employees. The end result? Increased productivity and employee loyalty under a more sustainable and fulfilling work environment.

  ❏ **Comp time:** How does the company compensate for overtime? Will you have to work late nights and weekends to implement new projects? How often? It is quite common for most large companies to implement technology changes very late in the evenings, on weekends, or both. Although the position you are applying for might not pay by the hour, many companies compensate for the additional work employees are putting in on evenings or weekends by granting "comp time" (additional time off). Try to understand where the employer stands with respect to compensation for overtime. Be aware that the position may offer comp time *or* a larger salary to compensate — and both, if you're lucky!

❑ **Telecommuting:** Telecommuting just might be one of the best benefits a company could offer because of the following advantages:

  ❑ It reduces stress on the employee from the daily grind of commuting.

  ❑ It reduces your auto insurance costs and general wear and tear on your vehicle.

  ❑ It drastically reduces your fuel costs.

  ❑ Employees can work free of workplace distractions and are generally happier as a result.

The telecommuting benefit can add up to thousands of dollars in annual savings; however, some employers are still adjusting to this new trend. Translation: They are stuck in the 1980s. Unfortunately, quite a few micro-managers survived the twentieth century and feel that they cannot effectively micro-manage you if you are sitting at home in your skivvies. Plenty of companies are huge proponents of this benefit, however, because it is a win-win scenario for both the employee and the company. The company no longer has to pay hundreds and hundreds of dollars per square foot for office space when you can do the exact same job in the comfort of your own home. In the past few years, the federal, state, and local governments have begun to recognize the benefits of telecommuting, such as reduced wear and tear on roadways and alleviation of traffic congestion. As a result, they have started offering tax incentives to companies that allow employees to work from home.

❑ **Flexible scheduling:** Have you taken on the role of a being a twenty-first century parent, student, or gamer? If so, this benefit is huge. Perhaps you have to take the kids to school on Monday and Wednesday, and pick up the little rascals on Tuesday and Thursday. Maybe you need an extra hour in the morning to study for certifications or classes. You may just want time for late-night instance runs with your World of Warcraft guild. If you can find an employer with flexible scheduling, you can have a much more fulfilling work and life balance.

❑ **Job-site benefits:** Although companies may seem to be offering more and more on-site incentives to their employees out of generosity, in reality, an employee who is offered on-site conveniences not only is a happy employee but also one with a diminished need to leave the office to take care of personal responsibilities. Make sure that you determine which on-site benefits are truly important to your work environment and which ones are "cool" but trivial benefits whose merits are, at most, bragging rights to your friends. Does the company have a gym or a small workout area? Does it hold on-site fitness classes? If the company does not offer an on-site gym, does it offer discounts at local gyms in your area? Does it reimburse you up to a certain amount (typically, 50 percent of the monthly fees)?

  ❑ Do they have on-site health care services at little or no cost to the employee?

  ❑ For families with kids, does the company offer company-sponsored (off-site is good; on-site is better) child care? Does it have a cafeteria that serves hot food? Is it edible? Is the food *free*? As much as we like our candy bars and Mountain Dew, vending machines do not count.

  ❑ Does the company have an open refrigerator of *free* health drinks, which will load you up with vitamin C and other nutrients?

  ❑ Does it have ping pong tables, air hockey, or other fun activities?

❑ Can you bring your kids to work? Every day? How about your dog?

❑ Does the company have ample *free* parking, or does the employee have to absorb a portion of the parking fees because of the company's location in a high-rent district? Perhaps the company offers reimbursement for mass transit.

❑ Is it an exciting place to work; is the place drab or fab? Is your office in the basement with gray, damp, musty walls or on an upper floor with a window and a great view?

❑ **Discounts and memberships:** My current company offers club membership to the big warehouse stores. It also offers 15 percent to 20 percent discounts at many of the retailers where we buy products. The savings can add up quickly.

❑ **Banking:** Does the company have an ATM or on-site bank? Does it offer membership to credit unions or other cost savings types of banks? These institutions can save you time, gas, and money.

❑ **Others:** There are many other unique and exciting benefits a company can offer. These companies will be proud to speak about their culture, so be sure to ask!

The Tangible Benefits

The following list of benefits have a quantitative value, meaning that you can place a dollar sign by each of these benefits when you include them in your analysis of the various job offers you have to consider.

❑ **Paid Time Off (PTO):** Synonymous with vacation, balance days (sometimes called "floating holidays"), and sick time clumped together. Many employers now prefer to give employees a block of personal time that can be used for any purpose. If you have children, sick days will be one of your more important benefits to consider. No, we aren't talking about time off for yourself; you will have to go to work when you are sick. You will have to save every possible sick day for the loving little tots who call you Mommy or Daddy. If you are contracting with your employer, you probably do not get any benefits other than an abnormally higher paycheck. If you are contracting, make certain that you calculate the cost of three to four weeks of PTO and health insurance before you quote an hourly rate to an employer.

❑ **Health insurance:** Make sure that you compare each of the major plans; specifically, you need to compare what is and what is not covered. One company may offer $5,000 more in salary than another but also may require you to absorb that much or more in out-of-pocket health care costs. If you have a family or are expecting or planning for a new family member, reviewing the health insurance is critical. Is your current doctor in the company network? Will you have to find a new doctor? It can be a real drag when the whole family has to find a new primary care physician.

Understand the difference between a PPO (Preferred Provider Organization) and an HMO (Health Maintenance Organization). For PPOs, the out-of-pocket costs are extremely varied, which might be challenging if you are trying to predict how much to deduct from your check each month if you are using a Flexible Spending Plan. With a traditional PPO, you typically pay a $10–$20 copay and then a percentage of the cost of the "provider-negotiated" rate for the visit (which can range from 0–30 percent) up to a yearly maximum out-of-pocket expense. The benefit, however, is that you may see any doctor or specialist of your choosing without having to make an appointment first with a primary-care physician for a referral. On the other hand, HMO plans typically cover 100 percent of your out-of-pocket costs at a lower monthly rate than do comparable PPO plans. The catch there is that you are typically prohibited from seeing any other doctor without a referral from your primary-care physician. If you forget to get a referral from your primary-care physician for a visit to the specialist, you may have to pay all the costs yourself.

It does not stop with medical insurance. Do not forget about dental and vision. Make sure that you compare the in-network and out-of-network coverage and determine whether your current doctor is in the network. Check out the various health insurance sites, and make sure that you can find your doctor or a new doctor in the area in which you intend to live.

The bottom line is that comparing the health insurance offered between one or more companies is not as easy as you think. Get the full details of the medical coverage and the monthly rates *before* you make your decision to accept an offer.

Life insurance is cheap. The only thing worth considering is the maximum coverage and the amount of hassle you must endure to attain the coverage you need to protect your family in case of a life-changing event. Typically, companies allow no more than six times the employee's salary as the target disbursement.

❑ **Long-term investment in the employee:** Unless you are working for the federal, state, or county government or the military, do not expect to retire after 20 years. The burden is on you to invest smartly with a 401(k), 403(b), Roth, or other investment account. Does the company offer a retirement package? Does it match your contributions? This match is *free* money and it would be downright foolish not to get every penny of that match. Make sure that you do the math properly when comparing offers.

As an example: We have never understood why some companies offer 100 percent matching on the first 2 percent of your salary, and 50 percent on the next 2 percent of your salary, and 25 percent on the next 2 percent of your salary up to a maximum of $6,000 per year. In other words, if you make $100,000 a year, the match is $3,500 a year, or 3.5 percent, not 6 percent. My current employer offers a match of 75 percent of the first 6 percent, or more accurately stated, 4.5 percent.

❑ **Commuter reimbursements:** Does the company encourage and compensate for commuting to and from work via public transportation? This benefit can drastically reduce your costs for your car, gas, wear and tear, and insurance. These costs all add up quickly.

❑ **Tuition reimbursements:** Many companies offer tuition reimbursement of all or a percentage of your tuition costs for classes taken during your employment. Make sure that you read the fine print, however, because these reimbursements often only kick in for "approved" curricula at accredited institutions and rarely cover books and materials. You may also want to inquire about job-specific training classes and certifications sponsored by the company that wouldn't normally fall under the standard tuition reimbursement benefit. In both cases, companies often require a continuing employment commitment.

❑ **Regular bonus compensation vs. signing bonuses:** Although a signing bonus might be an attractive benefit because you'd have money in your pocket immediately, regular bonuses (quarterly or annual) will result in a higher total compensation package year by year. Although detailed conversations regarding compensation can occur later, try to find out whether the position to which you are applying carries the opportunity for a regular bonus. Later in the chapter, we discuss how signing bonuses can often be an effective tool during the negotiation process to compensate for an offer that is lower than your target salary range.

Job Search

You may be open to relocation to a new city or state. Perhaps you want to stay right where you are and simply find a new employer offering better benefits or opportunities for growth. There are many ways to find a job using some of the techniques discussed later in this section, but your overall success in securing your ideal job will always depend on the solid foundation you have created with your résumé.

The Résumé

The résumé, also known as the curriculum vitae (CV), *must* be no more than three pages long — even better is one to two pages. We say this first because if you learn nothing else from this section of the book, you must remember this cardinal rule:

> **Your résumé should be three pages or fewer regardless of years of experience or number of former jobs.**

Now that we are clear on this rule of thumb, let us talk résumé content. What should be on your résumé? How much detail do you include? Should you list your education first or last? The answer to each of these questions changes as your career matures.

You have to stand out in a crowd to be noticed. The same applies to your résumé. Regardless of your accomplishments or what magical talents you can wield under stressful situations, your résumé has to catch the eye of the first line of defense for the employer: the recruiter. The recruiter, does not, in most cases, fully comprehend the many acronyms, technical jargon, and technologies in this field. Therefore, you have to give the recruiter a little something to get his or her attention.

> **You have approximately 30–60 seconds to grab the recruiter's attention! Tick tock!**

Spice up your résumé with a bit of word processing magic. Add a subtle border here and there, or a little shadowing around your name and each of the section titles. Google "résumé writing" for more information on spicing up your résumé.

If you have many years of experience, focus on that by placing your professional experience near the top. On the other hand, if you are just finishing school, place your relevant education and any related internships near the top. The most important thing to emphasize in your résumé is your relevant experience. If you worked at the pizza parlor preparing the Americanized version of the Italian flat-bread dish for four years while you attended school (which does demonstrate a level of responsibility), it is not considered relevant professional experience. Put it at the bottom of your résumé as additional experience. The résumé should include, but not be limited to, the following:

- ❑ Name
- ❑ Objective
- ❑ Professional certifications
- ❑ Professional experience
- ❑ Education

The jury is out on whether to include a skill-set section. The primary reason that most recruiters ignore it is the "stretch" factor. Show of hands: How many of you have listed something in your skill-set section after being briefly introduced to that particular technology or product? If you raised your hand, then you should consider revising your skill-set section.

> **Question: Can you discuss, in-depth, everything you have listed on your résumé?**

Take note: You should be willing and able to discuss anything listed on your résumé in detail. When one of the authors of this book conducts technical interviews, the first thing he does is toss the corporate "canned" list of questions into the trash. He formulates his technical questions straight from the candidate's résumé. When he asks a question about a specific technology or product, regardless of whether he knows it, he looks for an immediate, thoughtful, and articulate response from the candidate. If there is delay or doubt in the tone of his or her response, a bit more digging on the topic will confirm his suspicion.

Company Recruiters

The traditional application process has multiple levels, starting with a recruiter from the company trying to fill the position. These folks look for keywords (Security, IPSec, CISSP, SANS, and so on) that they have as requirements for open positions. They are the company gatekeepers. They filter applicants who are potential matches to hiring managers, who, themselves, quickly scan résumés to find the top three to five candidates.

We always talk about making that great first impression. Newsflash: The first impression you should be most concerned about starts with the recruiter. The recruiter will take note of your phone conversations, your speech, your vocabulary, your writing, and anything else he or she can "observe" to gauge you. These observations are funneled back to the hiring manager if you get through the first line of defense. Keep this thought in mind before you sign e-mails with "Ciao, baby!"

The recruiter, in most cases, is responsible for scheduling interviews, providing benefits information, soliciting salary history from you, sending your additional questions to the hiring manager, and ultimately making the job offer both verbally (informally) and in writing (formally).

Professional Networking

If you are like one of the authors, you have moved around a few times. Not to worry; it is quite normal and accepted in the IT field. One of the best methods of finding a job is through previous contacts made at other jobs. Hence, it is imperative that you *not* burn any bridges on your way out the door. Make it a point to keep in touch with all your former co-workers. The IT community and specifically the IT Security community can be rather small.

If you have burned a bridge once or twice on the way out the door, you may want to think about a career change. We heard in a movie once that truck driving can be quite lucrative. The bonus plan includes all the interesting scenery while driving 500 miles a day, every day of the year.

If you hold a government security clearance or plan to get one in your next job, that is something else to keep in mind. The background investigation process requires that investigators talk with each of your former employers from the previous 10 years of your career.

It is always a tough decision to leave a company that has treated you well, but our experiences have revealed the importance of the following:

> **Your decision-making process should consider what is best for you, your career growth, and your family, in the order of priority that suits you personally.**

Headhunters

First and foremost, you should never pay for a headhunting service. Many agencies provide this service free of charge to the job seeker. When working with one of the free headhunting services, do not hesitate to tell them exactly what you want in a job, benefits, ideal manager, ideal work environment, and so on. Think of headhunters as corporate matchmakers. Sometimes they work for large IT placement firms and sometimes they work independently. In either case, they are providing a service that's free to you; the headhunter is paid by the hiring organization after a successful match is made. Use that knowledge to your advantage to find the perfect job with the perfect benefits.

> **Remember: You should never pay for a headhunting service!**

On occasion, you run across a headhunter who is new to the business or does not fully appreciate (translation: comprehend) the skills required in the IT Security field. So, you may be referred to a few jobs that are unrelated to your job search. For example, the headhunter may send you a posting or two for a programming job or a network engineering job requiring Microsoft AD experience. It happens on occasion. Remember that sometimes you get what you pay for! Just thank the headhunter for his or her efforts, and share some key words that the headhunter can use in the search. If you are interested in an IDP/IDS job, provide relevant search terms along with a certification or two that may be related.

Now you may ask, "Where do I find a headhunter?" If your résumé is posted on any of the job boards, headhunters will almost certainly find you. Otherwise, point your browser of choice to Google and search for "IT security placement."

Tools

You have two primary ways to find a job using online tools:

❑   The first method is a more passive approach, meaning that you let the employer find you by registering and building a résumé on one or more of the big job boards (DICE, Monster, Hotjobs, Tech Expo USA, and so on.) This online résumé is your master copy, so make sure that you keep it updated.

❑   The second method is a more active approach, meaning that you are scrubbing the job boards every day looking for a reprieve from your current employer. This method requires a bit more effort.

The trend for most companies is to contract with the big job-posting companies. These companies provide internal and external job postings for a particular company's Web site. Fewer and fewer companies are allowing you to apply for or express interest in a position without first filling out their respective résumé builder. In the old days, you could apply for a job with the click of a button from most — if not all — of the big job boards.

Interviewing

The interview process has several stages. Generally, the larger the company, the more complex and time-consuming the process. Keep this in mind if you are intentionally trying to get job offers from multiple companies.

What Employers Want

Hundreds of surveys have been conducted to determine what employers are looking for in a potential candidate. Many attributes appear consistently in these surveys. What is the most critical attribute employers are looking for in an employee? It is not job knowledge, as many would suspect — instead, it is a *good attitude*. This finding falls in line with the popular management philosophy, "Hire for attitude; train for skills." Employers want to know that you are emotionally balanced, eager to apply your skills, compatible within a team, and adaptable to change, without being difficult or negative. The common thread and foundation of these key attributes is a good attitude — never underestimate how powerful this can be!

Attributes cited high on the list of importance also include the following:

❏   Professional communication skills

❏   Sophisticated analytical and problem solving skills

❏   High degree of product/industry knowledge

❏   Hard-working and highly reliable

For those of you who are already in the workplace, you probably remember the usual "nontechnical interview questions" from your last interview. Several more of these questions appear at the end of the chapter. You should carefully consider a response to each one, because your new potential employer is bound to ask one or more of them. They may be along the following lines:

❏   Describe a problem you encountered in your current position and how you handled it.

❏   How do you keep yourself current professionally?

❏   How would you describe your work performance?

❏   What are your strengths and weaknesses?

Now you probably see why these are so popular: They tap into the important attributes the employer is seeking in the candidate. The more examples you can provide that demonstrate the important attributes listed previously, the better positioned you are to obtain an offer. Keep in mind that the individual with whom you are interviewing may have already seen several other candidates who already know these strategies. Assume that such is the case and practice in advance your ability to recall work performance based on the skill or skills you want to exhibit. Your job is to make sure that the interviewer gets the information he or she needs to make the right hiring decision where you are concerned!

Phone Interviews

Phone interviews, like taxes, are a necessary evil. More often than not, employers are conducting phone interviews because they are looking to narrow the candidate pool for the on-site phase of the interview process as well as to minimize travel costs for out-of-state candidates. These may be positive benefits for employers, but the prospective candidate is placed at a disadvantage. You no longer have the benefit of eye contact, gestures, or nonverbal cues to help guide the tone, pace, and direction of the interview.

Because phone interviews can happen at a moment's notice, be prepared in advance! Prepare for the possibility of phone interviews in the same manner you would for an on-site interview. If you are contacted by a recruiter or hiring manager for a phone interview, it is perfectly acceptable — and expected — that you clear your workspace of any distractions before beginning. It is not advisable to ask for an alternative date or time for the phone interview; this is your chance to get your foot in the door before the next person the recruiter contacts. Do not squander this opportunity!

The first phone interview is often arranged by the recruiter and in most cases can be technical in nature. The technical phone interview is sometimes delegated to a senior member of the staff to evaluate your knowledge based on what you have listed on your résumé. These types of interviews typically last no fewer than 30 minutes and can sometimes go as long as two hours.

If you are lucky enough to know about the phone interview in advance, it is always best to get some idea from the recruiter or hiring manager of what will be discussed so that you know how to prepare. If you do not know the technology or product, do not pretend that you do. This is the quickest way to fail an interview. No one is expected to know everything during an interview; the most important and simplest lesson when interviewing is as follows:

When you do not know the answer, say, "I do not know."

Most interviewers respect the fact that you are willing to admit that and will move on to the next question.

Ask a question if you have one. You may want to ask about a typical work day, the job requirements, the technologies or products the company has deployed, and so on. Your questions should demonstrate a genuine interest in the company, products, or technologies. Keep in mind that this person is most likely going to be your peer if you get the job, so avoid personal preferences or discussing likes and dislikes for a particular technology or product.

While you are speaking with the interviewer, be aware of the following:

❑ **Your diction:** It is essential that you speak clearly and at the right volume and pace so that the interviewer can clearly understand your responses. Pay close attention to your verbal pauses such as "um" and "uh" so that you can minimize them as much as possible.

❑ **The length of your answers:** Without eye contact or nonverbal cues to guide you, rambling on and on during your response is an easy trap to fall into. If you practice your answers to sample interview questions in advance, you increase your chances of providing concise, accurate, and to-the-point responses.

❑ **The information being presented:** Nervousness or self-consciousness during a phone interview can take up valuable space in the "processing" department of your brain, which means that you run the risk of missing important information! Do your best to relax and listen; when it is your turn to speak, dazzle the person on the other end of the phone with the information he or she needs.

❑ **The prospect of an on-site interview:** Under the assumption that phone interviews are a precursor to (not a replacement for) on-site interviews, be sure to ask the interviewer about the possibility of meeting on-site for an interview.

On-Site Interviews

After you progress past the phone interviews, you'll be asked on-site for a face-to-face interview. You will need all your wits about you for this meeting. Preparation, dress, manners, and an ability to tactfully discuss salary requirements will assist you here.

Preparation

"The dog ate my homework!"

That excuse may have worked in elementary school once or twice, but now you are all grown up. So do your homework and do it before you go on-site for the interview. Ideally, you should have prepared some questions regarding the company, benefits of interest, the typical work day, the IT products the company uses, and possibly how it has implemented them. If you are able to ask the recruiter or hiring manager questions in advance of the interview, take the knowledge you gained from that interview and hit the Internet. Learn all you can about the company. You should already know the job-specific products, but it does not hurt to brush up on the basics.

Check the company Web site. Web sites always have "About Us" and "Press Releases" sections. Absorb all you can and write down a few questions about what you learned. Asking a question or two during an interview about a recent press release or company announcement says much about you. (That is, that you did your homework.)

You probably already know about the "Careers" page, but check it out again. This time, look at the jobs you may not be interested in. You can learn what most companies deploy in their networks simply by looking at the job listings. We think that companies put too much detail in their job postings. It gives the social engineers of the world too much information to form their attack. Perhaps that could be a topic of conversation during the interview . . . if it is appropriate!

Dress for Success

Now that you have succeeded in scheduling face time with the hiring manager, you should take the initiative to dress appropriately for the visit. The answer to this enigma is really quite simple. Ask the hiring manager or recruiter (during the phone interview) about appropriate attire. With the combination of the IT field and the new age of the twenty-first century, wearing a three-piece suit to an interview is not usually required or expected.

For others, dressing to the nines increases their self-confidence. If you fall into this category, then unzip that zoot suit garment bag and knock 'em dead. Whatever your selection, make sure that you are comfortable in your attire by the time you arrive for the interview so that you can focus on the interview questions and not your appearance. For those of you equating "comfortable" with your favorite seven-day-old shirt that can practically drag itself to the laundry room, that would be considered inappropriate!

Salary Discussion

Make it a point to avoid discussing quantitative salary numbers with anyone other than the hiring manager or the recruiter — and save that discussion for conversations following the interview, not during. If the recruiter or hiring manager insists that he or she needs to know your salary requirements, simply state that you expect to be compensated at fair market value for the skill set that you can offer in the area you are expected to work and reside. With luck, the person will accept this response for the time being, but unfortunately, most people will not. If he or she insists on having a number on the spot, say that you will need some time to research a number based on the new job responsibilities and location. You also want to review the benefits package to fully understand the value offered by the company.

An alternative response might be to inquire about a salary range for the position, which might help you respond to the request more quickly. If the range is within your target but on the low side, you might mention that although the range is "very similar" to what you are looking for, you were "expecting a different range." This is your opportunity to offer a range with your target number on the low side of the stated range. For example, if your target salary is $80,000 per year and the recruiter offers a range of $65,000–$75,000, you might counter with $80,000–$85,000, keeping your target salary at the low end of the range.

Mind Your P's and Q's, Please

If you are not familiar with the basic P's and Q's, you can get a refresher from Mom or Dad. They reminded you on a daily basis for 18 years for a reason. Here are a few suggestions that you should use consistently before, during, and even after the interview:

- ❑ Say "Yes sir/No sir" and "Yes ma'am/No ma'am": Shows respect and a good upbringing.
- ❑ Say "please" and "thank you": These are obvious.
- ❑ Wait to sit until asked, and then sit only after the recruiter does, and say "thank you."
- ❑ When sitting at a table, you should stand when someone enters or leaves the room or table. Guess who just scored brownie points? Be careful not to make the other people in the room look bad.
- ❑ Send a thank-you note (via e-mail) to the hiring manager and the recruiter. Let them know how much you appreciate the opportunity to interview with them, knowing how precious their time is. Mail the note the same day as the interview. Include the appointment time and something you talked about that will help them remember who you are.
- ❑ Finally, call Mom or Dad and say "thank you" for the 18 years' worth of helpful reminders.

Most important, make sure that you have done the best "sell job" on your qualifications as possible. It would be smart to ask the interviewer if he or she has any questions or concerns about your background, which would give you the opportunity to address any objections before you leave. If you have fully expressed why you are interested in the job and what you have to offer, you have done all that you can!

Money Talks

At what point in the search do you talk money? How much do you ask for? How much can you get? How much are you worth? We have all pondered upon these mysteries a time or two in our careers. You should have a basic idea of your bare-minimum requirements. A basic number is required to keep the lights on, gas in the car, a roof over your head, and meet your long-term savings goals.

> **Important: This is your "target salary"; try not to accept a salary offer lower than that basic number. If the offer is not within your target salary range, consider negotiating a sign-on bonus. Alternatively, you could negotiate a semiannual review with the opportunity to get an increase based on your individual performance. Just make sure that whatever you successfully negotiate, you get in writing, preferably along with your offer letter!**

You might be surprised how many folks "settle" on a number lower than this magic number for fear of a 10-minute negotiation. Remove all emotion and extraneous personal matters from the "money talks." There is room on the table only for the skill set you offer and what the company is willing to pay you for it. Show no fear and play your best hand of poker ever. Do not be afraid to call the company's bluff, because it is a hiring manager's job to get the best skill set he or she can for the lowest annual salary. Knowing this tidbit of information is half the battle.

> **If you need help finding a target salary, check out SANS Salary Survey:** www.sans .org/surveys/ **or check out** www.salary.com.

When you conduct a salary search, find the job description that closely matches what you can offer to an employer. Do not forget to include your years of experience. If you are transitioning from one job to another, consider whether it is a step up to a position of greater responsibility or a lateral move; if it is a lateral one, certainly aim, at minimum, to make your current salary. If it is a move "up," consider what percentage a promotion would be with your current employer and use that as a benchmark for your new minimum salary with the new employer. When you have your basic, "must have," minimum number, keep reading: The following sections offer more information on how to make an accurate assessment of one or more offers.

Cost of Living

Before you start getting excited about a higher salary and a new city, you should *fully* understand and appreciate the cost-of-living index for that target salary number in the city you plan to reside. You should know the cost-of-living index for the new job location and adjust accordingly. Moving from one city to another can be drastically more expensive. Check out the Cost of Living calculator under the "Personal" section at www.salary.com and click Relocation, or check out HomeFair at www.homefair.com for more information.

Uncle Sam always has his hand out. With a new pay raise comes the possibility for a new tax bracket. If you are so inclined to buy the most house you can afford, as one of the authors did, you may also find yourself in a situation you never thought possible.

> **One of the authors moved from Indiana to Northern Virginia in 2003 (internal job transfer). He knew the cost of living was higher, and he asked for an adjustment in his salary to compensate. His employer looked at him as though he were crazy. His wife was also transferring, so he didn't really have a choice.**
>
> **They are now the proud owners of a typical home in Northern Virginia, which, to their dismay, costs four times more than their home in Indiana. They could make the payments, so they were not too worried. Besides, they could benefit from the tax deduction on the mortgage interest, property taxes, and all those little tax deductions they like to call their kids. However, they overlooked something!**
>
> **Because of the higher-than-normal tax deductions, they qualified for something called the Alternative Minimum Tax (AMT). Congress invented this beast of legislation in 1969 to keep the rich in check with their taxes. Well, in 1969 dollars, they were apparently considered "rich." More to the point, they had to dip into their savings to pay the tax bill that year.**

Comparing Locations

Scenario: You are married and have three kids and two job offers on the table, one in Northern Virginia (Company X) for $100,000 and one in Indianapolis, Indiana, for $92,000 (Company Y). You compare the offers and come up with the figures in the following table.

Company	X	Y	X – Y (Diff)
Income			
Salary (base)	$100,000	$92,000	$8,000
401K Match	$2,500	$5,520	($3,020)
Gym	$0	$500	($500)
Transportation	$0	$600	($600)
Total Comp	$102,500	$98,620	$3,880
Expenses			
Health	$6,000	$1,800	
Dental	$600	$300	
Vision	$180	$360	
Life Insurance	$300	$300	
Vision	$60	$60	
Total Expenses	$7,140	$2,820	$4,320
Total Package	$95,360	$95,800	($440)

Do you (A) pack your bags for the Beltway, or do you (B) brush up on the latest cow-tipping techniques and the top 10 uses of corn?

The answer is (B). According to CNN, $95,800 in Indianapolis, Indiana, is equal to $136,592 in the D.C. metro area. According to our math, Company X needs to increase its offer by $41,232 ($136,592–$95,360) to keep you in the D.C. metro area. Good luck with that challenge!

You should understand your expected tax liability before you jump at that new job opportunity. You may also want to check out http://paycheckcity.com to see what your paycheck would look like after all deductions, taxes, and so on are withheld from your base salary.

Relocating

If you are a homeowner and thinking of moving to a new city, you should check out www.zillow.com and www.realtor.com to get an idea of housing costs. Search for the same type of home you have now (number of bedrooms, bathrooms, square footage, lot size, and so on) and document a few numbers. Zillow will help you target a realistic price for the home based on several key factors: the tax-assessed value of the home and a list of comparables. So much for the realtor doing that work and collecting 6 percent from the seller. You can find the right number in about 30 seconds. They call it a Zestimate. Zillow is great for both buyers and sellers. Make sure that you set up your Zillow account and add any major changes to the house, which may increase the value. Throw in a picture and a "Make Me Move" price, and you are set. The "Make Me Move" prices that most people are asking are typically 17 percent higher than the Zestimates, according to a recent CNN "Money" article.

If you need to sell your home to move quickly, it is imperative that you price your home right the first time. If you price it too high, you risk having it sit on the market too long — a very bad thing. There is a little something called History on the Multiple Listing Service (MLS), to which all realtors have access. If you must continue to drop your price just to get a bite, you priced it too high. If you price it too low, buyers might wonder what is wrong with the house.

Make sure that you look at the property taxes on the listing. Also, Realtor.com has a built-in mortgage calculator that enables you to quickly calculate principal and interest payments. Check out www.bankrate.com to get the current mortgage interest rates. Also, check out www.homefair.com to see how much house you can afford. If you are not sure whether to buy or rent, Homefair also has a buy-versus-rent calculator to show the pros and cons of each.

> **Note to potential new homeowners: The principal and interest payment is only half the picture, or perhaps 66 to 75 percent of the picture. You are still missing escrows (also known as property taxes and insurance).**

Accepting or Rejecting the Offer

In previous sections, we discussed the skills of successful negotiations. Assuming that you have not jumped prematurely at your first offer and have met your job and salary requirements, you are ready to accept the job offer. Make sure that you have an offer letter in hand that is accurate according to the terms you have established with the prospective employer, and respond as quickly as possible. At this point, you can consider that you officially "have the job." You will be required to sign and fax your offer letter back to the hiring company with a proposed start date. Again, make these minute but important details a priority!

If you are currently employed and plan to leave the company for your new offer, start with a baseline of two weeks notice to your current employer. This is professional courtesy. Beyond that, extenuating circumstances may require you to adjust your official resignation date. Use your best judgment to make sure that you are satisfying the needs of your new employer, your own personal schedule, and the schedule of your current employer, in that order. But whatever you do, do *not* engage in any of these activities until you have that offer letter in hand!

Important: Offers sometimes have strings or contingencies attached. Very often, these contingencies must be satisfied before you can report to work or receive a paycheck. Don't be surprised if the fine print requires you to do the following:

- ❑ Pass a physical examination, a drug screen, or both
- ❑ Document your citizenship or immigration status
- ❑ Obtain or keep a security clearance as a requirement to keep your job
- ❑ Undergo a thorough background investigation, in which your credit history, police records, and travel history might be examined
- ❑ Verify your academic credentials
- ❑ Provide proof of your past employment, salary, or military service

If you are rejecting the offer, it is presumably for one of two reasons:

- ❑ You have learned through the interview process that you are no longer interested in the position.

  If this is the case, you can politely and professionally notify the recruiter and hiring manager that you respectfully decline their offer of employment. You can do this via e-mail or a phone conversation. If they ask for a reason, it is advisable that you be as general — and generic — as possible, because you may be interested in a different position in their company under different terms at a later date. Along the lines of "not burning your bridges," this is the time when less is indeed more.

- ❑ You are interested in the position; however, your terms have not been met.

  If this is the case, again, thank them for their offer. However, you may let them know that it is not in line with your minimum requirements. At this point, the process will likely go in one of two directions: the employer will end the process there or else open the floor for additional negotiations.

If your unmet terms are any of the *intangible* benefits described in this chapter, be specific about what did not meet your requirements. There may be some level of flexibility; however, do keep in mind that you are not completely in the driver's seat just because they are willing to discuss your requirements.

If your unmet terms are any of the *tangible* benefits described in this chapter — specifically, those related to salary — this step circles back to the "Money Talks" section of this chapter. Review your requirements with them. Perform any necessary negotiations, and close the conversation. Politely and respectfully, request that they generate a revised offer.

The bottom line is to always keep the value of your potential contributions in sight — throughout the entire interview and job acceptance process. Unless you are desperate for a job, use your time, effort, and negotiation skills to make sure that you are compensated for the skills you have to offer. Keep in mind that although you are employing strategies and resources to secure your perfect job, your prospective employer is investing just as much to make sure that it hires the best candidate for the position out of the candidate pool available. Patience and perseverance are key, and you just might be pleasantly surprised at the outcome!

Summary

The job search can be a daunting task if not done carefully and thoughtfully. It all starts with what you want out of a job — that is, your requirements. Benefits are an important aspect of the job that will keep you happily employed and productive, which in turn will continue to keep you employed. After you have clearly defined what you are looking for in a job, the next task is to spice up your résumé. The résumé is the key to gaining access to the hiring manager, which kicks off the interview process. Remember that your first impression starts with the recruiter, so keep this in mind during your communications with the company. The recruiter is the gatekeeper. If you are not careful and considerate, you may never get past this critical person.

Headhunters are a great resource for locating the job of your dreams. They are motivated to get you placed with a company because they don't get paid (by the company) until you get paid by your new employer. Typically, headhunters have to wait it out for a defined probation period (30–90 days after you start) before being paid. Keep this in mind when asking them to do your bidding. Always show respect for both headhunters and recruiters. It is a very small community, and they take their database of names with them everywhere.

You have many resources. Use some of the techniques discussed in this chapter and you are sure to find a win-win situation for both you and your new employer. Negotiating a salary offer can be worse than reading *Moby Dick* in Russian. It really isn't a big deal at all, and you need to remind yourself of that before, during, and after these conversations. Remember, 10 minutes' worth of poker face negotiations can mean winning a hand worth thousands of dollars.

The remaining chapters of the book introduce you to topics that are more technical. You should be somewhat familiar with some or most of the technical chapters in this book at this point in your career. If some of these concepts are foreign to you, don't worry — the book has plenty of references to other resources to bring you up to speed.

Nontechnical Interview Questions

You should practice answering some of these questions in the shower or while you stare at yourself in the mirror. Some of these questions can be downright insulting, so take note of your tone and articulate a thoughtful response. A few of these questions are meant to push your buttons.

Q: Why should we hire you? (This insult can frustrate the best of us, so note your tone when you answer it.)

Q: Why are you leaving your current job?

Q: What are your top three strengths?

Q: What are your top three weaknesses?

Q: What is an example of a difficult situation with a peer, and how did you resolve it?

Q: What is an example of a difficult situation with a supervisor, and how did you resolve it?

Q: If I asked your current or previous supervisor about your greatest strengths, what would he or she say?

Q: If I asked your current or previous supervisor about your weaknesses, what would he or she say?

Q: Do you like working in a team environment?

Q: Do you like working alone?

Q: How do you keep up-to-date on the latest technologies and best practices?

Q: What are your hobbies?

Q: What do you want to do? What are your short-term goals? Long-term goals?

Q: Tell me about one of your proudest accomplishments.

Knowing Networks:
Fundamentals

You are dressed in your best business suit, feeling confident about the upcoming interview. Already making it through two rounds of phone interviews, you are now walking into the building for a face-to-face panel interview with a few of the company's techies. You were told that these folks are on the team you would be joining. And they are watching to see whether you are "compatible." But most of all, they witness your ability to react to pointed and exacting technical questions. They see how much you sweat, how you keep your composure, and how well you know your stuff. You are led to a conference room, where you meet three of your peers. Introductions are made, pleasantries are given, and they ask you not to be seated. They instead ask you to go to the whiteboard. On the whiteboard are their "Top 10" topics. They ask you to rank your knowledge of each topic, with 1 being Expert and 5 being Can Barely Spell. Based on your self-ranking, they ask you questions.

At that point, you start to sweat. . .

Introduction

Have you ever wondered why you can study and nail your certification tests but go in to interviews and get tripped up on the most basic of networking questions? You have seemingly done all the preparation for the interview, but come that day, you second-guess yourself after the first few questions and your confidence fades. So what went wrong? Did you go on the offensive or did you wind up soft?

We do not have to answer these questions immediately. Instead, we should look at the foundation that will ultimately determine the success of your interview. Honing your knowledge for the technical interview should include a checklist of network fundamentals in order to eliminate any guesswork. For a technical interview, your network fundamentals checklist must address these key areas:

❑ **Understanding the models:** Specifically, you should understand the OSI, TCP/IP, Cisco, and Defense-in-Depth network models. This understanding will provide you with the cornerstone information you can always rely on in an interview.

❑ **Understanding the issues relevant to Layer 2:** Specifically, these include the traditional topics of collision domains, broadcast domains, switching versus hubbing, port security, and spanning tree.

❑ **Understanding the issues relevant to Layer 3:** These include IP as *the* routed protocol, internal routing protocols such as RIPv1/v2 and OSPF, external routing protocols such as BGP, subnetting/supernetting (or more accurately Classless Inter-Domain Routing), network address translation (NAT), and IPv6.

❑ **Understanding the issues relevant to Layer 4:** These include TCP and UDP, session building, headers and options, port address translation (PAT), and well-known ports.

❑ **Understanding the issues relevant at Layers 5-7:** These include application vulnerabilities, Trojans/worms/viruses, content filtering, and IDS/IPS/IDP.

Most of these areas are covered in depth in the following chapters. However, in this chapter we provide an idea of the types of subjects you will be asked about and some of the basics that you have to know going into your interview.

In today's technical interview, via phone or in person, candidates are questioned on how well they know networking. This is not new. Today, it is not uncommon for recruiters to pitch out a few fundamental questions to vet you for a position. At each step of the job-prospecting path, you have to be ready to draw from your experience and, most important, know how to convey your answers in the best way. To do this, you must be confident about the fundamentals. It is critical that you build a base of knowledge for the technical interview. This base will consist of building blocks that you may always rely on. Should you not have the exact answer to a question, you can still explain to the interviewer that you have the foundation and can easily build up to the answer given some research. To be able to do this with confidence, it is imperative that you understand network models.

Questions

The following questions provide a basis for the foundation you should build on when preparing for technical interviews. The first two sections are dedicated to the OSI (Open Systems Interconnect) and TCP/IP network models. These two models will help you conceptualize the protocols you may be quizzed on. We would be remiss if we did not throw in a brief discussion of Cisco's network model. Then we quickly cover how the defense-in-depth concept applies to the model. Defense-in-depth is the idea of approaching network security as a system of components, with each component mitigating a particular subset of threats. Following the model discussion, we cover more questions and answers from real interviews that we have conducted or been asked ourselves. Again, by relating the questions back to the OSI and TCP models, you will do yourself a great service in breaking down the question and formulating your answer. And as you go through these sections, think of clarification questions you can ask the interviewer. It is perfectly acceptable to glean as much information as you can from the interviewer regarding the job. Just remember to exercise extreme caution. Asking too many clarification questions may give the interviewer reason to think you do not know a subject very well.

What Is the OSI Model?

This is a very broad question, but it has been asked. It is hard to answer this one briefly and also nail down what the interviewer would like to hear. In our experience, the answer has to discuss the seven layers, including the function of each layer and example protocols for each layer. Most important, the answer must include a discussion of encapsulation. The Cisco certification exams always have questions referring to the OSI model, so if a position you are after requires a CCNA, be aware that they could just pull a few exam questions out to prove that you did more than cram for the test.

For a quick history refresher, the International Standards Organization (ISO) began work on a standard reference model for network protocols and applications in the early 1980s. This model was named the Open Systems Interconnect (OSI) Reference Model. The goal of the model was to provide an abstract collection of protocol descriptions in a layered approach. This was counter to what had been a world dominated by vendor-specific protocol stacks — think IBM's SNA. Do you need to know when ISO ratified the model? No. You just need to know that the OSI Reference Model still serves as a useful tool for understanding network protocol design and is commonly referred to in industry and academia all over the world.

As mentioned earlier and shown in Figure 2-1, the OSI model consists of seven layers. These seven layers address the numerous functions that make networked applications possible. Being a layered model, the lowest layer performs its function first, followed by the next higher layer, and so on through to the highest layer. Each layer of the model communicates with its neighbor layers only. This layered approach is the key to interoperability in a multivendor environment. With each layer encapsulating data from the higher layer, there is built-in insulation.

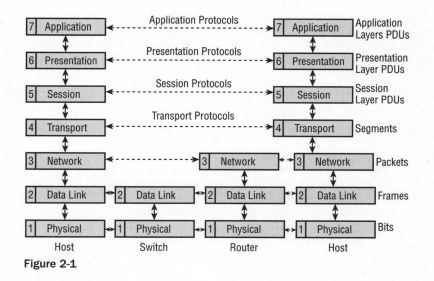

Figure 2-1

In the following sections, we briefly describe each layer's functionality as well as the security vulnerabilities at each layer. The OSI model's seven layers from bottom to top are the following: physical, data-link, network, transport, session, presentation, and application. Keep in mind that the purpose of this section is just to provide you with a reference for interview questions. Interviewers will not expect you to be an expert in all the layers, but you should know where a certain protocol would fit in the layers.

Physical Layer: "Bits"

As the name implies, the physical layer defines the physical facilities used in the network. These facilities include the cabling (coax, twisted-pair, fiber, copper, and so on), media converters, cable pin-outs, jacks, interface connectors, transmitter and receiver signal levels, bit-to-signal processing, line-voltages, and let us not forget wireless interfaces. Example electrical standards for the physical layer include DSL, Ethernet (10/100/1000BT), DOCSIS, RS-232/449/530, V.35, USB, Firewire, IEEE 802.11x/Vi-Fi physical layers, Bluetooth physical layer, SONET/SDH, and so on. Threats include physical access, wiretaps, and frequency interception ("WarDriving").

Data-Link Layer: "Frames"

The data-link layer is concerned with getting the data onto the physical layer. It does so using various bit-level encoding/decoding mechanisms. In other words, the data-link layer takes the bits from the physical layer and forms a data packet or frame. It also does the reverse: takes the packet from the higher layer and breaks it into a bit stream. Critical to the data link layer's function is the formatting of the data. The format of the frames it creates includes addressing (source and destination), the data itself, and a checksum. The checksum is used to ensure that the data was transmitted properly. Also in the data link layer is the concept of a maximum transmission unit (MTU). This defines the maximum size of a packet that can be sent reliably on the network medium. Example data link layer framing is Ethernet. Ethernet uses 48-bit addresses to define unique devices on the physical network. This address is called a Media Access Control (MAC) address. MAC addresses are split into two parts. The first three octets make up the vendor code, better known as an Organizationally Unique Identifier (OUI). The last three octets form a unique identifier locally assigned by the vendor. The address is represented as six colon-separated pairs of hex digits; for example, 00-12-3F-EB-4C-06. In this example, the 00-12-3F represents a Dell computer. The EB-4C-06 is a unique number assigned to the NIC. This MAC address is used in the frame header along with the destination MAC address. There is also a broadcast address for the data link layer. This address (FF:FF:FF:FF:FF:FF) is used for a packet intended for all hosts. Threats include MAC address spoofing, sniffing/snorting, and WEP/WPA hacking.

Network Layer: "Packets"

The OSI defines the network layer as the layer where higher-layer data segments are "wrapped," addressed, and sent on their way. The network layer is responsible for inspecting these addresses and forwarding the packet onto the next hop after consulting its routing table. Using the MTU (maximum transmission unit), the network layer is also responsible for breaking large packets into smaller packets for transmission. The end device will perform the reassembly. It is important to note that the network layer does not guarantee any reliability of packet transmission — that is, error checking. Error checking is a function of the transport layer. Internetwork Protocol (IP) is *the* Layer 3 protocol. Threats include fragmentation attacks, routing protocol attacks, ping attacks, and ARP poisoning.

Transport Layer: "Segments"

The transport layer is responsible for reliable transmission of data. The reliability is provided using a checksum on packets, controls to request retransmission of errored packets, and overall flow control of the traffic. TCP (Transmission Control Protocol) is the well-known transport protocol for reliable transmission. But not all traffic requires a reliable service. For instance, some application traffic cannot tolerate the delay caused by the retransmission of packets — for example, streaming content. So for this type of traffic, another transport layer protocol is suitable. Known as the User Datagram Protocol (UDP), it has lower overhead from not carrying a checksum and is therefore quicker to process. The transport layer is also the first layer that uses the concept of an end-to-end connection. Managing these connections using well-defined ports (or sockets when combined with the source IP address) is vital to the transport layer operation. Threats include denial-of-service (DoS) attacks, port scans, SYN/ACK/FIN attacks, and man-in-the-middle attacks.

Session Layer: "Session Protocol Data Unit (PDU)"

Because the transport layer provides the connection between two devices, the session layer is responsible for handling how those connections are used. Session layer protocols define the format of requests over these connections. Examples include the secure sockets layer (SSL), remote procedure call (RPC), and NETBIOS. Threats include password attacks, session hijacks, DoS attacks, and NETBIOS attacks.

Presentation Layer: "Presentation PDU"

The presentation layer is responsible for providing a common interface for higher-layer applications. To do so, the presentation layer may perform protocol conversion, data compression, or character translation. There are not many examples of the presentation layer other than the X protocol used in X-Windows. Some could argue that Java and ActiveX controls have presentation layer qualities. Threats include HTML code inspection and corrupt or malicious controls.

Application Layer: "Application PDU"

The application layer is the direct interface to the network programs executed on the device. Excellent examples of application layer protocols include SMTP/POP, HTTP, and FTP. Threats include Trojan horses, worms, viruses, cookie corruption, buffer overflows, phishing, Web server hijacking, spyware, and keyloggers.

For more information on the OSI Reference Model, refer to ISO standard 7498-1:1994. Another great resource is "OSI Reference Model — The ISO Model of Architecture for Open Systems Interconnection" by Hubert Zimmermann (available at `http://www.comsoc.org/livepubs/50_journals/pdf/ RightsManagement_eid=136833.pdf`).

What Is the TCP/IP Model
and How Does It Relate to the OSI Model?

The TCP/IP model and the OSI model are not directly aligned. Although the OSI model is referenced most often, the TCP/IP model has actually been around longer (since the 1970s). It was developed by the Department of Defense and DARPA. It is a simpler design and is a four-layer framework. The reason it has fewer layers than the OSI model is that many of the functions are not separated in the TCP/IP Model. To quickly review what you should remember, the four layers of the TCP/IP are the application, transport, Internet, and network layers. Figure 2-2 shows how the OSI and TCP/IP model compare.

The network layer is a combination of the OSI's data-link and physical layers with the same features. Here the model defines the hardware and network access behavior. The Internet layer is analogous to the OSI network layer. At this layer, addressing and routing are the key functions. The transport layer is analogous to the OSI model's session and transport layers. Here, the model defines peer-to-peer or host-to-host behavior. The application layer is analogous to the presentation and application layers. At this layer, the model defines application protocols.

For more information on the TCP/IP model and TCP/IP in general, be sure to check out *Internetworking with TCP/IP, Vol. 1* (5th Edition) by Douglas E. Comer.

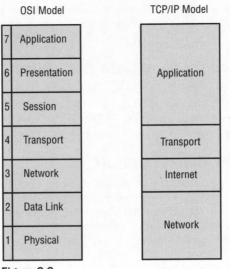

Figure 2-2

Tell Me about Cisco's "Standard" Architecture

Cisco continues to be the dominant vendor in today's networked world. It is a given that you will be asked at least one Cisco-specific question during your interview. Therefore it is imperative that you understand Cisco's design model and architecture. Although we are by no means Cisco evangelists, it is important to state fact. Cisco's architecture was originally created as a guide for network engineers to scale their Cisco networks. It also assisted in conceptualizing the family of routers that Cisco sold. It was critical for engineers to properly place routers that had the requisite resources (that is, processing power, memory, interfaces, and so on). Today, the model helps engineers in many ways:

❑ **Performance:** It helps the engineer design high-performance networks by eliminating or minimizing chokepoints in the network.

❑ **Scale:** The network model scales well for most organizations as the organization evolves.

❑ **Policy:** Network policies and filters can be applied at key distribution points in the network.

❑ **Troubleshooting:** The model helps engineers organize and therefore simplify the network — decreasing the time to troubleshoot problems when they happen.

Core Layer

Cisco presents its network model as a three-tiered architecture. As shown in Figure 2-3, at the top of the architecture is the core layer. This layer is commonly referred to as the backbone. This layer includes the high-end switches with high-speed interfaces. Backbone equipment provides for rapid and reliable transfer of packets across the network. High data transfer rates are imperative. Low packet latency and reliability are also critical. With these requirements in mind, Cisco rightfully positions high-speed switches in this layer. It is much easier and faster to do switching in hardware than route lookups in memory. Backbone equipment will have multiple paths and circuits to route or, more accurately, switch around problems. It should also have fault-tolerant features such as power supplies, route engines, and common logic processors. The core layer will have fewer network elements but much faster systems to handle the volume of traffic. Example core Cisco equipment includes Cisco switches such as its 7x00 series and 12000 series for WAN design, and Catalyst switches such as the 6000, 5000, and 4000 series in LAN design. Interfaces in the core would include leased-line circuits (T1/T3) and SONET/SDH.

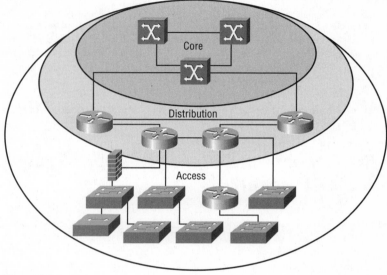

Figure 2-3

Distribution Layer

Because the core is more of a switching layer, the distribution layer is chiefly responsible for routing. This layer has tight control over the network resources. Common in this layer are packet filtering and firewall controls. There is also more of an effort to categorize packets and prioritize them. The distribution equipment essentially serves as a gatekeeper or control gate for traffic entering from the access layer and destined for the core. Examples of Cisco's distribution layer equipment include the 2600 and 4x00 series of routers.

Access Layer

The access layer is the point of entry into the network. This layer contains all the devices that directly connect to an end user or host system offering service. This layer undergoes the most rapid changes, and the equipment used has the highest port density. The access layer is made up of Ethernet switches, hubs, media converters, and repeaters. The concerns of the access layer include managing the collision domain, VLAN (virtual LAN) management, and port security. To briefly review, a collision domain is a concern in shared media where device traffic has the potential to "collide" when transmitting simultaneously. In the context of Cisco's architecture, the primary concern is proper network segmentation. Switches create separate collision domains through the use of VLANs. Port security is a function of the access switch. Most switches today can be configured to allow only a static MAC address on a given port.

A great analogy to use for the Cisco three-tiered architecture is the typical road system in America. Residential roads access all homes and are the ultimate source and destination for most of us. Common intra-city or town streets connect to residential streets. Then, intercity and interstate roads connect the towns and cities. So in this analogy, the access layer is analogous to residential roads. Intra-city and town roads are analogous to the distribution layer. And the core layer is similar to our interstate/intercity highway system. The speed limits on the roads are analogous to the relative bit-rates at each layer. Residential roads are generally slower because the vehicle and population density is highest. The interstates are faster because access points are few and multiple lanes and alternate routes provide reliability. Reliability at the city level is also worth noting. Cities in many cases have a beltway, or loop, that offers excellent traffic distribution around the city. One can argue topology advantages and disadvantages here.

For more information on Cisco's three-tiered architecture, Google "internetworking design basics site:cisco.com."

How Does the Concept of Defense-in-Depth Security Work with the OSI Model?

This is a great question for a prospective network security engineer. Before diving into the layers, you should establish that defense-in-depth is more about policy and procedures than actual security mechanisms protecting resources. Part of defense-in-depth includes physical security (a secure facility) as well as human security (background checks). But as the question was framed, the OSI layers are a great start to explaining the defense-in-depth concept. As you should know already, defense-in-depth means protecting more than one avenue of approach and protecting those avenues with multiple prevention methods. The best way to discuss this is by addressing each layer of the OSI model and what mechanisms are used to protect each. Companies may employ a security perimeter for the physical wiring (Layer 1), port security in their workgroup switches (Layer 2), access lists at their border routers (Layer 3), creating demilitarized zones (DMZs) and packet filtering at their firewalls (Layer 4), IDS/IDP monitoring/blocking (Layers 3–7), SSL tunnels (Layer 6), content filtering (Layer 7), AAA services (Layer 7), vulnerability scanning (Layers 4–7), virus scanning (Layer 7), and so on. Later chapters cover these topics in depth. But one item to mention now is the need for personnel to know the security measures in place and what threats they mitigate and vulnerabilities they protect against. Too often, companies rush to protect a network resource, only to gain a false sense of security because that mechanism may pose a security risk itself if not configured or managed properly.

Why Do We Think of Networking in Terms of Layers?

This is another good, fundamental question. You know that all the models are based on layers, but why are they? Essentially, ISO introduced layering in order to view the network functions logically. Each layer is independent of the next, provides a specific service, and therefore has its own overhead (header/trailer). As shown in Figure 2-4, at each layer processing is done on the corresponding header and trailer, and the contents and data are passed up the stack. It was also necessary for creating a certain degree of independence for the purposes of a multivendor environment.

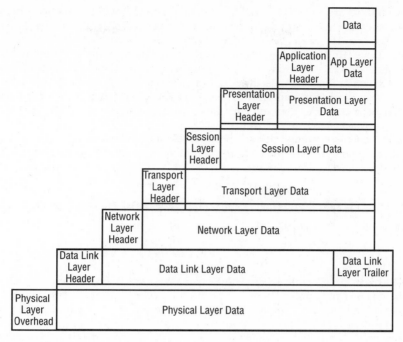

Figure 2-4

How Does the Spanning Tree Protocol Work, What Is Its Purpose, and What Are Some of the Types?

The Spanning Tree Protocol (STP) operates at Layer 2, and its purpose is to eliminate loops in networks. It does this by selectively blocking some ports and allowing other ports to forward traffic. You should understand how the election of the root node is accomplished in STP. All bridges and switches in the LAN will pass messages (bridge protocol data units, or BPDUs) to elect a root. The bridges and switches use the Bridge Identification (BID) to perform the election. The BID is made up of the switch MAC address and priority number. Unless configured otherwise, usually the lowest MAC address will be elected as the root. The second lowest will act as a secondary root.

All other switches will use that spanning tree to calculate their own shortest path to the root. All traffic will flow along the shortest path to the root bridge/switch. All ports will fall into one of the following modes: Listening, where the switch will process BPDUs and establish the network topology; Learning, where the switch will build the MAC to port translation table; Blocking, where this port could cause a loop if active but is still needed in the event of a trunk failure; Forwarding, where the port normally operates, transmitting and receiving data; and Disabled, where the port is administratively or physically disabled.

IEEE Standard 802.1D first defined the STP protocol. Basically, the STP protocol operation works by electing a root bridge first and then finding a least-cost path to the root bridge, followed by the disabling of links not in the tree. The most prevalent types of spanning tree implementations include Cisco's Per-VLAN spanning tree (PVST/PVST+), Rapid Spanning Tree Protocol (RSTP), and Multiple Spanning Tree Protocol (MSTP). Cisco's PVST and PVST+ are proprietary and work with ISL and 802.1Q VLAN trunks, respectively. Part of 802.1w, RSTP was introduced in 2002 as an extension to 802.1D. This extension provided a faster convergence time, and RSTP has since made STP obsolete. MSTP came out in 2003 under the work of IEEE 802.1s workgroup and added the function of multiple VLANs to IEEE802.1q-2003.

For more information on spanning tree protocols, check out *Interconnections*, Second Edition, by Radia Perlman (Addison-Wesley Professional. 2000), and the standards IEEE802.1d-2004 and IEEE802.1q-2003. On the Web, Google "STP site:cisco.com."

What Is the Difference between a Broadcast Domain and a Collision Domain?

Although not as relevant with the pervasive use of Ethernet switches, this question is still a classic. A collision domain is simply a group of hosts directly connected to a hub or repeater and is part of the Ethernet protocol design. Specifically, this protocol is the CSMA/CD (Carrier Sense Multiple Access/Collision Detection) and a Layer 2 — Data Link Layer function. Essentially, it allows devices sharing the same media to communicate fairly. You should remember the basic steps:

1. The network device listens for other transmissions measuring voltage. If there's a relative voltage change, the device waits.

2. After the device detects "silence," it will attempt to transmit.

3. Other devices still may try to transmit at the same time, so a collision occurs.

4. After the devices all detect the collision, they back off for a unique amount of time and then try to retransmit.

Frames that are corrupted from a collision are called runts. But most important, collisions can be avoided through the use of Ethernet switches, which separate collision domains or minimize the number of devices sharing the same segment. A broadcast domain is an area in which any network device can transmit directly to another device. This could be another device off a directly connected hub or switch. Only routers break up a broadcast domain. To reach all devices in the broadcast domain, devices use the all-1s MAC address (FF:FF:FF:FF).

Explain How Port Security Works on a Switch

Port security use is on the rise in today's private-enterprise networks, and this question comes up often. Port security refers to a feature that allows a switch to cache the Ethernet MAC address used on a given port. Only traffic originating from that cached address will be allowed to communicate through the switch. If a device with a different MAC address attempts to connect, the switch is capable of disabling the port and notifying the network administrator. Although some may see port security as constricting the mobility of a workforce, it does provide an excellent security mechanism to control physical access to the network.

Explain the TCP Three-Way Handshake and Relate It to the TCP State Diagram

The purpose of this question is to probe how well you know basic fundamentals. The first part of the question is relatively easy. The second part is the kicker. The TCP three-way handshake establishes a TCP session, or connection, and is the foundation for all reliable communication on the Internet today. As shown in Figure 2-5, the originating client will send the first packet with a SYN flag and a sequence number (X). The destination server replies with a SYN/ACK, its own sequence number (Y), and an acknowledgment of the clients' sequence number (X+1). The client returns an ACK and increments its own sequence number (X+1) and the sequence number of the server (Y+1). The connection is now established and the client can begin transmitting the data. The connection will remain open until one of the following happens: The client or server sends a FIN packet to finish or an RST packet to reset the connection, or the connection times out. All this exchange is referenced in the TCP state diagram shown in Figure 2-6. It is well worth the time to understand and be able to draw this diagram from memory. It is impressive to see candidates who understand the inner workings of the protocol.

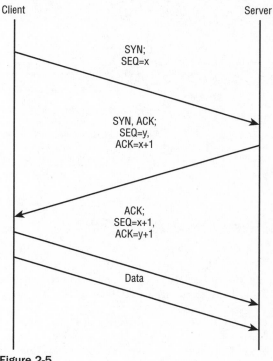

Figure 2-5

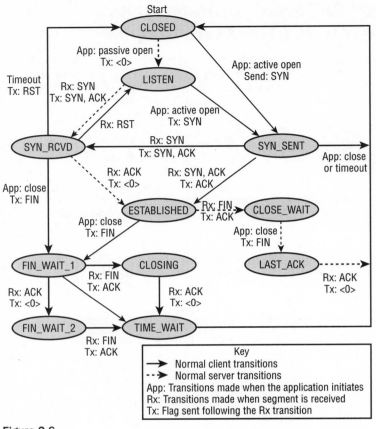

Figure 2-6

Briefly Describe the TCP and UDP Packet Headers

Interviewers love to throw this question in to see how well you know the fields in the TCP and UDP headers. RFC 791 defines the standard TCP header. RFC 768 defines the standard UDP header. The TCP header has a minimum size of 20 bytes and a maximum of 60 bytes, and it uses the IP protocol number of 6. The UDP header has a static size of 8 bytes and uses the IP protocol number of 17.

Following is a list of the fields in the TCP header (shown in Figure 2-7):

❑ **Source Port (16 bits):** Defines the source port of the connection.

❑ **Destination Port (16 bits):** Defines the destination port of the connection.

❑ **Sequence Number (32 bits):** Identifies the byte count relative to the initial sequence number established in the first SYN packet during the three-way handshake.

❑ **Acknowledgment Number (32 bits):** Contains the last sequence number of the current transmission as well as those received correctly by the host.

❑ **Data Offset (4 bits):** Identifies the number of 32-bit words in the header portion of the packet.

❑ **Reserved (6 bits):** As the name implies, this field is not currently used and is reserved for future use.

❑ **Flags (6 bits):** These are a series of 1-bit fields that are controls for the connection, as follows: Urgent (URG); Acknowledgment (ACK); Push (PSH); Reset (RST); Synchronize (SYN); and Finish (FIN).

❑ **Window (16 bits):** This field defines how many packets can be sent before an acknowledgment is received. This is critical to the performance of a connection, and the window size is adjusted accordingly.

❑ **Checksum (16 bits):** This field is a simple ones-complement function of a pseudo-header, the TCP header, and data that is computed by the client and recomputed by the server for integrity. If these do not match, a packet retransmission occurs. The pseudo header is the source and destination IP addresses and the TCP header.

❑ **Urgent Pointer (16 bits):** This field is the byte location of any urgent data that signals to the destination host to process immediately as opposed to buffering.

❑ **Options and Padding (32 bits):** These fields are used to pad the length of the TCP header so that it results in a multiple of 32 bits.

❑ **Data:** This is the data passed from the application layer (of the TCP/IP model).

0 1 2 3 4 5 6 7 8 9 10 11 12 13 14 15 16 17 18 19 20 21 22 23 24 25 26 27 28 29 30 31

Source Port							Destination Port	
Sequence Number								
Acknowledgment Number								
Data Offset	RSVD	URG	ACK	PSH	RST	SYN	FIN	Window
Checksum							Urgent Pointer	
Options							Padding	
Data								

Figure 2-7

As stated earlier in the chapter, UDP is used by applications that are not concerned with reliability or packet loss. These applications just need to transmit quickly and with as little overhead as possible. The UDP header has four 16-bit fields (see Figure 2-8), making the total overhead 8 bytes. Similarly to TCP, the Source Port and Destination Port fields define the ports to be used. The Length field is the length of the entire packet (header and data). As is the TCP checksum, the UDP checksum field is a ones-complement of a pseudo header, the UDP header and the data. One important note is that the UDP checksum is optional and can be set to 0.

0 1 2 3 4 5 6 7 8 9 10 11 12 13 14 15 16 17 18 19 20 21 22 23 24 25 26 27 28 29 30 31

Source Port	Destination Port
Length	UDP Checksum

Figure 2-8

What Well-Known Port Numbers Are You Familiar With?

This is always a good question to probe how often a candidate deals with specific higher-layer protocols. There are too many ports to mention, but the critical ones are the following: FTP (20-21/TCP:UDP), secure shell (22/TCP:UDP), Telnet (23/TCP:UDP), TACACS (49/TCP:UDP), DNS (53/TCP:UDP), SMTP (25/TCP:UDP), TFTP (69/UDP), HTTP (80/TCP), SSL (443/TCP), POP3 (110/TCP), RADIUS (1812-1813/UDP), SNMP (161-162/UDP), BGP (179/TCP), LDAP (389/TCP:UDP), RDP (3389/TCP), and IKE/ISAKMP (500/TCP:UDP).

What Is the Difference between Classful and Classless Routing?

This is another softball question and one that CCNAs are often asked. Classful routing protocols are ones that strictly follow the Class A (8-bit prefix), B (16-bit prefix), and C (24-bit prefix) address boundaries. Examples include RIP and IGRP. Classless routing protocols are ones that throw out the traditional rules of classful routing and allow summarization of routes into smaller, more manageable groups. Classless routing is also known as supernetting and formally known as Classless Inter-Domain Routing (CIDR). For example, with the traditional Class C address of 192.168.16.0/24, a classful routing protocol would advertise only the /24. Every network device on the network would share the same subnet. If you had subnetted your network to use 192.168.16.16/25, you would have to advertise this more specific route using a classless routing protocol. The same applies to summarization or aggregation. If you have multiple Class C networks such as 192.168.16.0/24 and 192.168.17.0/24, using a classless routing protocol, these routes could be written as 192.168.16.0/23. Classless routing protocols include EIGRP, OSPF, RIPv2, and BGP.

Describe Variable-Length Subnet Masking (VLSM)

Similar to the previous question, this is another favorite fundamental question. VLSM is a feature of OSPF, RIPv2, and BGP that enables classless routing. With classful routing protocols such as RIPv1 or IGRP, every autonomous system uses the same subnet mask. For example, 192.168.16.0, 192.168.17.0, and 192.168.18.0 are all Class C networks and therefore have a /24 or 255.255.255.0 subnet mask. VLSM allows an autonomous system to support different subnet masks such as 192.168.18.0/26 and 192.168.18.128/25 to support subnets. VLSM also supports "supernetting," such as describing 192.168.20.0/23 to include all hosts in 192.168.20.0 and 192.168.21.0. Do not be surprised if you are asked to perform a few subnet and supernet examples.

For more information on VLSM, Google "VLSM site:cisco.com."

What Is the Difference between a Routed Protocol and a Routing Protocol?

This is another "softball" question but you would be surprised by how it trips up candidates. A routed protocol is one that defines the header within a network layer packet and is used at each Layer 3 packet inspection. For example, IP addresses are used to forward packets from device to device in the network. A routing protocol is one that shares routing information between routers. Routing protocols use messages to exchange routes and network health information. Examples of routing protocols are Routing Information Protocol (RIP), Border Gateway Protocol (BGP), Open Shortest Path First (OSPF), Interior Gateway Routing Protocol (IGRP), and Enhanced Interior Gateway Routing Protocol (EIGRP).

Draw the Diagram of a Typical OSPF Network and Explain Generally How It Works: DR, BDR, Election, ASBR, ABR, Route Redistribution, and Summarization

This question is a great one and often makes the interviewee wonder where to start. Intentionally open-ended, the responses vary widely. What you should convey in your answer is an in-depth knowledge of OSPF. Scratch the surface and dive in deeper if you see positive responses from your interviewers. Preferably using a whiteboard, start with the hierarchy of OSPF — a two-level model — and draw a diagram like the one in Figure 2-9.

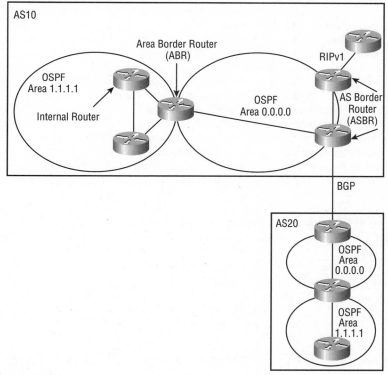

Figure 2-9

Discuss having a backbone Area 0 (or 0.0.0.0) and that all areas must connect to the backbone area. Other area types include the following: stub area (an area that does not receive AS external routes); total stubby area (an area that does not allow summary routes or external routes); and not-so-stubby area (an area that can import AS external routes and send them to the backbone area, but will not receive AS external routes from the backbone or other areas). You want to include the type of routers contained in the hierarchy: internal routers, area border routers (ABR), backbone routers, and autonomous system boundary routers (ASBR). Mention that the shortest path first (SPF) calculation is performed independently on each area. You should state that the time to converge is faster than distance-vector routing protocols (DVRPs) such as RIP. Include a brief statement on the low bandwidth requirement for LSAs. Also mention support for classless routing, Variable-Length Subnet Masking (VLSM), authentication, and multipath statements. Describe the OSPF algorithm and generally how it works: Changes in the network generate LSAs, routers exchange the LSAs, and each router builds and maintains its own database. So if the network is in a steady state, there will be refresh LSAs only every 30 minutes. You want to cover the five types of routing protocol packets: Hello, Database description, Link-state request, Link-state update, and Link-state acknowledgment. Hello packets are multicast on 224.0.0.5 and routers use them to form adjacency relationships. You want to cover the types of Link State Advertisements (LSAs): Router link (LSA type 1), Network link (LSA type 2), Network summary (LSA type 3), ASBR (LSA type 4), External (LSA type 5), and NSSA external (LSA type 7). Do not neglect a discussion on IPv6 and that OSPFv3 supports it. You might want to discuss briefly how vendors implement OSPFv3 using a ships-in-the-night approach to support both v3 and v2 simultaneously. OSPFv3 distributes IPv6 prefixes and uses the same interfaces and nearly the same LSA types as OSPFv2. It uses the same methods for neighbor discovery and adjacency forming. The only differences are that OSPFv3 has to use a network link rather than a subnet. And there can be multiple instances of OSPFv3 on a given link. You should mention that the topology in OSPFv3 is a bit different as well — using a router ID and Link ID. And because OSPFv3 uses links, there's a new Link LSA type as well as an Intra-Area Prefix LSA for the IPv6 prefixes.

To fully answer the question, you have to go through the process of neighbor finding and adjacency creation. Routers sharing a common network segment or link will become neighbors using the Hello protocol. Routers send Hello packets out each interface with the multicast address of 224.0.0.5. When a router sees its own primary address in a Hello packet from another router, the routers are then neighbors. As neighbors, the routers have to agree on the following things: the area-id (of the area they belong to); a preshared password (for authentication); hello and dead intervals (how often hello packets are sent and how long to wait to for a neighbor's hello); and a stub area flag (whether the router is in a stub area). Neighbor routers then form adjacencies. When the routers exchange their databases, they are adjacent. To limit the volume of information exchanged on a network segment, routers go through an election process. This election nominates a designated router (DR) and a backup designated router (BDR). The DR is the sole source for updates on the segment. All other routers on the segment exchange route information with the DR and BDR. Area Border Routers (ABRs) collect all the routes for the area and combine/summarize them into a single advertisement to the backbone area (inter-area route summarization). The backbone routers then forward these summarized routes. External route summarization may occur as well when distributing the routes to another protocol.

For more information on interior routing protocols, check out *Routing TCP/IP, Volume 1* (2nd Edition) (CCIE Professional Development) by Jeff Doyle and Jennifer Carroll (Cisco Press. 2006).

Explain BGP, the Differences between BGP and OSPF, What Prefixes Are, and What Attributes and Types Are Used in BGP

The Border Gateway Protocol (BGP) is a favorite subject for many technical interviewers. It is the exterior routing protocol of choice in today's networks and is quite different from interior routing protocols such as OSPF. BGP fulfills the role of mediating between two "administratively controlled" networks. These administratively controlled networks are known as autonomous systems (ASs). BGP, requiring a reliable connection between peers, uses TCP port 179. Each peer session gets a single TCP session. BGP is an application layer protocol, so it requires the TCP session to be established before exchanging any route information. BGP sessions can be authenticated using MD5 signatures when exchanging updates. An UPDATE message can have a variable number of attributes; however, they cannot be repeated. As for the prefixes, an UPDATE message can advertise only one route. It can, however, list routes to be deleted. BGP is considered a path vector protocol because it stores route information in addition to path attributes. The route selection is done in a deterministic fashion based on best route policy. The policy is based off the path attributes. Where interior routing protocols use metrics such as delay, link utilization, or hops, BGP does not. Understand that BGP is capable of running in two modes: exterior and interior. EBGP is used for peering between different autonomous systems (AS). IBGP is used for routers within the same AS. Path attributes are different for the two modes; these are discussed shortly.

There are two key differences between BGP and OSPF (or any internal routing protocol). The first difference is how the protocols scale up to accommodate large numbers of routes. BGP scales up well because it sends a complete route update only once when a session is established with a peer. After that, the BGP speaker will send only incremental changes. Even though OSPF mostly sends link state information, there are still periods in which all its routing information is sent. The second key difference is the support for path attributes in BGP. BGP uses path attributes to form routing policies. This works well when you have to route between separately owned and maintained networks (autonomous systems). The routing policies allow you to make a decision as to whether to accept, reject, or change (summarize/aggregate) routes from a peer network. This helps protect the network and control how routes are propagated throughout the internal network.

A prefix is the network portion of the IP address and implies the use of classless addressing. BGP uses prefixes in the Network Layer Reachability Information (NRLI) field in the UPDATE messages. The path attributes convey the prefix characteristics to the peer router. Another hot topic in BGP is the ability to perform route dampening. Route dampening is a feature that controls the frequency of routes changing state — up, down, up, down, and so on. This frequent changing of state is called route flapping. Most routers today can sense the flapping and remove the offending route. To do so, they monitor how often the flapping occurs and penalize the route each time. After the penalties exceed a set threshold, the route is removed and updates are ignored. The route can be reused after a certain amount of time.

One of the greatest arguments in BGP is which attributes should or should not be used when sharing information between two networks. (Just a quick definition note: The words *update* and *advertisement* are used interchangeably.) In BGP, there are numerous path attributes that accompany an update between two BGP speakers who wish to exchange routing information. We draw from RFC 4271/1771 for the following information. There are four defined categories for BGP attributes:

- ❑ Well-known mandatory
- ❑ Well-known discretionary
- ❑ Optional transitive
- ❑ Optional nontransitive

As the name implies, any vendor who wishes to implement BGP must have the well-known attributes. The mandatory attributes are ones that have to be included in every update. Discretionary attributes do not. Optional attributes are ones that some BGP speakers may use and others may not. The transitive bit in the update determines whether a BGP neighbor propagates the attribute or simply deletes it.

It is always good to review the well-known mandatory attributes first. There are three mandatory attributes that are well-known: ORIGIN, AS_PATH, and NEXT_HOP. There are two well-known, discretionary attributes: Local Preference, and Atomic Aggregate. All these attributes are described in the following list:

❑ **ORIGIN:** The Origin code is how the route originated, or the source of the route. The choices are internal gateway protocol (IGP), external gateway protocol (EGP), or incomplete. A great follow-up question is, "What is the cause of an unknown/incomplete?" Some of the most common reasons are route aggregation/summarization and redistribution.

❑ **AS_PATH:** The AS_PATH attribute is simply a list of all the autonomous systems (AS) that the given route in the update transits through. As the update passes through each AS, each BGP host adds its own AS to the list.

❑ **NEXT_HOP:** The NEXT_HOP attribute is the IP address of the first router in the next AS. And this first router may be more than one hop away. When this is the case, the interior routing protocol will compute a route to the BGP NEXT_HOP IP address. Just remember that Internal BGP sessions will not change the NEXT_HOP attribute — only external BGP sessions do.

❑ **LOCAL_PREF:** The local preference attribute is used to inform internal BGP peers of the preferred AS egress point for the included route.

❑ **ATOMIC_AGGREGATE**: The atomic aggregate attribute is used when a BGP speaker has overlapping routes from one of its peers. The BGP speaker will set the attribute when it makes a less-specific route selection. Aggregation, also known as summarization, hides network reachability and topology information. The atomic aggregate attribute is the mechanism used to hide the AS path.

Examples of the optional transitive attributes are the Aggregator, Communities, and Extended Communities attributes.

❑ **Aggregator:** The Aggregator attribute is a way for a BGP speaker to notify its peer that it has aggregated a given route and provides its own AS number and IP address.

❑ **Communities:** Communities are the "catch-all" attributes. In most large networks today, BGP communities are used to enforce policy. They do not directly affect the route selection algorithm of BGP, but they can shape how routes are treated when received in an update. There are three communities that are commonly used: NO_EXPORT, NO_ADVERTISE, and NO_EXPORT_ SUBCONFED. The NO_EXPORT community attribute is a tag that notifies the peer whether the route can be exported to an external AS. The NO_ADVERTISE community attribute notifies the peer to not advertise the route at all. The NO_EXPORT_SUBCONFED community extends the NO_EXPORT attribute to include confederated ASs.

❑ **Extended Communities:** Extended Communities extend the BGP attributes further. There are a number of Extended Communities in draft and used in some BGP implementations. Ones to mention include the Autonomous System Specific, Route Target, Route Origin, and Link Bandwidth.

❑ **MULTI_EXIT_DISC:** The MED attribute is an optional, nontransitive attribute that provides a means to advertise multiple exit points for the local AS. Each exit point is given a metric, and the lowest metric will be the preferred exit point.

Much has been written on BGP but the great references for BGP are still the RFCs. There are many and they all deserve attention: RFC 4271 - A Border Gateway Protocol 4 (BGP-4); RFC 4272 - BGP Security Vulnerabilities Analysis; RFC 4273 - Definitions of Managed Objects for BGP-4; RFC 4276 - BGP-4 Implementation Report; RFC 1772 - Application of the Border Gateway Protocol in the Internet; RFC 1773 - Experience with the BGP-4 protocol; RFC 1774/4274 - BGP-4 Protocol Analysis; RFC 1997 - BGP Communities Attribute; and RFC 1998 - An Application of the BGP Community Attribute in Multi-home Routing as well as Internet-Draft document draft-ietf-idr-bgp-ext-communities, BGP Extended Communities Attribute.

Describe Routing Filters and What They Accomplish

Route filters are used in several routing protocols. Most common are the OSPF and BGP implementations. OSPF uses route filters, or route maps, to restrict summary routes and prevent routes from being imported into the route table. Most route maps use match clauses to match prefixes that they wish to accept or deny.

BGP routers use route filters to enforce policy. There are three filter types that can be applied to match updates exchanged between BGP speakers:

- ❑ **Path filters:** Using the AS-PATH attribute, if the update matches the filter criteria, the update is accepted or denied.

- ❑ **Prefix filters:** Using the prefix in the NRLI, if the update matches the filter criteria, the update is accepted or denied.

- ❑ **Route maps:** As with the interior routing protocols, route maps can have more actions associated with the match criteria. Routes can be accepted or denied, but attributes can be changed as well.

There is also work being done in the field of exchanging the route filters between BGP speakers.

For more information on OSPF and BGP route filtering, check out *Routing TCP/IP, Volume 1* (2nd Edition) (CCIE Professional Development) by Jeff Doyle and Jennifer Carroll (Cisco Press. 2006). For more information on BGP outbound route filtering, check out "Outbound Route Filtering Capability for BGP-4 - draft-ietf-idr-route-filter-16.txt," by E. Chen and Y. Rekhter.

Recommended Reading

BGP by Iljitsch Van Beijnum (O'Reilly Media. ISBN: 978-0596002541).
BGP Design and Implementation by Randy Zhang and Micah Bartell (Cisco Press. ISBN: 978-1587051098).
CCIE Routing and Switching Official Exam Certification Guide (2nd Edition) (Exam Certification Guide) by Wendell Odom, Jim Geier, and Naren Mehta (Cisco Press. ISBN: 978-1587201417).
Cisco LAN Switching Fundamentals by David Barnes and Basir Sakandar (Cisco Press. ISBN: 978-1587050893).
Illustrated TCP/IP (Wiley Illustrated Network Series) (Paperback) by Matthew Naugle (Wiley. ISBN: 978-0471196563).

Interconnections, 2nd Edition, by Radia Perlman (Addison-Wesley Professional. ISBN: 978-0201634488).

Internet Routing Architectures (2nd Edition), by Sam Halabi (Cisco Press. ISBN: 978-1578702336).

Internetworking with TCP/IP, Vol 1 (5th Edition) by Douglas E Comer (Prentice Hall. ISBN: 978-0131876712).

OSPF Complete Implementation by John T. Moy (Addison-Wesley Professional. ISBN: 978-0201309669).

OSPF and IS-IS: Choosing an IGP for Large-Scale Networks by Jeff Doyle (Addison-Wesley Professional. ISBN: 978-0321168795).

Routing TCP/IP, Volume 1 (2nd Edition) (CCIE Professional Development) by Jeff Doyle and Jennifer Carroll (Cisco Press. ISBN: 978-1587052026).

Knowing Security: Fundamentals

Of all the chapters in this book, this is the most general in nature. That's because we consider this content to be foundational; it contains information that all security professionals should have locked away in their toolbox for later use. Many of these topics are picked up through formal education, on-the-job training, or simply through the expertise you gain from experience. Interviewers will expect you to already have a clear understanding of each topic presented here and how it affects your work and the organization. We have limited space to share these concepts with you, so we encourage you to do your own additional research. To aid you in that effort, we provide some Web links at the end of the chapter that you can use as a starting point.

Adjust Your Thinking

Your role as a security professional is to provide protection for an organization's critical information types — that is, information that the organization *must* have that is correct and available to conduct business. This is true whether you are a consultant with a client organization or you work as a security professional for your own organization. To protect the organization's assets in the most effective manner, you need to be clear on the concepts discussed in this section. This is not intended to be a comprehensive list, but instead highlights concepts considered most important by industry professionals and security certification organizations.

Every organization has a mission — the reason it exists. The mission can be something as simple as generating profits for investors, or something slightly more complex, such as achieving 100 percent customer satisfaction. The information you are tasked to protect is used on a daily basis to accomplish this mission. Each risk to an information type is also a risk to the organization's mission. If this critical information is compromised, the result can range from something as mundane as fines or inconvenience to the organization to something much more dramatic, such as the loss of customer confidence.

When you begin your work as a security professional, you should understand that you actually have multiple job functions. One of these additional duties is as an ad hoc linguist. Yes, a linguist. You'll be responsible for translating technical security discussions into language that is easier for managers and decision makers to understand. Never underestimate the value of this function. Failure to communicate with managers and achieve their full buy-in on the information assurance process can lead to a good many issues. Some of these include lack of security budget funding, failure of the organization to take information security seriously, and deficient levels of user awareness regarding information security. Each of these issues can potentially put the organization at risk. It is your job to help communicate and ensure management buy-in for the security processes.

Many organizations struggle with keeping information security a priority because of the perceived lack of *return on investment (ROI)*. Because of this perception, organizations sometimes combine job roles and responsibilities. A dangerous example of doing so is when a system or network administrator is given full responsibilities for also securing the network. This situation creates a conflict of interest for the worker in question. The administration side of that worker's duties requires the administrator to keep the services available and easy to use for the other employees of the organization. In contrast, however, the security side attempts to limit services and restrict access in order to ensure the protection of the critical information. If a single person carries both titles, the operational side nearly always takes precedence over the security side.

Core Values

Security professionals have a number of values to integrate into the core of how they conduct their business. This section provides a general overview of these values and what they mean to you.

Access Control

One of the foundations of information security is *access control*. To understand basic access control, consider information as a physical asset. A variety of information types exist within an organization, and each one is in its own room, behind a door. Access control mechanisms allow you to specifically control who or what can get in, or out of, that door. In this case, perhaps you've put a different lock on each door and given keys only to those individuals allowed in the room. By controlling the movement or use of your information assets, you help limit the risk to your organization.

From an electronic information perspective, the doors, and their keys, are security mechanisms that you'll put into place to guard the organization's information. The main goal is to understand where the doors should be and who should have the keys. To help make these decisions, security professionals refer to the concept of Least Privilege.

Least Privilege is the concept that people should not have access to information not required to achieve their job functions. Someone who was hired as a human resources representative most likely won't need access to sensitive research and development data. This individual needs access to employee records, corporate strategy, and benefits information, whereas someone in research and development does not. As a security professional, one of your concerns will be controlling access to critical information, ensuring that only authorized individuals with a real need have access.

Be aware that ensuring appropriate access may prove difficult to implement in some organizations. You may discover that employees have a sense of family, or a default culture of trust, especially in organizations that were once small businesses. For example, you may hear, "I don't mind if John has access to my research data; I trust him. This is Organization X, after all."

Most security professionals agree that a default policy of Deny All/Allow by Exception is most effective for protecting information resources. This type of policy restricts all access to information and network traffic by default. Access to specific information resources is granted by exception to this policy and is based on the needs of the organization. These exceptions are granted only to those whose job duties require the access. The decision regarding who should have access to each information type is made by the upper management of the organization and typically is defined within corporate policies.

Dealing with the CIA

Another core value of information security is protecting information from a variety of basic compromises. These include protecting the *confidentiality*, *integrity*, and *availability* of the organization's information assets. These three items are collectively referred to as *CIA*.

Confidentiality sets the goal of protecting information from unauthorized disclosure or viewing. You want to ensure that only those individuals who need to see particular information will be capable of viewing that information. The security mechanisms and policies that you put into place should address the need to maintain confidentiality of critical information. Unauthorized disclosure of information could result in a number of negative results for the organization, including fines, loss of sensitive research and development, loss of customer confidence, or loss of strategic advantage.

Integrity sets the goal of ensuring that critical information cannot be modified by unauthorized processes or individuals. Bear in mind that this modification could be intentional or unintentional, or based internally or externally. The security process and policies put into place should protect the organization's information from intentional or accidental modification. Such modification could result in poor corporate decisions, loss of financial control, changes to customer information, or a failure to respond appropriately to organizational issues as they arise. Imagine if your bank lost the integrity of your bank accounts, resulting in a large number of bounced checks and fines.

Availability addresses the need for critical information types to be available at exactly the moment you need access to that information. There will always be pieces of information within any organization that are more important to the organizational mission than other information. Based on the importance of the information, you need to understand what information needs immediate availability and which pieces can withstand a slight delay in access. For example, a hospital that prides itself on saving lives will need to access patient information quickly, whereas a slight delay in the availability of billing information may be acceptable. The patient information provides data about blood type, allergies, known medical conditions, and medications the patient may be taking. If a patient becomes ill, the hospital will need this data to help the patient. The billing information does not need to be immediately available to save a patient's life.

Additional Core Values

You need to be familiar with two additional core values. The first is composed of two related concepts: identification and authorization. Identification ensures that you know without a doubt who is accessing your information resources, and authorization allows people access to only those pieces of information to which they need access. To some extent, you use Least Privilege to achieve these goals. The end result is that you, as the security professional, must help ensure that you can identify who is trying to access corporate information and control what information they access.

The other addition is nonrepudiation. By enforcing nonrepudiation, you ensure that individuals within the organization are accountable for their actions and cannot deny involvement at a later date. This particular aspect of information security will likely be more important in some organizations than it will be in others. For example, a hospital will want to ensure that when a prescription is made under a doctor's name, the signature was indeed placed by that doctor. Sarbanes-Oxley, which is discussed in Chapter 4, is also concerned with ensuring nonrepudiation. For example, executives with publicly traded corporations can no longer deny knowledge of decisions made by the organization that may impact investors or the financial state of the company, as long as mechanisms of nonrepudiation have been put into place.

Basic Concepts

Up to this point in the chapter, we've covered the core values of information security. In this section, we cover some basic concepts of information security that will help you make decisions about how to implement the appropriate security mechanisms within your organizations. We want you to walk away with an understanding that security has to be addressed at a variety of levels in order to provide a layered defense. If a compromise occurs at one level within the organization, mechanisms will still be in place at other levels to stop a compromise of sensitive information.

Defense in Depth

We look at this concept from two perspectives. First, we look at a higher-level view of layered security, also called Defense in Depth (DiD). DiD is a standard methodology that addresses security from three perspectives: management, technical, and operational. The National Security Agency specifically uses the categories of people, technology, and operations. For our purposes, "people" is equivalent to "management." The National Institute of Standards and Technology also uses the management, technical, and operational categories when considering security controls.

Security controls should be considered with respect to these three areas to ensure that an organization has full coverage for its security program. A hole in one of these areas should be compensated by controls in one of the other two areas. For example, if the virus protection at the firewall fails to stop a virus from propagating across the organization via e-mail, the users should be trained to avoid double-clicking foreign attachments or opening potentially malicious documents. This security training should be based on corporate security policies that identify the dangers to the organization and lay out procedures for dealing with those dangers. We take a brief look at each of these three areas.

People can make the difference between a mildly secure and a highly secure organization. Where technical and operational controls fail, people should be trained to step up and respond appropriately. Much of the reliance on human response that we work toward is based on management decisions regarding policies and procedures. In organizations in which the management doesn't adequately support the security process, the people in the organization will have less guidance and training. Management support in the security process is vitally important to ensuring that the security program is successful.

Technology has come to be wrongly viewed as somewhat of a "fix-all" for organizations looking to become more secure. Vendors don't help when they introduce their products as the key to good security. However, the impact of technology on an organization's security policy depends more on the requirements of the organization than on the quality of the product. As an example, buying the best new intrusion detection appliance isn't likely to help in an organization in which the people don't know how to interpret the results or may lack the resources to respond appropriately. Technology must meet the needs of the organization. You wouldn't buy a shoe that was several sizes too large just because it's the "hot new thing"! The same concept applies to security purchases.

The other thing to understand about technology is that it's created by humans, and humans make mistakes. It's one of the things we're best at. So, because they're created by humans, even security products have inherent vulnerabilities. There is no such thing as a silver bullet. It's important to understand this and be prepared to manage your technology.

The operational aspect of DiD concerns those security processes that ensure our continued ability to conduct business in a secure manner. How is information secured during transmission, storage, and processing on the network? How do users and customers interact with the systems and the data? The operational aspect encompasses a broad variety of areas that include enforcing security policies and ensuring that systems meet required security guidelines. Operational concerns may seem vague at first, but they encompass a plethora of areas important to organizations. Disaster recovery and business continuity are two very important areas that fall within this aspect of DiD. Responding to suspected incidents or intrusions also falls into this area.

Layered Defense

At the core of any organization is a certain amount of data, or information, used to conduct business or meet mission objectives. That information needs to be protected through the use of multiple security mechanisms. The key concept here is that if an attacker compromises one security mechanism that was in place during the attack, other mechanisms should step up to deny further access, alert the organization of the intrusion, or both. This is known as a layered defense.

As an example of this concept, consider Figure 3-1. At the center, you can see the critical information the organization is trying to protect. Each security mechanism you implement around the information provides another level of protection through which an attacker must pass to compromise that information. The more layers you have, the better protected your information is, in theory.

Bear in mind that a layer is only as useful as the quality of its implementation. For instance, if you were to use a poorly configured firewall to protect the network perimeter around your information, that firewall would provide a much weaker boundary through which the attacker must pass. A more securely configured firewall has a better chance of stopping an intruder. This concept is true with all security mechanisms or products you implement. But as you consider these layers, please remember that even security products have vulnerabilities associated with them.

The outermost ring around the information in Figure 3-1 is the router. Since the router was first introduced, professionals have viewed it as a vital component to the networking function. Over the last 10 years, however, the role of the router has expanded dramatically and now provides the first line of defense. The access control lists (ACLs) implemented on routers can provide approval or denial of network traffic traversing into or out of a network.

Firewalls provide the second outermost ring. Firewalls can be hardware or software based, but the basic premise is the same: control traffic at a more granular level. These devices allow you to control not only network address filters but also protocol filters. Organizations can now allow certain computers in or out of the network based on what protocol or host they are attempting to reach.

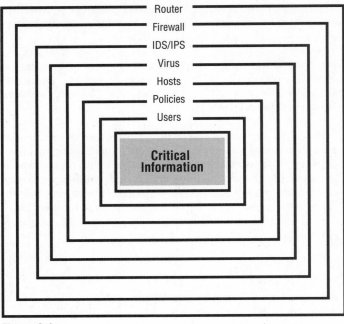

Router
Firewall
IDS/IPS
Virus
Hosts
Policies
Users

Critical Information

Figure 3-1

Intrusion detection systems (IDSs) and intrusion prevention systems (IPSs) are the next layer, providing a mechanism for administrators and security professionals to monitor attempts to bypass the defenses they have put into place. A huge number of these products are cropping up on the market, but the key is that an IDS passively monitors traffic and simply alerts, and logs, when it detects nefarious traffic. An IPS, on the other hand, provides this same capability, along with the added bonus of actively stopping the offending traffic.

We've included virus protection as the next layer because it operates on both a network level and host level. Border firewalls and other security devices now have the ability to scan for viruses in incoming and outgoing e-mails and file exchanges. Host-based virus detection provides this same protection on the various computers in the organization. With the huge numbers of servers and workstations that have been plagued by virus attacks over the last 10 years, this layer is considered a normal cost of doing business at most companies.

The secure configuration of the hosts and servers on the network provides the next layer of defense in our example. Disabling services that aren't required and ensuring that applications are patched appropriately are big pieces of this layer. This layer could also include local host-based firewalls or intrusion-detection mechanisms.

Policies are the second innermost ring in our defense example. In contrast to the previous layers we've discussed, this one is not technical in nature. Instead, security policies define what the security goals and objectives of the organization are at the current time. These goals mostly relate directly to the mission of the organization and how it conducts its business. These documents include such items as Incident Response Procedures, Security Policy, Acceptable Use Policy, and Configuration Management documents, just to name a few. The documents in question should be endorsed and supported by the upper management within the organization; otherwise, they aren't worth the paper they're printed on.

Users are the innermost layer because they provide the absolute last layer of defense within your organization. In case all other layers fail, an organization needs to depend on knowledgeable and ethical users to protect the critical information. To do this, the users must be informed and trained concerning the security policies and how the loss of critical information could impact the organization. Education is key here. This layer also relies quite heavily on hiring the correct personnel through the use of background checks.

Remember that the defense processes you put into place within your organization should be based on your needs. Some organizations may need fewer layers, whereas others may require many more layers. Use what you need based on the value of the information and the threats to that information.

Managing Risk

Regardless of how many layers you have protecting your organization, you need to know that those layers are implemented to manage the variety of attack vectors that intruders might use to access your critical information. Understanding the threats to your organization and the attack vector that those threats might use is crucial if you want a clear understanding of the total risk to your organization.

Risk can be defined as your exposure to potential loss or harm. For example, in the business world, this relates back to those things within your organization that make you money. Every organization needs to be aware of its potential risk and how to make effective decisions to address those risks.

We need to clarify something right now: *Risk* is not the same as *threat*. Risk has three components: *threat*, *impact* (value of the asset), and *vulnerability* (see Figure 3-2). If one of these three components is missing, risk does not exist. To provide a better understanding, we look at each of these in detail.

Figure 3-2

Threat

Threat can be defined as the knowledge that someone or something intends to cause you harm or damage your assets. The threat can be something clear-cut, such as a hacker trying to get at your customer's credit card information, or something more obscure, such as a foreign intelligence agency attempting to gain access to classified information. Threats are different to each organization and can be determined based on the organization's mission, the information it uses, and the industry within which it operates. For example, a travel agency most likely does not consider foreign intelligence to be a threat. In contrast, the agency is likely to be very concerned with having its online reservation Web site taken down or defaced by a malicious hacker.

Impact

The impact of an attack on an organization is directly related to the value of the assets being attacked. For this reason, the term *impact* is often used interchangeably with the phrase *value of the asset*. If an attacker gains access to public information, the impact on your organization is not likely to be negative in nature. However, if an attacker gains access to proprietary research and development information on the newest product line, the organization will feel a direct negative impact.

Protection mechanisms should be considered in the context of the value of each asset. For instance, a company won't spend its entire security budget protecting public information. Instead, more resources will be spent to protect the sensitive research and development information. We discuss more on categorizing and classifying your information assets in a later section of this chapter.

Vulnerabilities

Vulnerabilities provide the ability for an organization to be affected in a negative manner. These vulnerabilities can be technical, programmatic, or human in nature. Regardless of the type of vulnerability, they still provide a means for compromising an organization and should be addressed.

Vulnerabilities can be eliminated, mitigated, or accepted. You cannot eliminate all vulnerabilities in an organization. If you could, then you could reach that goal of 100 percent security. Some vulnerabilities need to be mitigated, which means that an organization will find other means to protect the asset from compromise because the removal of the vulnerability is either impossible or would have a detrimental effect on how the organization conducts business. In some cases, mitigating the vulnerability may not be worth the required resources — if, for example, the information were public in nature. In such cases, the organization may decide to simply accept the vulnerability.

Limiting Risk

If you consider risk in the context of a triangle, as shown previously in Figure 3-2, you can more effectively demonstrate the change to an organization's risk by addressing vulnerabilities. Note that the ability of an organization to limit the threats to its organization or to change the value of its assets is very limited. Any organization has the best opportunity to reduce risk by removing existing vulnerabilities. It's still important to understand the threats to your organization; otherwise, you're running in the dark. And if you never take the time to understand the actual value of your information assets, you'll never truly know what the impact would be on your organization if an attacker succeeded in compromising those assets. It's critically important to understand all aspects of risk, but you should also know that vulnerabilities are typically the easiest, if not the only, aspect that can be directly affected by your actions. Figure 3-3 provides an example of this effect.

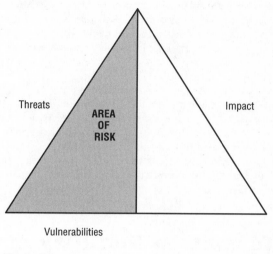

Figure 3-3

Data Classification and Labeling

Not all types of information within an organization are the same. Some pieces of information simply have a more dramatic impact on business operations than others. For instance, in a company that provides medical care to patients, the medical records are likely more important to conducting daily operations than is the human resource information maintained about current employees. Although both types of information have an obvious degree of importance to the organization, they are not equal. The following sections discuss recommended ways for differentiating and identifying the importance of various information types.

Data Classification

Data classification allows organizations to clearly define the importance of information types to the organization. Based on those classifications, an organization can determine the appropriate level of protection for each information type. Using our previous example of a medical care facility, the organization will likely decide that more stringent security mechanisms need to be in place for the patient medical records than for the human resource information. From a budgeting perspective, this approach aids organizations in planning for annual security budgets and security purchases. From an operational perspective, it allows the organization to create procedures for labeling pieces of information, based on their classification, and procedures for handling those various classifications of information.

Data Labeling

Although similar to data classification, data labeling actually uses your defined differences between information types to communicate to employees how important the information is and how they should protect it. For instance, a common classification structure used in the military includes designations such as For Official Use Only, Confidential, Secret, and Top Secret. But classifications are specific to the industry or organization. As an example, in a more commercial setting, the military classifications we just showed won't be such a good fit. A commercial business might choose classification levels as simple as Public, Sensitive, and Confidential.

The key to creating these classifications is the simultaneous creation of handling procedures for each classification level. For the Public classification, the organization might create handling procedures that state "Information marked at the Public classification level is considered to have very little negative impact on our organization if disclosed. Information at this classification level may be stored in normal, unlocked file cabinets." An example of the Sensitive classification is, "Information marked at the Sensitive classification has been determined to potentially have a detrimental effect on the organization if disclosed to unauthorized individuals, modified, or destroyed. This information should be stored in locked file cabinets when not in use and kept under strict control when in use."

Ethics in Information Security

There are some industries for which the public sets a higher standard for ethical behavior. Information Security is one of those industries. In much the same way that your local police are held to a higher standard because they make decisions affecting the welfare of the local public, information security professionals are responsible for ensuring the protection of not only their organization but also their organization's customers. To be cliché, the buck stops here.

As evidence of this, consider most of the world's current security certifications. Institutions such as ISC(2) and ISSA have implemented ethics clauses for individuals wishing to be members or hold their certifications. Having such clauses is a result, in large part, of the access that security workers have to the organization and its informational assets. The last thing the organization needs is for you, a trusted individual, to be pilfering information or working against the organization in the background.

The following sections cover some basics of your ethical obligations. We can't possibly cover every contingency here, so use your judgment to do what's correct in each situation. Whether you're in this industry for the money or you enjoy the work, or both, the responsibilities are the same.

The Hack Back

One of the biggest issues to come up, time and again, is the desire to strike back against targets that may be attacking your organization. It's frustrating to see your organization targeted by someone you don't even know, for reasons you don't understand. For example, a remote site in a foreign country starts running brute force attacks against your Secure Shell (SSH) service in an attempt to get into the computer. These attacks show up in your audit logs as repeated failed logins from the same IP address. You've reported these types of incidents to the attacker's service provider and to law enforcement before, but it never seems to do any good, does it?

Now, let's assume that you're pretty smart in the technical department, so you decide to create a script that monitors for the log entries that provide evidence of these attacks. When an attack is detected, the script starts a scan of the remote target, looking for potential vulnerabilities and then feeding that information into Metasploit's command-line feature to allow an automatic remote compromise. What are the ethical concerns here? Bear in mind that you're supposed to be one of the good guys, which, by definition, says that you need to act ethically and correctly.

Reacting to an Incident

How you react to an incident defines how mature you are as a security professional. Such professionals cannot, and do not, guarantee 100 percent security. There may be cracks in your armor that you have yet to discover. Therefore, the occasional compromise may slip through and disrupt your organization. The amount of disruption, however, is totally dependent upon how prepared you are for the incident and how you handle the situation.

Always be prepared for an incident. Know the handling procedures. Do you unplug the network cable or turn off the compromised host? Are these procedures defined and documented? The manner in which you handle these situations could prove to be a valuable lessen to the organization and stop further compromise of informational assets.

Communication and Knowledge Transfer

A less frequently considered, but equally important, ethical dilemma is that of communication with the other employees in the organization. How many security workers have you found who were anti-social and preferred not to deal with other people? The truth is that you have a responsibility to share your expertise with the rest of the organization — to train and communicate with your managers and co-workers.

Managers

Communicating effectively with your managers and corporate leadership could be the difference between an effective security program and an ineffective one. The leadership of most corporate organizations think in financial terms: How much revenue are we projected to make this quarter? What are our obligations? What is the shareholder percentage? That's their job — to manage the firm and help ensure its success.

From their perspective, you work with the technical details required to keep the organization operational and secure. You speak a different language. And although your managers may respect you highly for this work, they still may have difficulty speaking your language.

Remember from earlier in the chapter that one of your primary job responsibilities is to be a linguist? A good majority of upper management gets paid to work in a finance-centered world, whereas you are paid to work with the technology. To help management understand the importance of information security to the organization and the potential impact of not addressing it adequately, you need to learn to communicate with managers in a language that they can understand. Now, with that said, every manager is different. You may have better luck communicating with one person than you do with others. But if you take the technical information you have and apply that to the risk diagrams we introduced earlier in the chapter, you will have a decent chance at success.

Also, be involved. Ask your managers for feedback into your process, and ensure that you're providing them with equally useful feedback. Stay involved in the configuration management processes and be prepared to provide guidance on the security policies. Be interested in the well-being of the organization, and management will be more likely to hear you when you provide input and guidance.

Users

Users are the keystone in any organization. They ensure the success of the organization by caring about their work and the customer. Additionally, they can ensure the security of the organization by paying attention to those actions within their everyday job roles that affect how information is handled.

But similarly to managers, users aren't always hired to fill information security functions or roles. An organization can have a plethora of functional users who have nothing to do with information security specifically. For example, you may end up working with architects, accountants, human resource specialists, receptionists, graphics design artists, software developers, network engineers, marketing folks, and managers.

In most cases, you won't be able to communicate with these users using your normal, day-to-day technical jargon. You need to bring your conversation up to a level that they can work with. Now, don't get us wrong: you have no reason to be condescending and talk down to the users. But because information security may not be their specific job function, it's helpful if you can meet them halfway in the conversation.

Training

One of the most useful means for communicating with an organization's managers and users is through annual security awareness training. This training provides an opportunity for the workers to temporarily step away from their normal job duties and spend a little time learning how they directly affect information security within the organization. It also provides you with a chance to reiterate those security responsibilities that everyone might have that get lost in the day-to-day operations. The key points covered in the following sections apply to all workers within the organization.

Make It Pertinent

Training needs to pertain directly to the audience. It should answer the question, Why should I care? If you address the user audience with the finer points of firewall configuration, you should expect some droopy eyelids and light snores. If, however, you present users with information they can use, such as avoiding social engineering tactics, they're more likely to pay attention.

Make It Useful

Training should apply to a worker's daily life and be fairly simple to implement. For example, in a military environment in which the work is all classified, you'll likely want to remind users to safeguard that classified information by being sure not leave it out on desks, locking it in approved containers when not in use, and avoiding conversations about classified information in nonsecure areas or with people who don't need to know the information.

Explain the Importance

Users are notoriously stubborn sometimes about adhering to new security rules or policies. Maybe they don't like someone changing the way they've always done their jobs. Perhaps the new security rules impact their ability to do something they like doing, such as instant messaging or surfing sports Web pages. Regardless of the reasons you encounter, there's only one way to overcome this issue and that's to explain, quite clearly, what could happen to the organization, and the user, if these policies are ignored.

For instance, if the user shows concern about the well-being of the organization as a whole, you might want to explain how small pieces of seemingly unimportant information can be gathered through social engineering and put together to form a clearer and more dangerous picture of the organization. You could even provide cues or evidence for the users to keep in mind when dealing with potentially untrusted individuals.

Train Annually

Training is great for reminding the general work population of the importance of information security. But as they go back to their normal jobs, that training will eventually fade into a dim memory locked deep within their minds. Annual training helps refocus the organization and provide a realignment with the corporate security vision.

Also, keep in mind that you can train your users without using a classroom! Putting up posters and reminders around the office place is a great way to keep users aware of their security responsibilities.

Documentation

Documentation is a great way to communicate with the employees about the views of the organization regarding information security. Documents such as the Security Policy, Acceptable Use Policy, training documents, configuration management guidelines, Business Continuity documents, and Incident Response documents provide a solid resource for users, managers, and yourself when questions arise.

Documentation Cooperation

Documentation cannot and should not be created in a vacuum. It's a joint effort requiring work on the part of the security professional, the management, and the organization's users. In order for the documents to be applicable and useful, all these groups should be involved in the creation and maintenance of these documents during their lifetime.

Managers have perspectives that are relevant to the documents. Their views on what functions within the organization have the greatest impact on the mission provide a focus and prioritization. The users who work to accomplish those functions will know what information, specifically, is required to meet their job functions and what happens if they lose that information. The security professional brings a more security-specific view and can provide input on attack trends in the current world and how to best protect the organization and its resources.

Documentation Isolation

Security professionals know that they need a team involved in the creation and maintenance of the documentation, but they have to take other policies, laws, and regulations into account as well. For example, if your organization does business online using a common merchant account, you likely have obligations to Visa or Mastercard to protect customer information that is being collected and transmitted. If you work in the medical field in the United States, you need to take the requirements in the federal HIPAA guidelines into account. Chapter 4 discusses international and federal security requirements in greater detail.

Documentation Enforcement

Creating good documentation is only half the battle. The other piece is getting people to read and adhere to it. Fortunately, if you create the training program mentioned earlier in this chapter, you'll have a mechanism to keep the users adequately informed about their responsibilities from a security perspective.

But keeping users informed and ensuring that they're adhering to the documents aren't the same. Upper management has to be willing to enforce the documentation, making it standard operating procedure within the organization. By showing their support of the policies, managers make them a priority with all users within the organization.

Daily Security Responsibilities

Security work is a continuous and daily process. You can't just install a firewall or an intrusion-detection system and say that you're suddenly secure. In some cases, you'll be lucky to enter an organization that already has a relatively mature security program. In these cases, most of the items discussed in the following sections will already be implemented and your job will be easier to manage.

In other cases, you may find yourself hired into an organization that has not had a security program in the past. In this case, you'll have the opportunity to build the program from the ground up. Although this might sound like more work, and a potentially bigger hassle, you may find it easier creating everything from scratch and ensuring that it's all done correctly. But let's look at some of the items you'll need to understand.

Patches and Hot Fixes

Both operating systems and applications have a single huge flaw: They are written by human beings. Because of that, they have bugs and security issues. Vendors release patches or hot fixes on a periodic basis to address security concerns that may have arisen since the last patch came out. To keep an organization secure, you need to ensure that these software patches are applied in a timely manner.

One important item to note here: Test your patches in a test environment before you implement them in production systems. In some cases, patches have caused more harm than good because of unexpected issues.

Backup and Restore

At this point, you're already aware that each organization has certain information it needs to accomplish its mission. Whether it pertains to customer credit cards or military strategy, that information is critical to the organization and must be protected. And because computer systems have been know to crash and hurricanes have been known to take out entire city blocks, you'll probably want to back all that information up to mobile media and store it elsewhere for safekeeping.

Backing up information is typically done in several ways, mostly automated. A *full* backup takes everything and backs it all up at one time. It takes longer and consumes more media space, but it backs up all the data. Full backups are done about once a week, on average.

Partial backups are done in between full backups, but not all the time. They're intended to ensure that a complete application or source tree is backed up more often than the full backups are run.

Incremental backups are run most days, in between the full backups. They include only those files that have changed since the last backup. These types of backups are short and consume much less media. But in most cases, they won't be enough to recover from a disaster.

But backing up your critical data is not enough. Testing backups by doing restores of sample data is very important. Test every tape and test every week. Ensure that all the information is still accessible. If you're not paying close attention to the backup software, you may never even notice that it's erroring out until it's too late. By doing periodic test restores, you can verify that the backups, and the media itself, are still valid.

Virus Protection

Virus protection helps protect the organization from malicious code by blocking harmful code either at the perimeter or on the host machine, where the user works. Unfortunately, too many users install virus protection and never update the signatures to reflect new threats. An outdated virus application is nearly as harmful as having no virus protection at all. As the security administrator, your responsibility is to ensure that the virus protection system is active and updated.

Perimeter Security

Defining the rules that protect the organization's Internet face is a huge responsibility and should not be taken lightly. It's best to implement a *deny all* type of rule set, through which you can allow traffic on a case-by-case basis. This type of system ensures that you always know what is allowed through the firewall or router, versus having some traffic slip through the cracks. Perimeter defenses exist on the router, firewall, switches, and intrusion-detection devices.

Summary

This chapter guided you through the basics a security professional should understand when interviewing for a job. From core values such as confidentiality, integrity, and availability to more specific concepts such as Least Privilege and data classification, we've covered a lot of material.

In your job, you will have a direct impact on how securely your organization conducts its business and whether customer information remains safe and secure. Keep in mind that information should be controlled based on the need for confidentiality, integrity, and availablility, or CIA. Also remember that, depending on your industry, you may need to gauge your security mechanisms against other topic areas, such as *nonrepudiation* and *authorization*.

Access control is the foundation for controlling who can view, edit, modify, or delete information within your organization. The best course of action in most cases is for you to use a system of *Least Privilege*. Using Least Privilege allows you to control access to information based on what users need to meet their job requirements.

Defense in depth means that information security should be addressed at three levels: *management, technical,* and *operations*. You need appropriate policies and management buy-in for the security process. You also need the correct technical tools and mechanisms that make sense for your organization based on your mission, and security mechanisms that keep the operations running smoothly.

At the center of the organization lies the information that keeps the mission alive. Security professionals build defenses in layers around this information to keep it safe and to augment any other security layers that may break down during a compromise attempt. This concept is called a *layered defense*. The number of layers you implement at your organization will depend on your needs and on how critical the information you're protecting is.

Along with these more obvious responsibilities, you have the responsibility of being ethical in your everyday actions. From your communications with the users and managers around you to your understanding of the correct line of action in each situation, the way you respond defines who you are as a professional.

Finally, at the core of your role as a security professional, you have a number of daily job duties that directly impact the security of the organization. These include virus protection, patches and updates, and backups.

Interview Q&A

Q: What is access control?

A: Access control provides the mechanism for ensuring that only authorized individuals can access organizational information. More stringent access control mechanisms are needed as the value of the information to the organization increases.

Q: What is Least Privilege?

A: Least Privilege states that users should have access only to exactly the information required to perform their job duties and nothing more.

Q: How do you define confidentiality?

A: Confidentiality basically means keeping private information private. You don't want outside competitors seeing your organization's work in research and development, and you don't want sensitive customer information being stolen and used for identity theft or fraud.

Q: What is integrity as it applies to information security?

A: Integrity is ensuring that information remains in the proper state while it's being used or stored. A loss of integrity occurs if information is modified in an unauthorized manner.

Q: What is availability?

A: Availability means that information is ready and waiting, right when you need to access it.

Q: How do you define risk?

A: Risk is a combination of threat, vulnerabilities, and impact to the organization (or value). Risk exists when all three of these elements are present simultaneously. For example, if an organization knows of a threat agent with a desire to steal its critical research information and a vulnerability exists that could allow that to happen, risk is present.

Q: What is the importance of classifying data?

A: Classifying data allows an organization to differentiate between routine information types and those types that have a critical impact on how it does business. Classifying also allows management to appropriately budget for the protection of varying information types, instead of protecting everything at the same level and wasting resources.

Q: How do you describe data labeling?

A: Data labeling is intended to aid with the identification of information. After information has been appropriately identified to users, steps can be taken to ensure the security of that information; such as storage and handling measures.

Recommended Reading

University of Wisconsin, Madison: Security Resource, `www.doit.wisc.edu/security/`.

University of Miami School of Medicine: Security Resource, `http://it.med.miami.edu/x904.xml`.

George Washington University: Data Classification Security Policy, `http://my.gwu.edu/files/policies/DataClassificationPolicy.pdf`.

Sun Corporation: Best Practices in Data Classification for Information Lifecycle Management, `www.sun.com` (search "Best Practices Data Classification").

National. Institute of Standards and Technology: Least Privilege Security Resource, `http://hissa.nist.gov/rbac/paper/node5.html`.

National Institute of Standards and Technology: Separation of Duties, `http://hissa.nist.gov/rbac/paper/node6.html`.

WindowsSecurity.com: Implementing Principle of Least Privilege, `www.windowsecurity.com` (search "Least Privilege").

University of California: Security Policy, `http://security.berkeley.edu/IT.sec.policy.html`.

SANS.org: InfoSec Acceptable Use Policy, `www.sans.org` (search "Acceptable Use Policy").

Carnegie-Mellon University: Handbook for Computer Security Incident Response Teams (CSIRTs), `www.sei.cmu.edu` (search: "Incident Response Handbook").

Understanding Regulations, Legislation, and Guidance

Your ability to impress the interviewing organization with your knowledge of relevant regulations, legislation, guidance, standards, policies, and procedures can greatly improve your chances of getting strong consideration for a position. When you are preparing for your interview, the research you do should turn up some very important information about the industry or primary functional areas that affect the organization or the customers it supports. This research specifically applies to what industry policies, procedures, legislation, and other guidance the organization will have concerns about. Depending on the position(s) you are interviewing for, being able to impress the interviewers with your knowledge of the areas about which they are concerned will help you improve your chances of getting the position.

With that end in mind, this chapter explains each of the following areas:

❑ **Regulation, legislation, and guidance definitions:** Provides a common understanding of the different types of requirements an organization is concerned about and why these things should matter to the organization's employees.

❑ **Government and DoD guidance:** Government entities face the need for compliance with multiple regulations, legislative requirements, and guidance. Understanding these needs will assist in developing a deeper understanding of the organization. Government guidance must be considered by federal, state, and local government entities, including military and law enforcement.

❑ **Commercial guidance:** Commercial industries also have to be concerned with regulations, legislation, and guidance. These requirements can come from industry regulators, federal requirements, state requirements, or international requirements.

Regulations, Legislation, and Guidance Defined

Different types of documentation serve different purposes. As the following list explains, some documentation is internally driven and some is externally driven. To prepare for the interview process for an information security position, you need to understand what types of internal security documentation the organization may have and what external security-related regulations the organization must comply with. Your understanding should include the differences between regulations, policy, procedures, legislation, and guidance, as follows:

❑ **Regulations:** Regulations are requirements that can come in many forms. They may be industry-specific regulations such as the Health Information Portability and Accountability Act (HIPAA), which addresses health care organizations. Regulations may also be wider in scope — for example, the Federal Information Security Management Act (FISMA). Regulations are basically the formal requirements that an organization must follow. Regulations can be either internally or externally generated, monitored, and enforced.

❑ **Policy:** Businesses create specific requirements that their employees and departments must adhere to. These requirements can include policies regarding the use of computers or the company's logo. The policy is basically a statement of what must be done. Policy is typically internally developed documentation but may be put in place to meet an external requirement, regulation, or legislation.

❑ **Procedures:** Procedures are generally put in place to show how to meet a policy. They are more detailed than policy statements. Procedures are typically internally developed documentation.

❑ **Legislation:** Legislation is an external directive that places specific requirements on a particular industry. It must be met in order for the business to be legally compliant. Legislation is put into place by the government. Legislation is typically an external driver, unless, of course, you are part of the government organization creating the legislation.

❑ **Guidance:** A set of recommendations or suggestions about things that should be considered when implementing security in the organization is referred to as guidance. Guidance is not a requirement but rather a suggestion and can originate internally or externally. For example, guidance might come as recommendations made by your manager or a senior member of your team, written up into an informal checklist or other document.

Why Does an Employer Care?

Employers are interested in compliance and guidance either because, as the following sections explain, they have to care or because they want to care. Honestly, the majority of organizations are interested in information security because they have to care. All organizations labor under the concept of "Due Diligence" or "Due Care." This concept, although not formally defined, is the concept of caring enough about the business, mission, or customers to implement at least a minimum set of security controls to protect mission-essential or sensitive information. Organizations that do not implement a level of "Due Diligence" or "Due Care" can be held accountable with or without formal regulations or legislation. This accountability typically occurs through lawsuits or loss of customers.

They Have to Care

Organizations must care about what regulations, legislation, and guidance they fall under. They are held directly responsible for the security of the information they deal with in support of their customers. In many cases, organizations will face fines or other sanctions if they violate certain rules associated with regulations, legislation, and guidance.

They Want to Care

Some organizations wish to implement good security programs, not because they have to but because they want to for the purpose of better supporting their internal or customers' needs. This idea comes down to *the right thing to do*. In many cases, this can be for competitive advantage or for market position.

Why Should You Care?

As someone looking for a position, you certainly want to impress the organization with your knowledge of the areas that affect and concern the organization. By showing a knowledge of and interest in the regulations and legislation affecting a company, you show that you have done your homework in preparation for the interview. You also show that you have the ability to gather knowledge and formulate solutions that will help the organization meet its needs internally as well as support its customers externally. Knowledge of the organization's specific regulations, legislation, and policies can set you apart from your competition and improve your chances of getting the position, or at least moving further along in the interview process.

> **A word of caution. Approach the interview with this information as a discussion point, but don't be convinced that you fully understand the organization or that other regulations and legislation might not be of a concern to the organization as well.**

There are so many regulations and legislation about which an organization may have to be concerned that some regulations may cross over into multiple industries. For example, an organization may have to deal with the Sarbanes-Oxley and Gramm-Leach-Bliley Acts, which may be fairly clear from your research. However, an organization may also have to deal with the Health Information Portability and Accountability Act (HIPAA) because of the customers it supports. This may not be clear from your research. So be prepared during the interview to be exposed to some new information. Besides, an interview is meant to be a two-way street: Your interviewers want to gather information about you, and you want to gather information about the organization. The following table represents a summary of the various standards and legislation to consider, depending on the area in which you are working. Please understand that this list is a representation of various standards and legislation, and does not necessarily represent all the possible standards that are in place today. Over time, the guiding legislation may change or be replaced by some new requirements. An example of this can be seen within the government, for which the DITSCAP certification and accreditation process is slowly being replaced by DIACAP.

Industry	Standards and Legislation
Federal Government (non-DoD)	FIPS 199, 200, FISMA, NIST 800 Series, OMB A130 Appendix III
Department of Defense and other National Security Systems	DoD 8500.1 & 8500.2, DCID 6/3, DITSCAP, DIACAP
All commercial industry	Industry-specific regulations; state-specific requirements and legislation
Health care	HIPAA, PCI
Financial institutions	GLBA, PCI
All publicly held organizations	Sarbanes-Oxley
Utilities	NERC, WISE
Education	FERPA, PCI
International	ISO 17799, ISO 27001, PCI

Now that you understand the basics, the remaining sections of the chapter cover in detail the specific information you need have well-prepared in this area for your interview.

Government- and DoD-Specific Information

Standards, regulations, and guidance play a critical role in the information security practices of government and Department of Defense (DoD) organizations. There are some overall federal government or DoD directives, but the military services (Army, Navy, Air Force, Marines) themselves have specific regulations.

United States Government Information Security

The Secretary of Commerce is assigned responsibility for defining standards and guidelines for the security of federal information systems, with the exception of national security systems. The Department of Defense (led by the National Security Agency) and the Director, Central Intelligence, are responsible for establishing standards and guidelines for national security systems.

In this section, we discuss standards and guidelines related to both national security systems and other federal information systems. Figure 4-1 represents a few of the different legislation and regulations that are considered as being part of a federal government agency.

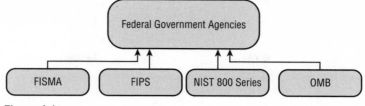

Figure 4-1

Non–National Security Systems

The following sections address the legislation, standards, and guidelines that govern non–national security systems under the responsibility of the Secretary of Commerce. The National Institute of Standards and Technology (NIST) is the agency within the Department of Commerce assigned the responsibility for managing the standards and guidelines associated with federal information and information system security.

Federal Information Security Management Act (FISMA) of 2002

FISMA is actual legislation passed by Congress as H.R. 2458-48. FISMA was passed primarily to force government organizations to implement security and remove loopholes organizations were using to waive the various standards, such as FIPS. In 2003, NIST started the FISMA Implementation Project to develop key security standards and guidelines that FISMA required. The required documentation includes FIPS 199, FIPS 200, and NIST Special Publications 800-53, 800-59, and 800-60. Additional documentation has been developed to support the overall FISMA implementation to include the other NIST 800 series documentation.

Part of the FISMA implementation is the FISMA scorecard. This scorecard rates an organization's current state of security against the FISMA requirements. Many government agencies are still struggling with the FISMA requirements even though as of this writing it has been nearly four years since it was passed in Congress.

Federal Information Processing Standards (FIPS)

NIST is responsible for the FIPS Publications, which you can find at `csrc.nist.gov` (Google "NIST FIPS site:csrc.nist.gov"). Two of the primary FIPS used are FIPS 199 and FIPS 200. The NIST Web site has additional FIPS that can be reviewed.

FIPS Publication 199 – Standards for Security Categorization of Federal Information and Information Systems

FISMA tasked NIST with the responsibility to develop a standard that would be used by all federal agencies to categorize all information and information systems in order to provide appropriate levels of security to the systems based on a risk level determination. FIPS199 provides this standard of categorization. The primary objective of providing categorization is to have a common framework that will ensure the effective management and oversight of federal government information security programs. The other objective is to provide consistent reporting of the adequacy and effectiveness of security policies, procedures, and practices to the Office of Management and Budget (OMB). FIPS 199 also attempts to provide coordination across civilian, national security, emergency preparedness, homeland security, and law enforcement communities.

FIPS 199 addresses the need for security based on confidentiality, integrity, and availability (CIA). It also addresses consideration of the impact to an organization based on the loss of confidentiality, integrity, or availability. FIPS 199 classifies the impact based on Low, Moderate, or High impact based on whether the loss has a limited, serious, or severe/catastrophic impact, respectively. FIPS 199 provides the baseline for the categorization process. However, it is a high-level publication, and other NIST publications help to define the application of FIPS 199, primarily NIST Special Publication 800-60.

FIPS Publication 200 – Minimum Security Requirements for Federal Information and Information Systems

FISMA directed NIST to develop a standard to address a minimum security requirement for federal information and information systems. FIPS 200 meets this requirement. The minimum security requirements established in FIPS 200 must be met by implementing controls as established in NIST Special Publication 800-53. Implementation of FIPS 200 requires that categorization be completed under FIPS 199. FIPS 200 defines 17 areas that must be addressed as part of the minimum security requirements. These areas are as follows:

❑ Access Control

❑ Awareness and Training

❑ Audit and Accountability

❑ Certification, Accreditation, and Security Assessments

❑ Configuration Management

❑ Contingency Planning

❑ Identification and Authentication

❑ Incident Response

❑ Maintenance

❑ Media Protection

❑ Physical and Environmental Protection

❑ Planning

❑ Personnel Security

❑ Risk Assessment

❑ System and Services Acquisition

❑ System and Communications Protection

❑ System and Information Integrity

You can find a description of each of these areas in the actual FIPS 200 document. We recommend familiarizing yourself with the definitions of these areas because the majority of them are applicable whether you are interviewing with a government or a commercial organization.

NIST 800 Series of Special Publications

NIST continues to develop and revise a series of special publications that address information security's many facets. As a part of the United States Department of Commerce, NIST has a broad reach to provide guidelines and requirements to federal government agencies. These special publications are developed by NIST but are made available for public comment to government and industry representatives to strengthen the special publications' applicability and accuracy across government and commercial organizations. You can find NIST documentation at csrc.nist.gov (Google "NIST 800 site:csrc.nist.gov"). To better understand these and other government documentation, you have to download the documents and look through them. The following sections provide a synopsis of some of the NIST documents with which you should be familiar; however, you can find other NIST Special Publications on the NIST Web site.

NIST SP 800-26 – Security Self Assessment Guide for Information Technology Systems

800-26 is a self-help guide for an organization to review its internal security. It also provides a good basis for collecting information in support of the overall certification and accreditation of the system. 800-26 has been revised to include direct references to the NIST SP 800-53 control requirements.

NIST SP 800-30 – Risk Management Guide for Information Technology Systems

800-30 was developed by NIST as key guidance for risk management within organizations, recognizing that organizations must use security as an enabler for accomplishing the organizational mission, not just to protect information technology assets. In the purpose section of NIST SP 800-30 (pg 1), risk and risk management are defined as follows:

Risk is the net negative impact of the exercise of a vulnerability, considering both the probability and the impact of occurrence. Risk management is the process of identifying risk, accessing risk, and taking steps to reduce risk to an acceptable level.

800-30 emphasizes that risk management is performed to allow organizations to accomplish their mission. By performing risk management activities, organizations can:

❑ Better secure their systems that process, transmit, and store organizational information

❑ Allow management to make informed risk management decisions

❑ Assist management in making decisions to allow systems to operate in their environment (accreditation)

NIST 800-30 provides a nine-step process that gives management the information they need to make risk based decisions. The steps are the following:

1. System Characterization
2. Threat Identification

3. Vulnerability Identification

4. Control Analysis

5. Likelihood Determination

6. Impact Analysis

7. Risk Determination

8. Control Recommendations

9. Results Documentation

NIST SP 800-30 is an excellent guide for understanding some of the basics of risk management, whether in government or commercial environments.

NIST SP 800-37 – Guide for the Security Certification and Accreditation of Federal Information Systems

800-37 provides federal government agencies with the necessary guidance to support the four phases of the certification and accreditation process. The four phases are as follows:

❑ Initiation Phase

❑ Security Certification Phase

❑ Security Accreditation Phase

❑ Continuous Monitoring Phase

Certification and accreditation existed before FISMA, but FISMA is the law that drove the development of 800-37. The federal government recognized the need for consistent processes to evaluate risks within federal government systems. NIST 800-37 is supported by other NIST publications to effectively implement the certification and accreditation process. These include 800-53, 800-53A, and 800-60.

NIST SP 800-53 – Recommended Security Controls for Federal Information Systems

NIST 800-53 defines the minimum security controls that need to be in place for a given federal government information system depending on the information system impact level (low, moderate, high). The four goals identified for 800-53 are the following:

❑ Provide a means for selecting and specifying security controls that is a consistent, comparable, and repeatable approach.

❑ Provide minimum security control recommendations categorized based on FIPS 199.

❑ Provide a security control catalog that is dynamic and extensible for today's dynamic environment.

❑ Create an assessment methodology and procedures that provide a foundation for control effectiveness.

NIST 800-53 breaks the security controls into three classes (management, operational, and technical) and 17 control families, with two-letter identifiers for tracking the controls through the entire process, as identified in the following table (taken from NIST SP 800-53, page 6).

Class	Family	Identifier
Management	Risk Assessment	RA
Management	Planning	PL
Management	System and Services Acquisition	SA
Management	Certification, Accreditation, and Security Assessments	CA
Operational	Personnel Security	PS
Operational	Physical and Environmental Protection	PE
Operational	Contingency Planning	CP
Operational	Configuration Management	CM
Operational	Maintenance	MA
Operational	System and Information Integrity	SI
Operational	Media Protection	MP
Operational	Incident Response	IR
Operational	Awareness and Training	AT
Technical	Identification and Authentication	IA
Technical	Access Control	AC
Technical	Audit and Accountability	AU
Technical	System and Communications Protection	SC

NIST SP 800-53A – Guide for Assessing the Security Controls in Federal Information Systems

NIST 800-53A is not yet in final form as of this writing; however, it is being implemented across several organizations in the federal government. The primary purpose of 800-53A is to provide the guidance for looking at the security controls that are defined in 800-53. 800-53A has four goals identified:

❑ Provide assessments of security controls that are more consistent, comparable, and repeatable.

❑ Provide assessments of security control effectiveness that are more cost effective.

❑ Promote a better understanding of the risks that impact operations, assets, or individuals.

❑ Provide decision makers with better information to make accreditation decisions.

NIST SP 800-53A has been designed to be used in support of NIST SP 800-37, Guide for the Security Certification and Accreditation of Federal Information Systems. 800-53A is a foundational document for examining a system for security risks and assuring that the appropriate mechanisms are in place to support the security of the system. As a guide, 800-53A identifies the assessment framework, the process for actually doing the assessment, and several templates for actually conducting the assessment based on the information system impact level (low, moderate, high). 800-53A is organized in direct support of the NIST 800-53 security controls including classes, families, and identifiers.

NIST SP 800-60 – Guide for Mapping Types of Information and Information Systems to Security Categories

FISMA requires federal government information systems to be categorized in order to determine the controls that must be in place to support the overall security of the system. 800-60 uses the FIPS 199 definitions, which include confidentiality, integrity, and availability. NIST 800-60 is intended to assist federal government agencies in mapping the security impact levels in a consistent manner based on the type of information and the information system's purpose (mission critical, mission support, administrative).

OMB Circular A130 – Appendix III: Security of Federal Automated Information Resources

A130 – Appendix III establishes the minimum security requirements that will be included with any general support system or major application used within the federal government. A130 was written before FISMA but is still referenced very heavily. The definitions set forth for general support system and major application are still recognized today. A130-Appendix III provides the following definitions:

General Support System. *"an interconnected set of information resources under the same direct management control which shares common functionality. A system normally includes hardware, software, information, data, applications, communications, and people. A system can be, for example, a local area network (LAN) including smart terminals that supports a branch office, an agency-wide backbone, a communications network, a departmental data processing center including its operating system and utilities, a tactical radio network, or a shared information processing service organization (IPSO)."*

Major Application. *"an application that requires special attention to security due to the risk and magnitude of the harm resulting from the loss, misuse, or unauthorized access to or modification of the information in the application."*

A130-Appendix III requires agencies with the federal government to ensure the following activities:

❑ **Plan** for security.

❑ **Ensure** appropriate assignment of security responsibilities.

❑ **Review** the security controls in the information systems.

❑ **Authorize** system processing before operations and then retest periodically.

Department of Defense and National Security Systems

DoD and National Security Systems fall under a different set of requirements in relation to applicable regulations. Figure 4-2 represents a subset of possible regulations that DoD and National Security Systems must consider.

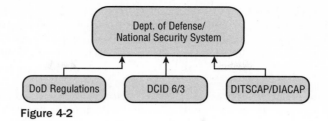

Figure 4-2

National Security Systems

A national security system is defined by 44 U.S.C. 3542(b)(2), which was established by FISMA, Title III, Public Law 107-347, December 17, 2002. The following criteria must be met for a system to be considered a national security system.

A national security system is any system or telecommunication system whose function, operation, or use

❑ Involves intelligence activities

❑ Involves cryptologic activities related to national security

❑ Involves command and control of military forces

❑ Involves equipment that is an integral part of a weapon or weapon system

❑ Is critical to the direct fulfillment of military or intelligence missions

❑ Is classified as established by executive order or act of Congress

It is important to note that the federal government does not allow for routine administration or business applications to be defined as national security systems. These include payroll, finance, logistics, or personnel management applications.

Security for national security systems is governed by Department of Defense requirements, Central Intelligence Agency requirements, and military service–specific requirements (Army, Navy, Air Force, Marines).

Director of Central Intelligence Directives (DCID) 6/3 –
Protecting Sensitive Compartmented Information within Information Systems

DCID 6/3 provides the requirements established by the Director of Central Intelligence for protecting certain types of intelligence information on any information system. In this directive, the Director of Central Intelligence is requiring all departments of the United States government, its contractors, and any allied governments processing intelligence information to follow the measures established in DCID 6/3.

DCID 6/3 establishes responsibilities of the many agencies and organizations that are involved with intelligence systems. These organizations include the Central Intelligence Agency, National Security Agency (NSA), National Reconnaissance Organization (NRO), Defense Intelligence Agency (DIA), and the remainder of the intelligence community. Because intelligence information can be processed on systems not owned by an intelligence agency, the actual responsibilities depend on the information and information system owners, as well as the types of intelligence information being processed. This also includes information and information systems on contractor locations or under contractor control. DCID 6/3 is concerned with protecting the confidentiality, integrity, and availability of this intelligence data.

DCID 6/3 provides the means to assure that systems containing intelligence data meet the minimum requirements of protection based ultimately on a formal certification and accreditation based on the DCID 6/3. The process identified within the DCID 6/3 includes the following:

❑ **Determine Level-of-Concern:** Three possible levels of concern are associated with confidentiality, integrity, and availability: Basic, Medium, and High. The higher the level of concern, the greater the requirement for protection.

❑ **Determine Protection Level (applies only to confidentiality):** Five protection levels are defined by DCID 6/3 for confidentiality. The higher the protection level, the greater the requirement for security measures and documentation to be implemented.

❑ **Determine Security Features and Assurances:** Using the level of concern and protection level, the necessary security features are to be implemented to assure appropriate levels of protection.

DCID 6/3 also establishes an entire group of Administrative Security Controls in addition to the security controls identified as part of the levels of concern and protection levels. These include the following:

❑ Security Education, Training, and Awareness

❑ Marking and Labeling

❑ Manual Review of Human Readable Output

❑ Media Accountability

❑ Media Clearing and Sanitization

❑ Co-Location

❑ Incident Reporting and Response

❑ Maintenance

❑ Records Management

❑ Communications Security

❑ Protected Hardware, Software, and Firmware

❑ EMSEC and TEMPEST

❑ Technical Surveillance Countermeasures

❑ Physical Security

❑ Personnel Security

- ❏ Access by Foreign Nationals
- ❏ Handling Caveats and Restrictions

The DCID also establishes the formal requirements for Risk Management, Certification, and Accreditation throughout the entire system life cycle. You can find a copy of DCID at `www.fas.org` (Google "DCID 6/3 site:fas.org").

Department of Defense Directive 8500.1

DoD 8500.1 was created by the Department of Defense as a directive that establishes the policy for information assurance within the Department of Defense. This directive implements a defense-in-depth approach that includes considerations for personnel, operations, and technology. DoD 8500.1 applies to all DoD-owned or controlled information systems. This directive does not supersede any requirements established for Sensitive Compartmented Information (SCI) and special assess programs, which are controlled by the policies of the Director of Central Intelligence. The directive establishes the Assistant Secretary of Defense for Command, Control, Communications, and Intelligence as the DoD, Chief Information Officer. This is a significant responsibility to ensure the information assurance functions are addressed within the DoD environment. The directive also addresses the requirement for maintaining appropriate levels of security for confidentiality, integrity, availability, nonrepudiation, and authentication within DoD systems. You can find a copy of DoD 8500.1 at the Defense Technical Information Center (DTIC) Web site, `www.dtic.mil` (search "8500.1").

Department of Defense Instruction 8500.2

DoD 8500.2 is the instruction that implements DoD 8500.1. This instruction provides greater detail on the roles and responsibilities of the various organizations within DoD. DoD 8500.2 covers a broad range of subjects to include organizational component requirements, application security, enclaves, outsourcing, and interconnections. The instruction also establishes the clearance requirements for individuals needing to work in the DoD environment. The instruction also establishes that a certification and accreditation is required for a system to operate in the DoD environment. DoD 8500.2 establishes eight IA Control Subject Areas. Each of these IA Control Subject Areas has specific controls associated with them. The IA Control Subject Areas are the following:

- ❏ Security Design and Configuration
- ❏ Identification and Authentication
- ❏ Enclave and Computing Environment
- ❏ Enclave Boundary Defense
- ❏ Physical and Environmental
- ❏ Personnel
- ❏ Continuity
- ❏ Vulnerability and Incident Management

You can find a copy of DoD 8500.2 at the Defense Technical Information Center (DTIC) at `www.dtic.mil` (search "8500.2").

Commercial Information Security

Commercial industries have their own sets of information security challenges that they must deal with to meet the requirements set forth by federal and state governments or industry-specific regulations. Depending on the industry, specific standards may exist. Where an industry specific regulation does not exist, the organization may be affected by other federal or state laws and regulations. When you are preparing to interview with an organization, it is essential to research the organization to understand what standards and legislation affect them. Figure 4-3 represents some of the legislation and regulations that commercial and public companies need to consider concerning information security requirements.

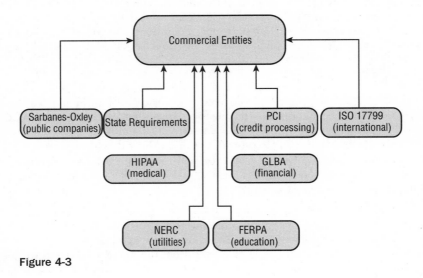

Figure 4-3

State-Specific Cyber Security Laws

According to the Cyber Security Industry Alliance, 34 states have passed cyber security laws, but the majority of the legislation has been focused on notification of consumers if their information has been compromised, instead of on prevention. Sixteen states have passed laws that specifically make phishing attacks illegal. Some industry experts and politicians argue that having so many state laws will create confusion and nonstandard application of the laws, and they recommend that a national cyber security law be enacted. A national cyber security law is being discussed in Congress as of this writing.

California Cyber Security Laws

California often is a leader in legislation related to interests of the people. Cyber security is no exception, and California has passed at least three specific bills related to cyber security. In many cases, California law is then used as a foundation by other states for building their cyber security laws. The California laws include the following:

❑ **SB 1386 – California Security Breach Information Act:** SB 1386 is an identity theft prevention act that requires organizations maintaining individuals' personal information to notify those individuals if the information is compromised, allowing them to take action to help stop identity theft from occurring.

- ❑ **SB 355 – California Anti-Phishing Act of 2005:** SB 355 explicitly states it is unlawful for any person to "solicit, request, or take any action to induce another person, through electronic means, to provide identifying information by representing itself to be a business without the approval or authority of the business."

- ❑ **AB 1950:** California Assembly Bill 1950, passed in 2005, requires organizations that own or license personal information about Californians to implement reasonable security measures to protect that information. AB 1950 points to national standards such as HIPAA and GLBA for guidance on what is considered reasonable security.

National Infrastructure Protection

Originally established as Presidential Decision Directive (PDD) 63 under President Clinton, the concept of requiring the protection of the critical functions that keep the United States operational has now been rolled into Homeland Security Presidential Directive (HSPD) 7. Critical infrastructure includes food supplies, water supplies, power, public health, national defense, national icons, and national financial stability. Each of these areas has its own sets of industry or legislative requirements that drive security within its environment.

Health Care

The health care industry has many challenges in relation to protecting the confidentiality of information for patients. Historically, health care professionals have been in the position of wanting to or needing to share information about patients to potentially provide better care. But the health care industry has a moral and legal obligation to protect private information of the consumers of health care services.

Health Insurance Portability and Accountability Act (HIPAA)

Passed by Congress in 1996, HIPAA was designed to address needs within the health care industry to improve efficiency and effectiveness of health care transaction processing and protection of privacy information. HIPAA ended up with three primary rules: the transaction rule, the privacy rule, and the security rule. HIPAA applies to any health plan, a health care clearinghouse, or any health care provider that transmits any health information. You can find more information on HIPAA at www.hhs.gov (search "HIPAA"). HIPAA is managed by the United States Department of Health and Human Services.

The transaction rule is of least interest to the security professional as it establishes standardization and common code sets for the processing of health transactions. This standardization assists the health care industry in preventing errors and also helps to reduce fraud in health care transactions.

The privacy rule focuses on protecting individually identifiable health information from improper use and allows some use of the information. The primary premise of the privacy rule is to implement reasonable safeguards of the information and minimum necessary standards for primary use and disclosure. This rule focuses on the control and proper use of the health information and patient rights as opposed to the actual security protections that are associated with the security rule. The privacy rule does give covered entities some flexibility in determining what is reasonable to implement based on their operation and size considerations. In some cases, "required" does not necessarily mean required if it is determined to be unreasonable for that organization. Unfortunately, HIPAA is not very specific on what is truly reasonable, therefore leaving what is "reasonable" open to determination by the covered entity.

The security rule was the last rule to be adopted within HIPAA and establishes a set of administrative, technical, and physical security procedures that need to be considered for a HIPAA-covered entity. The security rule is intended to protect the confidentiality, integrity, and availability of electronic protected health information. This is done through a set of standards that are either required or addressable. "Required" means they must be done; "addressable" means that they must be considered and implemented if reasonable. Again, this ambiguity leaves the definition of "reasonable" open to interpretation. The following table represents some of the key HIPAA-required and -addressable standards.

Safeguards	Required or Addressable
Administrative	Required: Risk analysis, risk management, enforcement, monitoring, assigned roles and responsibilities, separation of functions, incident response and reporting, data backup plan, disaster recovery plan, security evaluation, HIPAA requirements in contracts
	Addressable: Personnel security, access control authorization, security training and awareness, application and data criticality analysis, contingency planning testing and revision procedures
Technical	Required: Unique user ID, emergency access procedures, audit controls, individual authentication
	Addressable: Auto logoff, encryption of access controls and transmission security, authentication of EPHI integrity
Physical	Required: Media use and reuse rules, workstation rules and security
	Addressable: Facility security plan, access control and validation procedures, maintenance records, accountability of media, data backup and storage

HIPAA provides a good baseline standard for protecting the privacy and security of electronic protected health information (PHI). The effectiveness of the HIPAA rules will be determined by the actual implementation and enforcement of the standard.

Financial Services

The financial services industry plays a key role in the critical infrastructure of the United States economy. To continue to provide the necessary financial services, financial organizations need to assure the confidentially, integrity, availability, and nonrepudiation of the critical data that is associated with financial transactions. One of the primary legislative acts for the financial industry is the Gramm-Leach-Bliley Act.

Gramm-Leach-Bliley Act (GLBA)

The GLBA is also known as the Financial Services Modernization Act of 1999 and affects a large cross-section of financial institutions including national banks, federal branches, federal agencies of foreign banks, savings associations, FDIC-insured banks, federally insured credit unions, brokers, investment companies, investment advisors, and insurance companies. The GLBA consists of seven separate provisions dealing with a spectrum of financial measures. Title V, "Privacy," is of special interest because it involves the safeguarding of customer information. Title V has two subtitles. Subtitle A addresses privacy responsibilities to customers and the safeguarding of private information. Subtitle B addresses obtaining customer information through false pretenses and associated penalties for violating GLBA's provisions.

The primary subtitle of Title V in which security is a concern is titled "Safeguard the Security and Confidentiality of Customer Non-Public Information."

This subtitle states that institutions are required to have the following:

- ❑ **A Written Security Program:** Each covered institution must have a comprehensive written information security program addressing administrative, technical, and physical safeguards suitable to its size, complexity, and operations.

- ❑ **Board of Directors Approval:** The Board of Directors or an appropriate Board committee must approve the security program and oversee its development, implementation, and maintenance. Reports to the Board on security must be made annually.

- ❑ **Risk Assessment:** Risk assessments must be conducted that identify reasonably foreseeable internal and external threats that could lead to unauthorized disclosure, misuse, alteration, or destruction of customer information. The risk assessment must also assess the likelihood and damage of the threats, and assess the sufficiency of policies and procedures to control risk.

- ❑ **Manage and Control Risk:** Each covered institution must design an information security program to control identified risks, commensurate with the sensitivity of the information and the scope of activities; train staff to implement the program; and regularly test security controls, systems, and procedures.

- ❑ **Appropriate Measures:** Appropriate measures must be implemented to address access control, access restrictions, encryption, configuration management, personnel security, intrusion monitoring, incident response programs, and system backups.

- ❑ **Oversee Service Providers:** Each covered institution must exercise due diligence when selecting service providers who can access customer information. This includes requiring service providers by contract to implement appropriate measures to meet the security guidelines and monitoring compliance. Any contract established prior to March 5, 2001, had until July 1, 2003, to comply. Any new contracts signed after March 5, 2001, must immediately comply with the safeguarding standards to which the institution is held accountable. These service providers are required contractually to implement appropriate measures to safeguard the institutions' outsourced customer information.

- ❑ **Monitoring of Program:** Each covered institution must monitor its program and make adjustments in light of changes in technology, risk, and business activities.

The GLBA has had a huge impact on financial institutions and how they deal with their customer information. When you receive a privacy notice from your bank or credit card company, it is a result of the GLBA. The costs can be high for organizations, so they are looking for cost-effective ways to implement the requirements.

Utilities

Utilities are critical infrastructure requiring protection to avoid issues of compromise of confidentiality, integrity, and availability of critical operational and customer information. Compromise of critical systems within a utility can result in severe impact to a large cross-section of a given area or region. There have been incidents of extended power outages due to mismanaged or incorrect information about the power output and the power on the grid. A major concern with this critical infrastructure is a terrorist's ability to disrupt, damage, or make unavailable the items that we expect and make us comfortable. (that is, consistent power, safe water, and so on). The major systems that have the highest level of concern within a utility are the Supervisory Control and Data Acquisition (SCADA) systems. These systems are used to gather and analyze real-time data about the operations and must be available and accurate to be effective.

North American Electric Reliability Council (NERC) Critical Infrastructure Protection (CIP) Standards

NERC is an organization that provides guidance for the reliability and security of the electrical systems throughout the United States. As critical infrastructure, the electrical industry must be concerned about the protection of confidentiality, integrity, and availability of the power systems and the information systems that support the overall power production. NERC is a focal point for coordination between the electrical industry and the federal government. NERC coordinates with the Department of Energy and the Department of Homeland Security. NERC adopted a series of Critical Infrastructure Protection standards (at www.nerc.com, search "CIPC"). They currently are the following:

- ❑ CIP-001 – Sabotage Reporting
- ❑ CIP-002 – Critical Cyber Asset Identification
- ❑ CIP-003 – Security Management Controls
- ❑ CIP-004 – Personnel and Training
- ❑ CIP-005 – Electronic Security Perimeter(s)
- ❑ CIP-006 – Physical Security of Critical Cyber Assets
- ❑ CIP-007 – Systems Security Management
- ❑ CIP-008 – Incident Reporting and Response Planning
- ❑ CIP-009 – Recovery Plans for Critical Cyber Assets

Water Infrastructure Security Enhancement (WISE)

WISE provides security guidance for water and wastewater/storm water utilities. There is a heavy dependence upon physical security in the water utilities, but WISE does address an entire process of risk assessment and risk management that can easily be transitioned into supporting information security needs. You can find more information on WISE at www.awwa.org (Google "WISE site:awwa.org").

Education

Educational institutions have been notoriously open in their information technology environment to allow almost any type of activity to occur. Because of the nature of educational institutions, the justification was that putting rules in place would stifle the free-flow idea creation that is expected to occur in an educational environment. Fortunately, some of this thinking has changed because of well-publicized security incidents that have occurred as a result of poor information security at educational institutions.

Family Educational Rights and Privacy Act (FERPA)

FERPA is designed to protect the privacy of student records at any school that receives funds under a majority of U.S. Department of Education programs. FERPA gives parents the right to inspect and review the student's records maintained by the school. These rights transfer to the student when he or she turns 18 or heads off to college. This means that parents don't necessarily have the right to review their children's student records after they're in college. FERPA also requires a process for requesting corrections to the records.

FERPA requires educational institutions to have written permission before it can disclose personal information outside the school. This implies a requirement to protect the confidentiality and integrity of student information to avoid unauthorized disclosure of that information. FERPA does allow exceptions for when student information can be shared without consent. These include the following:

- ❑ School officials with legitimate educational interest
- ❑ Other schools to which a student is transferring
- ❑ Specified officials for audit or evaluation purposes
- ❑ Appropriate parties in connection with financial aid to a student
- ❑ Organizations conducting certain studies for or on behalf of the school
- ❑ Accrediting organizations
- ❑ Compliance with a judicial order or lawfully issued subpoena
- ❑ Appropriate officials in cases of health and safety emergencies
- ❑ State and local authorities, within a juvenile justice system, pursuant to specific state law

You can find more information on FERPA at the U.S. Department of Education Web site, www.ed.gov (Google "FERPA site:ed.gov").

International Standards

The international community plays a critical role in information security. The technology that exists today and the connectivity we have through the Internet make almost every system internationally accessible. Without appropriate controls and sufficient education, the potential exists for a worldwide influx of insecure systems. The international standards assist in providing an educational tool and a foundation for basic information security practices and implementations.

International Organization for Standardization (ISO) 17799 and ISO 27001

ISO 17799, the Code of Practice for Information Security Management, originally grew out of British Standard (BS) 7799. It became an ISO in 2000, and the most current update was in 2005. ISO 17799 is organized into 11 sections and identifies more than 120 main controls and more than 500 detailed controls. ISO 17799 is a foundational document that starts by educating readers about what information security is and why it is important. It then discusses areas that are considered critical to an information security program and areas that are considered best practices. The ISO then goes into detail on the 11 major areas. The 11 major sections are the following:

- ❑ Security Policy
- ❑ Organization of Information Security

- ❑ Asset Management
- ❑ Human Resources Security
- ❑ Physical and Environmental Security
- ❑ Communications and Operations Management
- ❑ Access Control
- ❑ Information Systems Acquisition, Development and Maintenance
- ❑ Information Security Incident Management
- ❑ Business Continuity Management
- ❑ Compliance

The standard evolved from British standards; however, it is truly international, with input from countries worldwide. Countries providing input to the latest version of ISO 17799 include Australia, Brazil, Germany, Norway, the United Kingdom, and the United States. ISO 17799 certification carries a three-year renewal requirement to stay current. ISO 17799 is a baseline document, and organizations and countries must build upon the baseline to meet their organizational needs.

ISO 27001 is basically part two of ISO 17799, with the focus on how to apply the ISO 17799 standard and build an information security management program. ISO 27001 grew out of BS7799 Part 2.

Unfortunately, the ISO standards are made available on a fee basis, so it is not as easy to obtain as some standards. You can purchase both ISO 17799 and 27001 through the ISO Web site at `www.iso.org` (search "ISO 17799" and "ISO 27001").

Payment Card Industry (PCI) Data Security Standard

The PCI standard requires any vendor that maintains credit card information to implement information security protections to protect the credit card information. VISA spearheaded the effort to create the PCI standard, which has been adopted as the standard for MasterCard also. The PCI Standard (v1.1) consists of 12 security requirements under six major headings. The following table reflects the major requirements in the PCI. You can find the entire document at `www.pcisecuritystandards.org` (Google "PCI Data Security Standard site:pcisecuritystandards.org").

Policy	Requirements
Build and Maintain a Secure Network	Install and maintain a firewall configuration to protect data Do not use vendor supplied defaults for passwords and other security parameters
Protect Cardholder Data	Protect stored data Encrypt transmission of cardholder data and sensitive information across public networks

Policy	Requirements
Maintain a Vulnerability Management Program	Use and regularly update antivirus software Develop and maintain secure systems and applications
Implement Strong Access Control Measures	Restrict access to data by business need-to-know Assign a unique ID to each person with computer access Restrict physical access to the cardholder data
Regularly Monitor and Test Networks	Track and monitor all access to network resources and cardholder data Regularly test security systems and processes
Maintain an Information Security Policy	Maintain a policy that addresses information security

Public Companies

Publicly held and traded companies have had a greater responsibility placed on them to be accountable to shareholders and the public in general. High-profile instances of corporate corruption and unethical behavior has driven the United States government to place greater controls and requirements on organizational accountability.

Sarbanes-Oxley (SOX) Act of 2002

SOX was signed into law with the focus of protecting investors through requiring and holding senior management of public companies individually accountable for accurate and reliable financial information about the company in accordance with securities laws. The accounting scandals of companies such as Enron and MCI/WorldCom were the primary drivers behind SOX. A portion of the SOX requirements pertain to the protection of the integrity of the financial records to ensure that the financials of the companies are reported accurately. To accomplish this, organizations must have an effective security program that includes audits of the information systems supporting the organization and implementation of appropriate access controls and protections to assure the integrity protection.

The two major sections of SOX that affect information security are the following:

❑ Section 302 – Certification of Disclosure in Companies' Quarterly and Annual Reports or Corporate Responsibility for Financial Reports

❑ Section 404 – Management's Reports on Internal Control over Financial Reporting and Certification of Disclosure in Exchange Act Periodic Reports

SOX requires organizations to provide, in their required management reports, the status and management of the internal controls used in financial reporting. This information, along with holding the CEO and CFO individually accountable for the financial reporting, assures management buy-in for implementing information security within an organization. Section 404 also contains a clause that requires the independent auditors to attest to and report on the internal controls that are in place within the organization.

SOX also has an international impact. A publicly held company that has offices or business units within the United States must meet SOX reporting requirements.

Using This Information in the Interview

Effective use of this information in an interview can impress your interviewers and improve your chances of obtaining a position. If an organization knows that you have spent the time researching and understanding its needs and the requirements that it falls under, it will likely have a greater appreciation for your potential to work within its organization.

Don't try to blow smoke about your knowledge of any particular regulation. Do as much research as you can to understand what is involved, but if you give the impression you are an expert in a certain process or regulation, the organization will test you on it. Be prepared to share what you know, but the key is to impress upon the organization that you are willing to continue to research and learn what information, processes, and procedures are needed to accomplish the job and support the organization's needs.

Summary

Information security regulations, standards, and guidance all play key roles in an organization's ability to manage risk, deal with external requirements, and support its customers. Nearly every industry is affected by regulations, and in some cases by multiple regulations. The most regulated industries are those that involve the federal government, Department of Defense, and the critical infrastructure of the United States. There are also international concerns that directly affect an organization's ability to support its mission and customers world wide. These various regulations and requirements must be understood and effectively implemented by the organization to assure both compliance and an effective security program.

As you prepare for your interview for the information security job of your dreams, be sure to research, read, and integrate your knowledge of relevant security standards and regulations into the interview discussion. Doing so shows knowledge of the organization's mission and needs. It also demonstrates your ability to take the extra steps in supporting the organization's information security needs. Best of luck in your job search.

Interview Q&A

Q: Why does my organization need to worry about regulations and legislation?

A: Two concepts drive this discussion: compliance and due diligence. If your organization falls under any particular piece of legislation or regulation, you must show that you are taking steps to be in compliance with the directive. If you are not in compliance, you may face fines or other sanctions against your organization. The other concept is due diligence. Due diligence addresses a logical, minimum, and necessary level of security within organizations to support and serve the customer and the employees. Failure with due diligence can result in customer dissatisfaction and employee loss.

Q: Don't all the regulations and legislation basically say the same thing?

A: Approximately 80 percent of all information security–related regulations and legislation basically say the same thing, which relates to the concept of due diligence. The remaining 20 percent relates to industry or governmental specific implementation requirements.

Q: What is the difference between a requirement and guidance?

A: A requirement is something you must do. Guidance is something you might consider doing and implementing if it makes sense in your environment.

Q: What federal law regarding computer security and compliance applies to all government agencies under the executive branch of the United States government?

A: FISMA (Federal Information System Management Act).

Q: What FIPS document provides the guidance on the categorization and classification of risk for federal computer systems?

A: FIPS 199 – Standards for Security Categorization of Federal Information and Information Systems.

Q: What two NIST Special Publications provide the listing of security controls for federal information systems and how to access the controls?

A: NIST SP 800-53 – Recommended Security Controls for Federal Information Systems and NIST SP 800-53A – Guide for Assessing the Security Controls in Federal Information Systems.

Q: What government agency has the authority to set requirements for systems that contain national intelligence information?

A: The Central Intelligence Agency (CIA). The Director, CIA establishes rules for intelligence systems working with DoD and the military services.

Q: What is considered to be national infrastructure?

A: Food supplies, water supplies, power, public health, national defense, national icons, and national financial stability.

Q: I am a publicly held health care organization. What regulations or legislation do I have to worry about?

A: HIPAA, Sarbanes-Oxley, state requirements, and possibly PCI.

Q: Why was Sarbanes-Oxley passed?

A: In the wake of financial scandals at Enron and other companies, Congress passed Sarbanes-Oxley in an attempt to get public companies to provide accurate and ethical financial results to protect shareholders and employees from being financially hurt by intentional actions of individual decision-makers in the organization. With Sarbanes-Oxley, CEOs and CFOs must account for the accuracy of the information in the financial statements and can be held individually accountable if they are not accurate.

Recommended Reading

DoD Information Technology Security Certification & Accreditation Process (DITSCAP) and DoD Information Assurance Certification and Accreditation Process (DIACAP), `http://iase.disa.mil` (Google "DITSCAP site:iase.disa.mil").

Defense Technical Information Center, `www.dtic.mil` (search "8500").

ISO/IEM 17799, `www.wikipedia.org` (search "ISO 17799").

International Standards Organization, `www.iso.org` (search "ISO 17799" and "ISO 27001").

Department of Defense Information Assurance Portal: Policy and Guidance, `http://iase.disa.mil` (Google "Policy and Guidance site:iase.disa.mil").

INFOSEC Assurance Training and Rating Program: Policies, Regulations, Guidelines, Circulars, `www.iatrp.com`.

Federal Information Processing Standards (FIPS), `http://csrc.nist.gov` (Google "NIST FIPS site:csrc.nist.gov").

Director of Central Intelligence Directive 6/3, `www.fas.org` (Google "DCID 6/3 site:fas.org").

NIST 800 Series of Special Publications, `http://csrc.nist.gov` (Google: "NIST 800 site:csrc.nist.gov").

Health and Human Services, `www.hhs.gov` (search "HIPAA").

North American Electric Reliability Council (NERC), `www.nerc.com` (search "CIPC").

Water Infrastructure Security Enhancement (WISE), `www.awwa.org` (Google "WISE site:awwa.org").

Family Educational Rights and Privacy Act (FERPA), `www.ed.gov` (Google "FERPA site:http://www.ed.gov").

Payment Card Industry Data Security Standard (PCI), `https://www.pcisecuritystandards.org` (Google "PCI Data Security Standard site:pcisecuritystandards.org").

5

Knowing Firewalls: Fundamentals

A firewall is the network device used to provide access control to your network. Every network today uses a firewall as a barrier between itself and the Internet. Often, firewalls are also deployed inside a private network to secure critical servers or clients. Firewalls are a key component to any network security infrastructure.

In this chapter, we look at firewalls from the ground up, leaving you with a basic understanding of several key topics about firewalls. First, you learn about the major firewall technologies and how they work. Next, you move to the major firewall vendors, focusing on the three major firewall vendors and the special technologies they bring to the firewall market. In that section, smaller key players also are discussed.

A firewall is more than just a software construct — it also needs a hardware platform to run on. We explore the major firewall device types that are used in the market today, and the good and bad parts of them. Next, we dive into the management strategies that are used with firewall devices. Finally, we discuss the different deployment strategies for firewalls.

This chapter should leave you with at least a basic understanding of the firewall marketplace and the technology contained within it. The firewall market is a diverse place, and you must understand at least the basics of the available technologies to get a foothold into it. To ensure that you are prepared for the interview process, you should know the technologies that your potential employer is looking for. Quite often, interviewers focus on specific vendors' products more than anything else. If you are looking to get a position where a specific vendor's technology is employed, ensure that you have experience with the product. Experience is always superior to certifications and book experience. (In an entry-level position, however, these things are likely to be enough to get you the position.)

When interviewing for a security position, first rely on your experiences in the industry. Highlight what you have done and how you came to the conclusions you did. Interviewers often look more closely at the process you took to get the result than just the result itself. They are looking for how you applied security principals to the task to achieve your result.

If you have no previous security experience except for what you have studied, do not worry. Just apply the security knowledge you've gained through study — including what you learn in this chapter and throughout this book — to any questions that the interviewer asks you.

Firewall Technologies

Not all firewall technologies are created equal. Throughout the development of these technologies, they were created to meet specific requirements and were based on the hardware capabilities of the time. The insight required when creating firewall technologies was to solve a particular problem specific to the time, not to solve all possible problems with it. As time went on, the need for stronger security services increased. As the Internet grew in popularity, so did the risks associated with it. As the Internet connected organizations, it also connected them to threats. Many companies did not realize that they connected themselves to thousands of potential attackers. Typically, each host in the network had an IP address that was accessible to the entire Internet with no security mechanisms in place. New groups of threats grew, and they overcame the firewall technology of the time. This led to new innovative products to counter these various threats.

In today's firewall market, dozens of vendors are using an amalgamation of technologies to provide the best products. As time passes, firewall technology grows and blossoms into new security strategies. The range of products and strategies makes it critical for you to understand what the best technologies are, which means that you must be familiar with the options and how they came to be. Even old technologies are still strong when deployed in the right environment. In this first section of this chapter, we look at the main firewall technologies available in the market today.

No technology is intrinsically better than another, but a particular technology might be best for a specific use. For that reason, the most important criteria for judging which to employ is the use case for the technology. Choosing the right technology or combinations of technologies depends on what the environment calls for. When you've finished this section, you will be familiar with each of the various technologies and what they are capable of — information that will come in handy if an interviewer asks what firewall solution you'd recommend for a particular application.

You can find a great article discussing the history of firewalls and its technology at www.cisco.com *(search for "Evolution of the Firewall Industry"). Another good review on firewalls is at* www.interhack .net/pubs/fwfaq/.

Packet Filter

The oldest firewall technology is the *packet filter*, which looks at each packet as it passes through a network interface. This technology originated on Cisco routers around the year 1985. The implementation of this technology was quite simple and its concepts have been passed on to all subsequent firewall technologies.

A packet filter does exactly what its name suggests — it filters packets. The technology is designed to either allow an individual packet or deny it based on the configured filter or Access Control List (ACL).

An ACL consists of several different criteria that you can configure. At the end of each ACL is an implicit deny. This will drop any traffic that is not explicitly allowed.

The original implementation of packet filters is allowed only for the combination of source and destination Internet Protocol, or IP, addresses.

Packet filtering is a fairly basic mechanism to control access into or out of a network. This model induced a strict allow or deny policy based upon IP address alone. If the source IP address were allowed to the destination, the source would have access to all services on the destination. In the beginning, this was sufficient, but it was far from ideal.

As new network-based services became available, the requirement to reduce the level of access between sources and destinations increased. Because hosts now served dozens of different services, restricting access to a specific service was required. New revisions of packet filters came into existence. The second iteration of filtering capabilities allowed for the inclusion of source port, destination port, and IP protocol type as decision criteria. This change created a much stricter security implementation. Access between hosts or networks could be restricted down to the service port and protocol such as Transmission Control Protocol (TCP), User Datagram Protocol (UDP), and IP. For protocols such as Internet Control Message Protocol (ICMP), the specific message types could also be selected.

A great Web site to use to learn more about TCP/IP is www.tcpipguide.com. *This information can also be found in book form (*The TCP/IP Guide, *No Starch Press, ISBN 159327047X).*

Although security capability increased, so did the complexity of the situation. Because the inspection of packets has now gone beyond just IP addressing, the problem of dealing with the bidirectional nature of communications comes into play. When two hosts talk to each other using TCP, for example, they use a set of ports. The initiating host talks to its destination host using a random port greater than 1025 to a static port of the destination host. When creating an access list, you must specify the static port of the destination host. You can see this in the following pseudo code:

```
From source IP X to dest IP Y with source port 1025-65535 to destination port 80
```

Although this ingress-based policy is very straightforward, creating a return policy to restrict egress traffic is not as easy. Because the nature of TCP communications involves the creation of two separate flows to create a session, you must configure an inverse policy to allow return traffic from the server back to the host. You can see this in the following pseudo code:

```
From source IP X to dest IP Y with source port 80 to destination port 1025-65535
```

The issue here is that the source IP address can now access the destination on any port. Although this does not seem like an issue, it ends up being a huge problem by allowing unsolicited connections back through the network to the destination host. The possibility thereby exists for an attacker to attempt to hijack sessions or exploit vulnerabilities on the OS or its hosted services. This situation created the need to monitor the state of the connection. The resulting technology is called a *stateful firewall*, which it is discussed in the following section.

Although this development may seem to render ACLs completely useless, the reality is quite the contrary. Packet filtering technology is still used today and it is considered best practice to do so. The technology is deployed in many locations where monitoring state is not required. You can filter out network garbage such as specific protocols or ports that you may not want your firewall to deal with. Some routers are capable of doing this in hardware-based processing, which allows for line rate filtering of network traffic.

The capabilities of a packet filter today are extended in many ways. In some devices, you can filter down at a very low level. The pseudo code that follows this paragraph is an example. You can now look deeper in the packet to make a match, which includes looking deeper inside of protocols to look at specific flags or options being set. Doing so extends the older firewall technology to keep it relevant today.

```
From source IP X to dest IP Y with TCP flag SYN and TCP flag FIN
OR
From source any to destination any where IP protocol is equal to 50
```

Stateful Firewall

A stateful firewall was invented to resolve the shortcomings of packet filtering. Originally called a circuit-level firewall, the stateful firewall is considered a second-generation technology. As its name implies, this firewall technology is aware of the state of the ongoing communications. This firewall technology is the most commonly deployed today in firewall products.

The ability to maintain state is crucial for almost all security deployments. Stateful firewall technology is based upon a few important concepts. In contrast to packet filters, stateful firewalls watch and maintain the entire state of a connection. A connection is made up of two separate flows. A client system initiates a connection to a remote server. This flow starts the session setup. At this point, the firewall must determine the beginning state of the communication. The determination is based upon the type of protocol being used.

We first look at the truly stateful transport protocol TCP (or transmission control protocol). TCP has a clear beginning, middle, and end to each of its network conversations. When a TCP connection begins, it marks the initial packet coming from the client with a SYN flag. This flag tells the remote host that the client system wants to initialize a connection. The server sends a SYN/ACK packet and acknowledges the original SYN packet. To confirm that this packet was received, the client system sends an ACK back to the server. This process is called a three-way handshake. During the communication, each packet is flagged with a SYN/ACK packet during the conversation. Figure 5-1 shows an example of a three-way handshake.

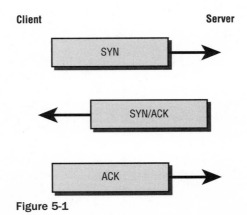

Figure 5-1

To close the conversation gracefully, the closing host sends a FIN packet and the receiving host sends an ACK packet back. The receiving host sends a FIN packet and the initial closing host sends an ACK packet. This process is called a four-way handshake. A four-way handshake is done to ensure that no data is lost, with both sides acknowledging the close. A host also can abruptly close a session by sending just an RST or reset packet. Figure 5-2 shows an example of the four-way connection close.

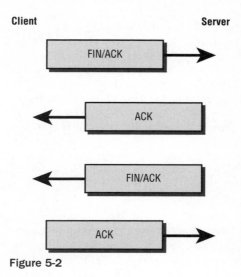

Figure 5-2

Now you can see that identifying the entire state of the communication for a TCP session is possible and allows a stateful firewall to keep track of the state of the session. When creating policies on a stateful firewall, you typically need to match only three components: the source IP, the destination IP, and the service you want to allow or deny. In contrast to a packet filter firewall, the return packets are automatically allowed if they are consistent with the state of the communications. After the session is closed, the return path that was dynamically created through the firewall is closed. This process is much more secure then leaving the return path open via a static ACL such as a packet filter.

UDP and Internet Control Message Protocol (ICMP) are different beasts to deal with, however. Neither of these protocols is truly stateful. Each firewall vendor uses different mechanisms to determine the state of the protocol. Vendors typically create short-lived sessions for these protocols, assuming that they will be short lived. However, the length of the session varies based upon the UDP or ICMP implementation.

Some applications do not act in a way that is firewall friendly, which typically means that the application uses another mechanism to communicate the change of state besides the underlying transport protocol. An example is the File Transfer Protocol (FTP). This protocol negotiates a port on which the client will connect to the server. This new port is random and unpredictable from just looking at the transport protocol. The firewall must look inside the application layer to determine this information. To do this vendors implement what is known as an Application Layer Gateway (ALG). An ALG looks at specific protocols at the application layer, thereby allowing the firewall to monitor for changes that are not done at the transport layer. The firewall can then create a pinhole in the firewall to allow the communication to continue.

Although stateful firewalls are the most popular firewalls and are considered the mainstream technology, they are not without their downside. The biggest challenge is maintaining the sessions. Each session takes up a specific amount of resources on the firewall. A network attack can attempt to overwhelm the firewall by taking up all the available sessions. Doing so can easily crash the firewall and create a service loss on the network. To fight against such an attack, a vendor uses both its hardware and software to mitigate the risk of this occurring.

The second drawback of a stateful firewall is that it is not the most secure type of firewall. A stateful firewall does not do a full protocol decode and typically operates only at the network and transport layers (TCP/UDP/IP). However, stateful firewalls implement several different technologies to overcome this limitation. A stateful firewall provides secure transport between two networks by securing the traffic and allowing the minimal number of ports to be open at any given time. This technology balances speed and security to create the most viable firewall for organizations.

> You can find additional information covering the concept of stateful firewalls at `www.answers.com/topic/stateful-inspection`.

An application proxy is considered the most secure firewall type and is discussed in the following section.

Application Proxy

An application proxy is the most secure firewall technology on the market today. An application proxy firewall operates as a middleman to all of the connections that attempt to pass through it. As the technology's name suggests, this type of firewall proxies an application's connection.

When a client attempts to make a connection through the firewall, the firewall terminates the connection to it. Then the firewall opens and initiates a connection to the destination host on behalf of the client. All the data can be inspected by the application proxy firewall as it passes between the client-proxy connection and proxy-server connection.

This type of separation, plus the capability to inspect all the data, is why the application proxy firewall is the most secure. The firewall must have a protocol decoder built in for each of the supported protocols. If it doesn't, it is possible to support any protocol with a generic proxy. A generic proxy, however, does not provide the same level of inspection as a custom protocol decoder. The generic proxy still can proxy a connection but is unable to understand the application inside the connection.

The application proxy must open a connection for each session passing through the firewall, which takes a great amount of work on the firewall's part. The slower performance that results from managing so many connections has led to the general disuse of this technology as the main firewall for an organization. However, many companies still use application proxy firewalls in limited-use scenarios and for environments in which performance isn't a factor.

Application proxy firewalls are most commonly used for providing Web-based services. This use includes an authenticated proxy for monitoring outbound Web access and application accelerator products. Application accelerator products sit in front of the Web servers and proxy connections while also providing SSL acceleration and content compression.

The two most notable vendors providing application proxy firewalls today are Microsoft and Secure Computing. Microsoft uses proxy technology in its Internet Security and Acceleration Server (ISA) product. The ISA server, although not used as a main firewall device, is still highly popular in Microsoft-focused organizations. Secure Computing's Sidewinder G2 firewall is also a widely deployed product. Secure Computing purchased the Gauntlet firewall in 2002. Gauntlet was the most popular application proxy firewall during the peak usage of the application proxy technology.

You can read more about ISA server at `www.microsoft.com/isaserver/`.

You can find more information about secure computing and the G2 firewall at www `.securecomputing.com`.

Unified Threat Management

Unified Threat Management (UTM) is a new term in the firewall industry — in fact, UTM is the hottest buzzword in the industry today. The term describes the combination of several security technologies on one device. The typical UTM technologies are the following: stateful firewall; IPS; antivirus; antispyware; antiphishing; anti-adware; antispam; and Web filtering. This technology is included typically on a firewall that employs a stateful firewall as its core technology. This technology is used in lower-speed deployments of a gigabit-per-second throughput or less.

UTM increases the security of a stateful firewall by adding different layers of inspection. It does this and still maintains the important throughput, which is one of the important benefits of stateful inspection. The Intrusion Prevention System functions implemented in UTM are usually subsets of full-blown IPS features. This form of IPS was formerly known as Deep Inspection or Deep Packet Inspection. The IPS feature looks for specific attacks inside flows. These attacks are usually divided into categories of severity. The IPS component is usually deployed to stop the most critical attacks that are active threats, such as worms.

A discussion of the IPS features of UTM can be found at `www.securityfocus.com/infocus/1716.c`.

Network-based antivirus technology is often limited to a small set of protocols. These protocols are the ones in which viruses are most commonly found, such as HyperText Transfer Protocol (HTTP), Simple Mail Transfer Protocol (SMTP), and Post Office Protocol version 3 (POP3).

Anti-*x* protocols (spyware, adware, and spam) block or at least limit the amount of incoming spyware, adware, and spam. These products can be developed by the firewall vendor themselves or they can be products developed by partners. As with the antivirus products, these products are used only on specific protocols, such as mail protocols in the case of antispam.

Web filtering allows you to block Web sites that are inappropriate for your organization. By including filtering on the firewall, you reduce the number of devices that need to be managed in your environment. The features for integrated Web filtering can be limited as opposed to using a full installation of a filtering product. Often, Web filtering is done by partnering with a major player such as Websense or Surf Control.

UTM features are often best deployed in low throughput environments with low user counts. Over the years, performance of such features has become much better. In the past, you would never want to deploy these features in environments with more than 50 people. Today, however, many products can support several hundred users. UTM is a great technology to add to your environment, and the future for it looks bright.

If you go to www.eweek.com *and search for "Unified Threat Management," you can find a few good articles on the impact of UTM in the security field.*

Intrusion Protection System

Intrusion prevention system (IPS) technologies have been deployed on stand-alone devices in the past. However, today you can run a complete IPS system on your firewall. You do so by combining (usually) a stateful firewall technology with an IPS engine. Throughput typically depends on the implementation. Some vendors choose to dedicate specific hardware resources to the IPS inspection. These devices have the highest throughput — much more than a completely software-based implementation.

This IPS technology deployment differs from UTM because it is much more feature rich and supports more protocols. A typical UTM deployment consists of a couple hundred signatures and supports a dozen signatures whereas a true IPS deployment consists of several thousand signatures and 40 or more protocols. A signature is a specific pattern or combination of patterns that match an attack. The inclusion of IPS on firewalls provides stateful firewalls with the security that an application proxy can provide yet at incredibly fast, multigigabit speeds.

You can find a more in-depth discussion of IPS at www.securityfocus.com/infocus/1670.

Network Address Translation

Network Address Translation (NAT) is a technology that allows you to change one IP address into another as a packet passes through a firewall. This can be done to the source IP, destination IP, or both. NAT gives you the ability to do several different things, the first being the ability to hide your network's IP address range, obfuscating what its true IP address range is. You can use a set of nonroutable IP addresses for your private network. These typically come from the Request For Comment (RFC) 1918 address set. Because these addresses are not routable on the Internet, you need to hide them behind public IP addresses.

Most organizations do not have the ability to provide one public IP address for each private IP address. In these cases, a combination of NAT and Port Address Translation (PAT) is used. PAT swaps the source port of the packet to a higher port and then uses a single IP address to hide many internal IP addresses behind. The firewall tracks the connection by mapping the original source port to the new PAT port. Doing so allows it to know which connection belongs to which internal IP.

To read more about NAT, go to www.tcpipguide.com *and search for NAT. You can find a more in-depth discussion there.*

Virtual Private Networks

A Virtual Private Network (VPN) is created by employing a protocol that allows packets to be transported between two endpoints yet seem as though they are part of the same network. Using one of several protocols such as Multiprotocol Label Switching (MPLS), IPsec, or Generic Router Encapsulation, you can create a VPN. Most firewalls create VPNs using IPsec. IPsec is a protocol suite that enables the secure transport of traffic between two endpoints. Most firewall products on the market today allow for the creation of IPsec VPNs. IPsec VPN and its technologies are fully discussed in Chapter 6.

Major Vendors

Three major vendors control more than 60 percent of the firewall marketplace, dominating both in technology and market share. Often raising the bar of technologies available to the enterprise, they provide an ongoing vision to the market. In addition to these large key players, some smaller vendors play a key role in the market as well. The smaller companies often drive innovation in newer technologies and force the larger manufacturers to increase feature velocity.

This section first looks at the three key players in the firewall market. Each of these vendors has specific technologies that are key to its success and are the reason these vendors are on top of the market share list.

Cisco

No networking technology exists in which Cisco does not have product placement today. When a new network technology comes out, Cisco typically develops or purchases a company to enter into that market. This is no different in the firewall space as well. Cisco was the first vendor to implement a firewalling technology with the introduction of ACLs in its well-known router technologies.

Cisco focused on the implementation of ACLs on routers in the early days of firewall technology. As time passed, and with the innovation of stateful firewalls, Cisco needed to increase its play in the market. The company started with a two-fold plan. The first step was the inclusion of a stateful firewall implementation on the Internetwork Operating System (IOS). The second step was to purchase the company's NAT products and introduce them as the PIX firewall. With the power of routers available at the time, Cisco was unable to provide significant stateful performance with the PIX firewall, so the company needed to look into a stand-alone appliance, which it did with its acquisition of NAT products.

Because of its experience in the creation of embedded systems, Cisco decided to stay with the appliance-based model. An appliance model allows for simple management and quick deployment. The PIX appliances were software-based devices running on Intel-based processors. Although the PIX appliances were great appliances at the time, they were not the highest-performing devices. Despite that, because Cisco was the largest networking player in the market, it still quickly gained market share.

PIX firewalls were originally managed from a command-line interface (CLI), using a completely different syntax than the IOS command set that administrators were used to. This was challenging to those who decided to adopt this technology. However, many organizations that were familiar with Cisco chose to deploy the appliances.

The long-term strategy, though, was to leverage layered security into all its products. The ultimate goal was to bring this into a chassis-based solution. A chassis differs from an appliance in that the system is completely modular. Both interfaces and management components can be replaced. An appliance usually has fixed management and interfaces. Some appliances, however, include modular interface cards. The large Catalyst switching chassis included modular interface cards, allowing Cisco to sell to customers that already had these chassis in their networks. Early iterations were not stable or easy to use. Today, Cisco continues to strengthen the firewall services module (FWSM) into the 6500 series chassis. Cisco's effort in this area has given it a strong presence in large enterprises that have an installed base of the 6500 chassis.

In the edge router market, Cisco is focusing on the migration toward a single router/firewall device. This focus would leverage the market share that it controls in the enterprise routing space, allowing Cisco to replace existing routers with the new integrated security devices. In this space, however, Cisco faced competition from the budding company Juniper Networks.

Cisco's new platform for the security space is the Adaptive Security Appliance (ASA) product. The ASA allows you to customize it with one of four security modules: a Firewall module, Anti-X or UTM module, IPS module, or VPN module. (The module takes up the single expansion slot.) This customization allows the appliance to be adapted to the environment you wish to deploy it in.

Although they are known for having some of the best routers and switches in the market today, Cisco is not considered to have the best security products. Although this might not be apparent when you consider that it has a large portion of the market share, it is something that is known in the security field. Cisco continually strives to maintain its market share by introducing new products and increasing quality.

A large criticism of Cisco security products is the lack of a central management solution. Large enterprises often deploy hundreds and even thousands of firewalls globally. Obviously, managing these devices individually is impossible. A central management system is required to provide effective management of this number of environments. Although issues still exist with Cisco's central management, Cisco is constantly updating its central management strategies and is growing stronger with every release.

> *Cisco's Web site is at* `www.cisco.com`. *You can find Cisco's security products by searching for "security and VPN."*

Juniper Networks

Juniper Networks originally focused solely on the core routing space. In 2004, Juniper acquired a company called NetScreen, which provided Juniper an entry into both the enterprise market space and the security space. NetScreen brought several security technologies to Juniper. The NetScreen firewall became the key technology for Juniper Networks. The NetScreen firewall is a hardware-based appliance much like the Cisco PIX. However, it has several technologies that make it an extremely strong product. The NetScreen firewall provided stable and scalable performance numbers with the inclusion of an application-specific integrated circuit, or ASIC. An ASIC was used for session lookup or forwarding based upon the device. At the time that NetScreen products used ASICs, most devices relied on a general-purpose CPU for performance. Using just a CPU provided dismal throughput compared to an ASIC-based platform. NetScreen is credited with bringing the first gigabit firewall to the market.

In addition, NetScreen implemented an easy-to-use Web interface to manage the firewall along with its CLI. The Web interface allowed anyone who could point and click to manage the firewall. This capability went a long way in the early firewall days. Many startups purchased the low-cost, high-performance devices, which increased NetScreen's market share quickly. NetScreen developed the first gigabit firewall, the NS-1000, a device that brought NetScreen credibility for its ability to develop new technologies.

Juniper firewalls use a concept called *zones*. A zone is a logical label that is placed on each network interface. When creating a policy, you include a source zone and destination zone in the firewall rule. Having these zones allows you to specifically determine the way traffic transverses through your firewall. This capability is unique among firewall products and speeds performance by limiting which rules the firewall needs to process when checking whether the traffic matches.

Juniper's first attempt at central management was called Global Pro. The software met with limited success and was replaced by the product NetScreen Security Manager, or NSM. NSM is modeled on Check Point's provider-1 platform. The cost is much less than that of any of the Check Point management products. The NSM product has made large strides over the years in its development. Early criticism by customers has turned to praise and wide adoption of the product.

Today, Juniper Networks is the only company that challenges both Check Point and Cisco in the marketplace. Recently, Juniper has introduced a new product line of security routers. These are traditional NetScreen firewalls; however, they now include the capability for WAN interfaces. These WAN interfaces allow this device to replace the router that would normally sit in front of it.

The secure routing space is a multibillion-dollar market in which only Cisco and Juniper Networks are competitors.

> *Juniper Networks' Web site is* `www.juniper.net`*, and you can find the security products at* `www.juniper.net/products/`*. You can also read more about Juniper firewalls in the book* Configuring Juniper Networks NetScreen & SSG Firewalls *(Syngress Publishing, ISBN 1597491187).*

Check Point

We cannot discuss the term *firewall* without also discussing the company Check Point Software Technologies, LTD. Founded in 1993, Check Point revolutionized the firewall market. The original flagship product, Firewall-1, brought several core enhancements to the firewall market. The most notable and recognizable is the Check Point GUI manager. The Check Point GUI is the standard on which all firewall management is based. The GUI provides an easy way for administrators to manage the firewall infrastructure. It also provides a straightforward interface that transcended the CLI-only world of firewalls of the time.

Check Point also came up with the option to provide Virtual Private Network (VPN) services. The VPN component was originally a software-license option but eventually became a standard feature. One of the co-founders, Gil Shwed, even wrote an encryption algorithm called FWZ that was included in the software until the 5.0 version was released. Creating a VPN and doing NAT was also done in the GUI.

The Check Point firewall product ran on third-party operating systems. Sun's Solaris operating system was the original platform of choice. Check Point also supported many other operating systems: HP-UX, Microsoft Windows NT, and AIX. However, as time passed and the market changed, customers wanted an appliance-based solution. Check Point partnered with the Finnish company Nokia to produce the IP series appliances. Nokia purchased a company named Ipsilon in 1997 and used its technologies, namely the IPSO operating system. The IP series ran the IPSO operating system that was based on FreeBSD. Nokia also provided software support for Check Point's firewall product line.

With the release of the NG 5.0 version of the software, Check Point introduced its own version of an operating system called Secure Platform (Splat). Secure Platform was a Linux-based system that came with Check Point preinstalled. It allowed you to insert the CD, boot, and install the OS with Check Point in about 15 minutes. This was a much lower-cost alternative to purchasing either a Sun server or Nokia appliance.

The biggest complaint about Check Point always has been its complex software licensing. Each software license requires a software subscription and support contract. Managing these was often tough enough, but renewing and keeping up-to-date with them was also a large challenge. Check Point introduced a Web-based license management system to ease the burden of dealing with all the available licenses. However, this system didn't reduce the cost of the licenses. Also, Check Point software is often run on third-party hardware, which increases the cost. Additionally, you will have to call the hardware vendor for hardware support and Check Point for software support. Many competitors used this inconvenience as leverage to argue for replacing aging installations of Check Point with their own products.

Check Point is the market leader among software firewalls vendors. Check Point and Juniper Networks are constantly battling for market share in the firewall space. As of the end of last year, Check Point was second in overall firewall market share, according to infonetics research. You can read more about Check Point products at its Web site at www.checkpoint.com.

Other Vendors

Although the three main vendors tend to dominate the market, some room is still available for the smaller companies to operate in. These vendors offer similar technologies to the larger vendors but provide some niche features as well. One of the big factors to point out is that these vendors also play as the lower-cost choice. They often attempt to price their products, with more features, at lower cost than the bigger vendors' products.

Three examples of smaller vendors are SonicWALL (www.sonicwall.com), WatchGuard (www.watchguard.com), and Fortinet (www.fortinet.com). Each of these vendors targets the consumer with a low-cost, appliance-based solution. They offer robust features and focus on places where the core vendors are weaker. An example of this is the UTM feature set; these vendors offer lower-cost versions of UTM.

SonicWALL was one of the first companies to offer some UTM features, such as integrated Web filtering. SonicWALL did this because the customer base, which consisted of small to medium businesses, called for this integration early on. The larger vendors offered these features in the long run, but larger companies take longer to create features than do these smaller, more nimble companies.

Choosing one of the smaller vendors isn't a bad thing. As is true of any decision, choosing the right product requires an accurate evaluation of the scenario at hand. If you are looking for a feature-rich, low-cost device, a smaller vendor may make the most sense. If you are looking for a feature-rich, low-cost device that also has a large company to back the technology, you may want to be cautious when choosing a smaller company's products. When choosing products, look at them from both a business and a technology perspective. An interviewer may choose to see whether you can distinguish between the two. Just because a company has the best technology does not make that technology the best choice for your organization. A business decision would focus on the strengths of the company behind the product as well as the costs of the product.

Open source technologies offer a low-cost alternative to commercial products. They provide decently rounded solutions for organizations on shoestring budgets. Extremely small offices that have no budget often deploy these solutions. The downside is support. If you are capable of taking the time to fully support a product for which you may be the last line of support, it is a good choice. Large organizations require the use of a product that is fully tested and have someone who can fix it in the event of any foreseeable problem. With an open source solution, this support typically isn't possible.

Device Types

Firewall technologies are only part of a complete solution. A firewall needs a strong hardware platform to host its software. Each vendor chooses a platform that allows for the best use of its software. The software is optimized to operate on specific hardware. In many cases, a vendor builds both the hardware and software that make up a firewall. Other times, a firewall software vendor will partner with a hardware manufacturer to create a hardware platform for the vendor.

Two classes of device can be used for a firewall: an appliance or a server. These are very broad categories, but they each have very distinct characteristics. An *appliance* is a device that is specifically designed to run a specified set of applications. A *server* is a general-purpose piece of hardware that can be used to run any software, whether a fileserver or firewall. Each device type has its benefits and drawbacks, and you will find out about those in the following sections.

Appliance

An appliance is a device that is built for a specific purpose or application. This is a very broad definition that includes several types of devices. We look at the most specific to the least specific types of devices to enable you to see the breadth that is encompassed in this category.

Some vendors such as Juniper Networks, Cisco, and SonicWALL create devices that are specific hardware appliances. These appliances are designed to run only code that is specific to the vendor. They often employ mechanisms that prevent you from installing other operating systems or code on them. Also, these hardware platforms have custom ASICs, processors, or other hardware that works only with the operating system designed for them. These appliances are designed to provide specific performance numbers and vendor-specific services. These are often the highest-performing devices available on the market. Because the hardware is specific to the vendor, it can be customized to provide specific services that the vendor wants to provide. An example of this customization are the UTM features we described previously. Many newer appliances are designed to provide high-performance UTM throughput.

These types of appliances also run a small, binary, image-based operating system (OS). The OS is loaded into a local flash memory– or hard drive–based storage system. Appliances have a great benefit also: Because of their design, they are easily replaced in the event of a failure. This means that there usually is a simple configuration either in the form of a text file or small binary file that can be saved and reloaded, enabling you to easily back up the system and restore the configuration on new hardware in the case of a failure. It removes the need to reload a base operating system and then load the firewall application on top of it.

Some appliances run other operating systems similar to those run on a server. The operating system may be Linux, Microsoft Windows, or a custom one. These devices then run a firewall application on top of the base operating system to provide firewalling services. These devices have a CLI or Web management console to configure the operating system and attempt to make the underlying system transparent to the end user. The firewall application is managed independently of the appliance. These devices are still classified as appliances because they are purpose-built devices that run a specific application. Examples of these devices are Crossbeam or Nokia appliances that are designed specifically to run Check Point firewall software.

Secure Router

Although a firewall is a device that directs traffic from one location to another and provides security services, it does not have a WAN interface. A router is a device that not only directs traffic from one location to another but also contains WAN interfaces. A secure router combines the features of both, and for this reason, the future of security devices is the secure router market.

Although this technology has been done before — most notably on the Nokia IP series Check Point– powered appliances — it was never a large success because Nokia isn't considered a powerhouse in the router marketplace. Today, Cisco and Juniper are focusing on this market and have created products specifically for the secure router space.

A secure router is an appliance-based firewall that contains WAN interfaces. Other components that are common among the secure router devices are a stateful firewall engine, UTM, routing protocol support, and WAN protocol support. Both Cisco and Juniper have used the underlying technologies that they have developed for the other products. In the long-term future, the concept of a router without full integration of security features will be a thing of the past.

Server Based

A server-based firewall is one that is run on a standard server. A server in this case is classified as hardware that runs a standard operating system and can be used to do other things in addition to running a firewall. Typically, an underlying operating system such as Solaris, Linux, or Microsoft Windows is loaded first. Then the operating system is patched and hardened to the level that is suggested by the manufacturer. After this is done, the firewall software is loaded on top of the base operating system.

This is how firewall products began. Initially, software companies developed firewall software on existing server platforms. Using an existing platform enabled companies to rapidly develop software features without needing to develop an entire operating system to run on. Early on, Solaris was the most popular choice because it was stable, provided a robust TCP/IP stack, and had many administrators already familiar with it. The only downside was that the hardware was more expensive than that for an Intel-based server. The most notable software to be server based was the Check Point firewall.

Today, however, many commercial firewall products run on Linux. The shift in development toward Linux came from the adoption of the OS for mainstream use and the fact that it could be more easily customized to fit the developers' needs. Also, Linux could be run on less expensive hardware than Sun Microsystems hardware and provided faster performance.

Management

Every firewall must be configurable. Many organizations choose a firewall product based on favoring its configuration capabilities over any other criteria. The more intuitive the design of the firewall's management, the easier it is to effectively secure your network.

Every vendor comes up with its own management strategy; however, there are three distinct classes of management. The first management type is called *stand-alone*. Stand-alone management allows the administrator to configure the firewall directly. The second management type is called *distributed management*. This architecture distributes the management tasks to two or more devices. The third type is *global management*. Global management allows for a management strategy that can encompass several hundred or thousand devices to be managed centrally.

Configuration Components

The three management types share three important concepts, each of which you should become familiar with.

The first concept is that of *object-oriented management*. With object-oriented management, each component of the configuration is an object. An *object* is a component that, after being created, can be referenced throughout the firewall's configuration. Take, for example, an address object. An *address object* is an object that represents an IP-addressed host or subnet. The address object can be used inside the firewall's security policy or in the firewall logs as an object that you can filter for. Another example of an object is a service object. A *service object* represents a service or protocol. This, again, is referenced inside firewall policies or used to filter in the logs.

The second concept for management is the device's configuration itself. This encompasses the interface addressing, routing table, remote management service, and any other settings that are specific to the device. Each device needs to have these components configured before it can operate as a security device.

The third concept is the security policy. A *security policy* is the configuration of the firewall that determines the action a firewall takes on the traffic when it enters the device. The most common options for a policy are the following: source IP, destination IP, service (protocol), action, and rule options. Each set of these options makes up an individual firewall rule. The security policy is a collection of rules.

Inside the rule, the source IP specifies the IP of the traffic entering the firewall. The destination IP specifies what IP the source IP address is attempting to connect to. The service or protocol is just that: the service or protocol that the source IP is attempting to connect to on the destination IP. When the source IP, destination IP, and service match, the firewall stops processing the policy and then performs the action on the traffic. This action could be to drop the traffic, reject it by sending a network message back to the source IP, or send it into a VPN tunnel. Rule options are flags that can be set, such as log the traffic or set a Simple Network Management Protocol (SNMP) trap when this traffic type is seen. This depends on the available options from the vendor.

These key concepts are applied to each of the management types that we look at in the following sections. These concepts are what make a firewall work.

Stand-Alone

Stand-alone firewall management means that management is performed on the firewall device itself. That is, you directly connect to the firewall and manage the device. The management includes not only the device management but the ability to create security policies. A stand-alone device is just as it sounds: a single device that provides enforcement without the need for any other system to operate.

This type of management can be done a few different ways. The original and still favorite stand-alone method is using a command-line interface, or CLI. The CLI allows for the direct input of commands into the device. Any device with a CLI would most likely have a console or serial port for access into the device. This is used for initial deployment and non-network–based access. For remote access to the CLI, most devices offer the less secure telnet and the more commonly used SSH, or secure shell.

Devices that are CLI based often have the capability to save the configuration as a list of CLI commands, making backup and restoration easy. These devices also give you the chance to prestage a series of commands for you to input when you want to make a change. It is very simple to script changes as well with a CLI. You can also create a perl, expect, or tcl script to send commands or backup device configurations. The most common CLI-based platforms are appliance-based firewalls.

Web-based management is another common management type for a stand-alone device and enables you to configure both the device and the security policy. An easy-to-use Web management system on a stand-alone appliance is a powerful tool for any administrator. Devices that have CLI management typically have a Web-based management option as well.

Examples of vendors that produce products with stand-alone management are Juniper Networks and SonicWALL. A drawback to stand-alone management is its difficulty in managing many devices simultaneously. Some vendors such as Juniper Networks or Cisco have management options for managing many devices at one time.

Distributed

Distributed management has two or more tiers within the management infrastructure. The classic example is the three-tiered model that Check Point created. In this design, the firewall or enforcement module is the device that the firewall or security policy is applied to. The management module is the software that holds all the configurations. This module also receives all the logging information from the firewall module. The graphical user interface (GUI) is the module you interact with. You use the GUI and then connect to the management module. Then you can create policies, modify polices, view logs, and push configurations to the firewall modules. The distributed management design can encompass dozens or hundreds of devices. (Larger-scale deployments are often done with a global management architecture. You would want to use global management in cases when you want to divide sections of your network into different administrative domains or group your network configuration into different containers. Global management is discussed in detail in the next section.)

Some firewall vendors such as Check Point require the three-tier architecture for their firewall deployments. Other vendors, such as Cisco and Juniper Networks, have the option to use a distributed deployment model, but it is not required.

Global Management

Global management architectures are similar to the distributed model; however, they are much larger in scale. A global management design provides two benefits. The first benefit is the capability to divide network management into separate administrative containers — that is, you can divide your firewalls into different groupings.

For example, you could put all the firewalls on the East Coast of the United States into a specific administrative group and the firewalls on the West Coast in another. Doing so can enable you to give administrators on the East Coast full access to only the firewalls in their territory, and give West Coast administrators access to only their firewalls. By dividing administrative control between the two groups, you give each group appropriate access to the proper firewalls, and restrict the groups from access to firewalls that they don't need to change.

The second use for global management is to separate firewalls into groups to divide the configuration into manageable pieces. In this scenario, you create smaller administrative groups just as in the preceding East Coast/West Coast example. In this case, however, all administrators get access to all groups of firewalls. This approach makes the firewalls more manageable because all the associated objects and logs are separated into the appropriate groups.

The first company to create a truly excellent product for this category was Check Point, with its Provider-1 product (`www.checkpoint.com/products/provider-1/index.html`). Provider-1 allows multiple instances of its distributed management system to run on a single server. This expanded Check Point's already dominant management capabilities even further. Juniper Networks introduced its global management product, called NetScreen Security Manager (NSM) (`www.juniper.net`; search for "NetScreen Security Manager"), a few years later. It is similar to Check Point's Provider-1 in concept; however, NSM does not run multiple processes but simply divides the configuration into multiple databases. Check Point's Provider-1 product, although a strong management system, is extremely expensive to purchase and support. Juniper Networks NSM software is considerably less expensive to implement.

Deployment Strategies

No matter which vendor you choose or which technologies you employ, you have several standard deployment strategies for firewalls. These designs are used throughout the world and are the most common deployment concepts. As with any type of networking, however, these deployment strategies can be used in many combinations. The combinations in firewall deployment are limitless, just as network configurations can be. The biggest challenge is to ensure that you keep the design as simple as possible.

> *Increasing the complexity of the design can actually lower your security because you may lose track of how to actually secure the network.*

In this section, we review the most popular firewall deployments. It is crucial to be familiar with these because you will see them in actual production environments. Most are not overly complex, but again, the strategy ultimately consists of the separation between two or more networks or network segments. These designs are generic and do not take into account any vendor-specific abilities.

> *An excellent book covering firewalls and firewall deployment strategies is* Building Internet Firewalls, Second Edition *(O'Reilly Publishing, ISBN 1565928717).*

Basic Deployment

The rationale for basic deployment for a firewall is simple: It provides separation between two separate networks. A firewall does this by providing both an ingress and an egress interface. An *ingress* interface is the interface where traffic enters a firewall. The *egress* interface is where traffic exits the firewall. Figure 5-3 shows an example of this.

Unprotected
Network

Protected
Network

Figure 5-3

A firewall typically acts as a router between the two networks that it is separating. The hosts on each side of the firewall need to access the other by passing through the firewall. This can be done by pointing to the firewall as your next routing hop or default route for the network on the other side of the firewall. Imagine that the network behind the firewall labeled Protected Network in Figure 5-3 is the local area network (LAN) of a small business. The other side, labeled Unprotected Network, is connected to the Internet. For this example, we assume that it's a public network with Internet routable addresses on the external segment. The firewall contains a default route pointing to its upstream router that is not depicted on the diagram.

For any host on the internal network to talk to a host on the outside of the firewall, it would need to pass through to the firewall. The traffic would ingress into the firewall on the internal interface. This is where the firewall gets to work applying the technology that it is built on, as described in the previous "Firewall Technologies" section.

The Balance of Security

Design in general is always a balance between extremes. In the case of security, it is a balance of many different pairs. Often, you want to do one thing — allow access for users — yet limit that accessibility, requiring you to compromise. This compromise could be necessary because of cost, management, application requirements, lack of knowledge, lack of time, or some other factor. Often, there is a better way that the security architecture could be designed, yet an external factor is causing you to change your design.

When creating a secure network design, always try to look at security as the most important part of the design. An interviewer may question you on the concepts of providing access versus providing security. You should always default to applying the most restrictive security measures while still allowing accessibility to the required services.

The value in this case is that the firewall allows everything outbound toward the Internet and does not allow any traffic back into the network. This ensures that the hosts are protected and invulnerable to attack. You may be inclined to share services with the rest of the world, however. To do so, you would need to allow access back into the network, which would require you to open a firewall rule or policy.

In the basic firewall deployment that we have been discussing, allowing inbound traffic is not a good idea. The risk here is that the host that is exposed to the Internet may be compromised, which would then allow an attacker to access all the internal resources of the network such as your critical data servers. Because of this risk, a different network design — A DMZ (demilitarized zone) — should be used. This design is detailed in the following section.

DMZ

The DMZ (or demilitarized zone) is a classic firewall implementation architecture. A DMZ is simply a network that is segmented from the other parts of the network. This segmentation ensures that the only access into and out of this network is through a firewall. The concept of the DMZ has changed over the years. In this section, we look at the concept of a DMZ — both its original implementation and the newest ideas about what makes up a DMZ.

Classic DMZ

A classic DMZ was originally a mix of a router and a dedicated firewall. The router provided the connectivity to the Internet by connecting to a wide area network (WAN) circuit. The router then provided, typically, an Ethernet link to the LAN. You can see this design in Figure 5-4.

Unprotected
Network

DMZ

Protected
Network

Figure 5-4

The router's Ethernet link connects to a switch that is also used for DMZ hosts. Also connecting to the switch is an Ethernet link to the firewall. The firewall then also connects back into the private, secured LAN. The various DMZ hosts that would be placed between the firewall and the router provide

Internet-accessible services. In the classic DMZ design, the Internet can access the DMZ for the specified services. The secured LAN can access the DMZ services as well. The LAN can also access the Internet. However, neither the DMZ hosts nor the Internet can access the secure LAN. The overall design is fairly strong. If the DMZ hosts are compromised, they can access only each other and not the secure LAN. Also, if the router is compromised, the secure LAN is still restricted and secured.

There are some drawbacks to the overall design, however. The first drawback is that typically the router provides only very simple security, such as a packet filter. A potential resolution to this problem is to implement a security router or a stateful firewalling router in this location. Doing so could increase your costs, which may be undesirable. Second, many of today's Internet services are tiered. A typical tiered structure contains a data server, an application server, and a Web server. With the classic DMZ design, you would potentially lose all these servers if a compromise took place in the DMZ.

Single-Firewall DMZ

The single-firewall DMZ is similar to what was discussed in the basic firewall deployment. The difference, though, is the addition of more network interfaces. Each interface provides an additional network that can be attached to the firewall. The most common example is a three-interface firewall device, which would allow for a secure LAN, an Internet connection, and a DMZ. The DMZ would contain hosts that you wish to secure from the rest of the secure LAN and from the Internet. This is the most typical deployment for a DMZ. Figure 5-5 shows an example of the typical single-firewall DMZ.

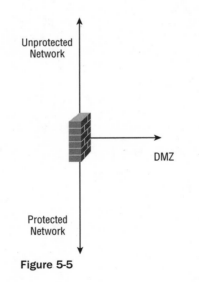

Figure 5-5

A great feature of the single-firewall DMZ is that you can always add DMZs by increasing the number of interfaces on the firewall. This would allow for multitiered applications to be spread across several secured DMZs, providing separation for each of the tiers.

High Availability

A firewall is placed at critical junctures throughout your network to enforce a security policy as it forces network traffic to go through it. This also makes the firewall a weak point in the network. If the firewall were to fail, the location where your firewall was placed would be broken. This is where the need for high availability is critical.

High availability (HA) is a requirement for many organizations because uptime is of an utmost importance. HA is achieved by having two or more firewalls providing redundant paths in the network. If a firewall fails, the other firewall will take over for the failed device. The mechanism for how failover occurs varies from vendor to vendor. It can also vary based upon your network topology.

Most firewall vendors offer the ability to perform stateful failover. For stateful failover, the primary firewall shares its known state of connections with the secondary firewall, which allows all the existing connections to failover to the second device. If you don't have stateful failover, you will lose all of your existing connections. This loss will occur because the second firewall is stateful and must understand the state of the connections going through it. If the state of the existing sessions is not known, they will be dropped and need to be reinitialized.

High Availability Types

Firewall HA clusters are deployed in one of two ways, as an active/passive cluster or an active/active cluster. An *active/passive* cluster uses two or more devices. One of the devices is active and passes all the traffic. The other devices in the cluster wait for the primary device to fail. During this time, the devices are passive and do not pass any traffic. The passive devices can be configured, based upon the vendor, to share the state information from the active device to the passive units.

In the event of a failure, one of the passive devices will take over. The mechanisms on how they failover also are based upon the vendor's implementation. For an active/passive cluster, failover is done with one of two technologies. The first uses gratuitous ARPs. The passive unit that takes over sends out gratuitous ARPs to tell the surrounding devices that it now has the IP addresses of the primary device. All the surrounding devices will then accept that the passive unit now has taken over for the active .

The second method uses a multicast MAC address. This address is used to represent the cluster's IP address. All the units in the cluster receive the packets intended for the primary firewall. If the primary device fails, the passive device then takes over for the now-failed active unit. Because the MAC address for the active IPs never actually changes, there is no need to change anything. The downside to the multicast MAC address is that not all switches can properly handle it. Sometimes you will have to make a static entry on the switch to tell what ports have the multicast MAC on it.

Multicast MAC addresses are also used in another type of HA deployment: the active/active deployment. In an *active/active* deployment, multiple devices pass traffic at the same time, allowing you to share the load across multiple devices. With a multicast MAC address, the firewalls determine what handles which traffic flows. This increases the amount of throughput by providing multiple firewalls and typically is done because the firewall vendor isn't capable of handling the total amount of throughput on a single device. Failover operates just as described previously. When one of the firewalls fails, the firewall that is left simply takes over the remainder of the traffic.

The other type of active/active deployment has two active units, both capable of passing traffic, and each device has its own unique IP address. To force traffic to each firewall, you would use either dynamic routing or static routing. In the event of a failure, the remaining device in a cluster would take over for both devices. Typically, this technology is used by vendors that offer higher-performing firewall devices.

How Many Devices in a Cluster?

Determining how many devices to use in a cluster is an often-debated firewall question. The most typical answer is to use two devices because if one firewall fails, the second device will take over for it. The logic here is very reasonable. You would deploy a single backup unit in the event of a failure.

Some administrators wish to deploy more than two devices so that the load is shared across multiple firewalls. The only time you would really want to do this is when a firewall vendor is unable to provide the required performance on a single device. When working with any HA design, you want to keep it as simple as possible. The more complex it is, the more issues you can run into when troubleshooting or when failure conditions occur.

Summary

In this chapter, we looked at the basics of the firewall. Today's firewall market is a complicated environment. The best advice for anyone looking to understand it is *learn the basics*, which are found in this chapter, and then do research. There is so much information available on vendors' Web sites and on the Web alone that you could never possibly read it all. On top of that, there is a slew of books on firewalls.

Focus on the fundamentals of the firewall technologies and then drill down to the vendors as needed. If you truly understand how something works, it doesn't really matter how a vendor implements it. You will be able to sit down and know what you want to accomplish; then, you just need to research the commands needed to implement it.

Never focus on just understanding how a single vendor does something. Learn the full technology around the vendor's implementation. This way, when you need to work with or understand another vendor, you just need to understand that company's implementation of the technology. You will be a much more valuable resource when you are not restricted to a single vendor.

Firewall technology constantly changes, and the biggest difficulty is keeping up. The Web is your best resource for this, followed closely by books. Books take time to write and publish. A technical book typically takes a lifecycle of three months to one year to write and another few months for printing and distribution. Books often cover established technologies and obviously are unable to change as fast as the Web.

Interview Q&A

Q: What is a packet filter firewall?

A: A packet filter firewall inspects traffic on a per-packet basis. It matches only on an individual packet basis. It is not capable of determining a packet flow or session. Packet filters can match a packet from the simple source and destination IP up to and including specific protocol flags such as TCP SYN and FIN. This varies based upon the vendor's implementation of a packet filter.

Q: What is stateful inspection?

A: In stateful inspection, a firewall inspects traffic based upon the state of the connection. The firewall is aware of the beginning, middle, and end of a connection. If the connection goes out of state, the firewall is able to detect it.

Q: What is an application proxy firewall?

A: An application proxy firewall proxies connections that attempt to go through the firewall. The client's request is always proxied to server. The server's response is proxied back to the client as well. This allows the proxy to completely inspect the connection.

Q: What does the term DMZ stand for?

A: This stands for demilitarized zone. It is a term that represents a segmented network to which access is protected by a firewall.

Q: Why would you want a high-availability firewall deployment in your network?

A: Because a firewall is often placed at a critical point in your network. If it were to fail, you would lose access to critical resources such as Internet access.

Q: What are the characteristics of an appliance firewall?

A: An appliance-based firewall is a device that is built for a specific purpose. The purpose in this case is to be a firewall.

Q: What is NAT?

A: NAT stands for Network Address Translation. With NAT, a packet has either the source or destination IP address modified as it passes through a firewall.

Q: What is Unified Threat Management?

A: Unified Threat Management, or UTM, is a collection of technologies that are bundled together to eliminate threats on the network. These technologies include deep-packet inspection, antivirus, antispam, and URL filtering.

Q: What are the main configuration components in a firewall?

A: The firewall's configuration (networking/routing), the firewall policy (the policy that restricts traffic for a device), and the firewall's objects (the components used during the firewall's policy configuration.

Q: What is a secure router?

A: A secure router is a device that couples the features of a router and a firewall, including the use of WAN interfaces, firewall services, and, often, a UTM feature set.

Q: What company was the first to implement firewall technologies?

A: Cisco Systems originally implemented firewall features in the form of packet filters on routers.

Q: Who are the three market leaders in the firewall technology space?

A: Cisco, Check Point, and Juniper Networks are the three market leaders. Cisco is the number one leader in firewall appliances. Check Point is the market leader in software-based firewalls. Juniper Networks is in second place behind Cisco for firewall appliances.

Q: What was Check Point's most important impact on the firewall market?

A: The creation of an easy-to-use central management tool. This tool contained easy-to-use GUIs and still sets the bar for user interfaces today.

Q: What is the most basic deployment for a firewall?

A: The most basic deployment for a firewall is placing a firewall between an untrusted network, such as the Internet, and the local area network. This placement limits the access that the Internet has to the local area network. The local area network has important services that should not be Internet accessible. These services include file servers and e-mail servers.

Q: Can you list the three core firewall technologies?

A: Packet filter, stateful inspection, and application proxies are the core firewall technologies.

Q: What are three technologies you can find in the UTM feature set?

A: Antivirus inspection, antispam, and deep-packet inspection. Antivirus technologies often focus on the inspection of Web and e-mail traffic.

Recommended Reading

The TCP/IP Guide: A Comprehensive, Illustrated Internet Protocols Reference, by Charles Kozierok (No Starch Press. ISBN: 978-1593270476. 2005).

Building Internet Firewalls (Second Edition), by Elizabeth D. Zwicky, Simon Cooper, and D. Brent Chapman (O'Reilly Media, Inc. ISBN: 978-1565928718. 2000).

Configuring Juniper Networks NetScreen & SSG Firewalls, by Rob Cameron, Brad Woodberg, Mike Swarm, Mathew Albers, Neil Wyler, Ralph Bonnell, and Mohan Madwachar (Syngress Publishing. ISBN: 978-1597491181. 2006).

Configuring Check Point NGX VPN-1/Firewall-1, by Robert Stephens, Barry J. Stiefel, and Simon Desmeules (Syngress Publishing. ISBN: 978-1597490313. 2005).

Cisco ASA and PIX Firewall Handbook, by David Hucaby (Cisco Press. ISBN: 978-1587051586. 2005).

The Best Damn Firewall Book Period, by Cherie Amon, Thomas W. Shinder, and Anne Carasik-Henmi (Syngress Publishing. ISBN: 978-1931836906. 2003).

Computer Security Basics (Second Edition), by Rick Lehtinen and G.T. Gangemi, Sr (O'Reilly Media, Inc. ISBN: 978-0596006693. 2006).

6

Knowing Virtual
Private Networks

The technical interview routinely covers questions regarding Virtual Private Networking (VPN) technologies. In this chapter, we briefly discuss the history, theory, and various uses for virtual private networking (VPN) technologies. We stress the word briefly, because we have approximately 20 pages to cover what would normally take hundreds of pages. Therefore, this chapter is limited to the practical applications, high-level configurations, and implementations. Specifically, we review IP Security, or IPsec. (Note the capitalization of IPsec. RFC 4301 specifically states that all other spellings of IPsec have been deprecated.) IPsec is used all over the world to provide confidentiality, data origin authentication, integrity, detection and rejection of replays, and limited traffic flow security of IP data.

Before we discuss the various uses and types of VPN technologies, we need to first review what makes it all possible: cryptography. The first few sections of this chapter should be familiar to most security practitioners. For those of you new to this material, we guide you to more in-depth discussions and reviews. We wrap up the discussion with an alternative approach for remote access users (client VPN) with a rapidly growing technology being widely adopted, which uses Secure Sockets Layer (SSL) or Transport Layer Security (TLS).

The chapter ends with a series of questions that can be used by either the interviewer (sitting behind the desk asking) or the interviewee (sitting in front of the desk answering). In either case, these questions are so detailed that they are sure to spark your interest in IPsec and the proposed alternative, SSL/TLS.

Goals and Assumptions

To get the most from this chapter, you should have a basic understanding of IPsec and the various encryption protocols and algorithms used to implement IPsec. You'll also find it beneficial if you're somewhat familiar with vendor implementations, although it's not required. IPsec, with its large number of possible configurations, can be a mind-numbing subject. The goal of this chapter is to review the high-level components of the cryptographic methods used in the IPsec suite in such a way that it is more easily retained. We also make an attempt to recommend a "best practice" configuration suitable for *all* organizations, corporate and government, except for protecting classified national security information.

The Cryptography of VPNs

Cryptography has been in use for thousands of years in one form or another. Governments and corporations alike use it to protect their sensitive data from prying eyes. Not to worry: It is not necessary to understand various cryptographic algorithms at the mathematical level, and it is certainly not necessary to understand differential cryptanalysis techniques to properly implement a sound and secure VPN solution. Terms such as rounds, S-boxes, and initialization vector (IV) may sound familiar, but rest assured — understanding the algorithms at the mathematical level is *not* required to get the job, unless, of course, you are applying for a cryptanalyst job at the National Security Agency (NSA).

There are many options with regard to choice of encryption ciphers, hashing algorithms, and key management protocols. We review only the NIST-approved cryptographic methods, which are more often than not deployed in both government and corporate environments.

Symmetric Key Cryptography

Symmetric key encryption uses a bi-directional or reversible encryption algorithm to provide confidentially of data. In other words, the sender and receiver of the sensitive data share a secret key. The sender feeds the secret key and data into any of a number of symmetric key algorithms to encrypt the plaintext data into cipher text. The receiver uses the exact same secret key to decrypt the cipher text back into plain-text using the same symmetric key algorithm. If Alice and Bob, to use the classic crypto characters, are sitting on different floors of the same building, then securely exchanging the secret key may not pose a risk. There is still a question of storage of the key, so compromise may still be an issue. However, if Alice is in Virginia, and Bob is on vacation in Singapore, then exchanging the secret key securely presents an issue and opens the door to potential comprise of the secret key.

There are currently three NIST approved symmetric ciphers. The newest addition to this list, the Advanced Encryption Standard (AES,) was added in November 2001. The Whitehouse Office of Management and Budget (OMB), responsible for the OMB circulars, delivered a notice shortly after NIST released AES stating that the new encryption method is expected to be valid for the next 20–30 years. NIST has stated that it will review AES every five years for continued use.

Symmetric ciphers are divided into stream and block ciphers. Block ciphers exercise their mathematical prowess on fixed-size chunks of data. Stream ciphers, on the other hand, operate on the data in a serial fashion or continuous stream — one bit at a time.

> *The two protocols we discuss in this chapter are block ciphers. Therefore, we focus our discussion on these block ciphers only. For more information on streaming ciphers, Google "Streaming cipher."*

One of the most popular streaming ciphers in use today is RC4, which is implemented in the original IEEE 802.11b, aka WEP. The current evolution of WEP is called WPA, which alleviates a key scheduler issue by using the Temporal Key Integrity Protocol (TKIP). The latest standard on the street is IEEE 802.11i, which introduces AES as the required encryption protocol. We cover wireless in much more detail later in the book. Your Internet browser also uses RC4 when connecting to most Internet sites using SSL.

Google "NIST Cryptographic Toolkit" to track the latest changes to the approved list. Warning: They do not change often.

Triple Data Encryption Algorithm (TDEA)

Triple DEA, known by many names (Triple Data Encryption Algorithm, TDEA, 2TDEA, 3TDEA, and 3DES), is an extension of the well-known and now defunct Data Encryption Standard (DES). It works by employing the now deprecated DES with two different keying options. These key options are referred to as *key bundles*.

Key Option 1, as outlined in FIPS PUB 46-3 and NIST 800-67, uses three unique keys: K1, K2, and K3. This option is known as 3TDEA and it has a key length of 168 bits. However, because of documented attacks against 3TDEA, its effective cryptographic strength is 112 bits. You may also see it referred to as EEE (encrypt, encrypt, encrypt). The operation invokes DES three times using the EEE method to create a ciphertext output. Check out NIST 800-57 or ANSX9.52 Annex B for more information on the effective strength of TDEA in either keying option.

Key Option 2 also uses three keys, K1, K2, and K3; however, only two are unique, because K1 and K3 are equal to each other. This option is known as 2TDES, and it has a key length of 112 bits. However, because of the same attacks documented against 3TDEA, 2TDEA has an effective cryptographic strength of 80 bits. You may also see it referred to as EDE (encrypt, decrypt, encrypt). The operation invokes DES three times — encrypt, decrypt, encrypt — to produce a stronger cipher text output.

Because of the iteration of steps necessary to create cipher text in TDEA (2TDEA or 3TDEA), it is considerably slower than newer ciphers such as AES, which is also cryptographically much stronger.

Google "FIPS PUB 46-3" for more information.

It is somewhat of a misnomer to refer to TDEA in either keying option as 3DES because it does have multiple key lengths. Vendors indicate which key length is used with AES, for example, AES-128, AES-192, or AES-256. For this reason, you should refer to TDEA by its keying method used, 2TDEA or 3TDEA. We won't hold our breath on getting the vendors to comply.

Advanced Encryption Standard (AES)

On January 2, 1997, NIST announced a contest to unearth a successor to the aging Data Encryption Standard (DES). The winner of the contest would be a freely available, publicly defined cipher, which must be implemented in hardware or software. The NIST opened the floodgates to the cryptographic community during a three-month comment period, requesting guidance on how best to select the next Advanced Encryption Standard (AES.) The proposed draft minimum acceptability requirements and evaluation criteria were outlined in the same notice.

Google "RIN 0693-ZA13 site:nist.gov" for more information on the selection process.

Following is the list of requirements as defined in the NIST release notice.

❑   A.1 AES shall be publicly defined.

❑   A.2 AES shall be a symmetric block cipher.

❑   A.3 AES shall be designed so that the key length may be increased as needed.

- ❏ A.4 AES shall be implementable in both hardware and software.

- ❏ A.5 AES shall either be (a) freely available or (b) available under terms consistent with the American National Standards Institute (ANSI) patent policy.

- ❏ A.6 Algorithms, which meet the above requirements, will be judged based on the following factors:

    a. security (that is, the effort required to cryptanalyze),

    b. computational efficiency,

    c. memory requirements,

    d. hardware and software suitability,

    e. simplicity,

    f. flexibility, and

    g. licensing requirements.

The winning candidate, Rijndael (pronounced "*Rhine doll*"), was developed by the Belgian cryptographers Joan Daemen and Vincent Rijmen. The name comes from a combination of the inventors' names. Following the design requirements, AES is a 128-bit block cipher with 128, 192, and 256-bit key lengths. However, AES is a modified version of Rijndael, which supports additional block sizes and key lengths. It requires very little memory to operate, and performs seven to 10 times faster than TDEA (3DES) in software. There is a slight performance increase in hardware on some vendor implementations.

Google "FIPS PUB 197" for more information on AES.

Asymmetric Cryptography

When you hear of asymmetric cryptography, the classic example of Alice and Bob comes to mind. Also known as public-key cryptography, it was developed in the 1970s to share messages between two or more persons in a secure fashion using a pair of keys — public and private. The private key is secret to each user, and the public keys are shared among interested parties. The public/private key pairs are initially requested by each user from a trusted agent or third party known as a Certificate Authority (CA). This process of establishing a third party (internally or externally) is known as a Public Key Infrastructure (PKI). Microsoft Active Directory (AD) integrates a Certificate Authority into its latest server operating systems at no additional cost, which makes it one of the more popular PKI software packages. Because of the sheer size of the U.S. government, the Defense Information Systems Agency (DISA) has one of the largest deployed PKI systems in the world.

Standards are critical to the success of public-key cryptography, or PKI. RSA Data Security Inc. received the patent on the RSA asymmetric key algorithm and the rights to several other key patents. Therefore, it has been awarded the licensing rights. RSA Security was interested in promoting and controlling the use of public key techniques, so RSA labs, a division of RSA Security, developed the Public-Key Cryptography Standards (PKCS). The word "standards" is somewhat misleading in this case because they are not industry standards. A few of the PKCS are now being developed under the IETF Public-Key Infrastructure (X.509) Working Group (PKIX).

Several of the PKCS are familiar to most security practitioners, specifically when requesting a certificate from a trusted authority.

The following list, from RSA Labs, is the PKCS maintained and controlled by RSA Labs.

❑ PKCS #1 defines mechanisms for encrypting and signing data using the RSA public-key cryptosystem.

❑ PKCS #3 defines a Diffie-Hellman key agreement protocol.

❑ PKCS #5 describes a method for encrypting a string with a secret key derived from a password.

❑ PKCS #6 is being phased out in favor of version 3 of X.509.

❑ PKCS #7 defines a general syntax for messages that include cryptographic enhancements such as digital signatures and encryption.

❑ PKCS #8 describes a format for private key information. This information includes a private key for some public-key algorithm, and optionally a set of attributes.

❑ PKCS #9 defines selected attribute types for use in the other PKCS standards.

❑ PKCS #10 describes syntax for certification requests.

❑ PKCS #11 defines a technology-independent programming interface, called Crypto kit, for cryptographic devices such as smart cards and PCMCIA cards.

❑ PKCS #12 specifies a portable format for storing or transporting a user's private keys, certificates, miscellaneous secrets, and so on.

❑ PKCS #13 is intended to define mechanisms for encrypting and signing data using Elliptic Curve Cryptography.

❑ PKCS #14 is currently in development and covers pseudo-random number generation.

❑ PKCS #15 is a complement to PKCS #11 giving a standard for the format of cryptographic credentials stored on cryptographic tokens.

Certificates

Digital certificates are used with digital signatures to bind a public key to an identity. The identity can be a person or a "thing" that requires the ability to exchange secrets securely. Common uses include verifying the identity of a network object such as a VPN appliance. Certificates are requested from a trusted Certificate Authority (CA) as discussed previously. The most popular type of certificate is the ITU-T X.509, which is developed and maintained by the IETF PKIX working group. It is documented in RFC 2459.

Google "RFC 2459 site:roxen.com" for more information on digital certificates.

Revoking Authentication

The certificate revocation list (CRL) is a list of certificate serial numbers that are no longer valid. They are no longer valid for one or more reasons, but the important point is, they are considered revoked and should not be relied upon.

As mentioned before, there are several reasons why a certificate may be revoked. The official list of reasons is maintained in RFC 3280. When maintaining a large number of certificates such as DISA or other large organizations, it is important to implement and configure a method to revoke CRLs quickly. The Online Certificate Status Protocol (OSCP) is a real-time method to revoke certificates. This feature is supported by every major vendor and documented in RFC 2560.

Google "RFC 3280" for more information about reasons a certificate may be revoked.

Google "RFC 2560 site:roxen.com" for more information about OSCP.

Hash Functions

Used for authentication, integrity, and nonrepudiation, hash functions are a one-way message digest that takes in an entire message and outputs a fixed-length (depending on the hash algorithm used), short hash. As set forth in FIPS 180-2: "for a given algorithm, it is computationally infeasible (1) to find a message that corresponds to a given message digest, or (2) to find two different messages that produce the same message digest. Any change to a message will, with a very high probability, result in a different message digest." In theory, of course.

Developed by the NSA, there are five approved cryptographic hashes as of this writing. They are SHA-1 and the newly adopted SHA-2 family, which includes SHA-224, SHA-256, SHA-384, and SHA-512. The list of approved hash functions is maintained by the NIST. The output of a hash function is sometimes referred to as a digital fingerprint.

Google "Crypto Toolkit site:nist.gov" for more information on each of these hash functions.

Practical applications of hash functions might include the following:

❑　IPsec employs hash functions to provide authentication and verification that data has not changed in transit between security gateways.

❑　Forensics experts employ hash functions to maintain a chain of custody on digital evidence to ensure that the data has not changed prior to a trial.

❑　Your favorite software vendor outputs a "fingerprint" for each of its software downloads so that users can verify that the software has not been changed either maliciously or accidentally during download.

Message Authentication Codes

There are currently two NIST-approved MAC algorithms. Message Authentication Codes (MAC), although somewhat similar to a hash function, are used to verify both the authenticity and integrity of a message by producing a cryptographic checksum. Similar to a standard checksum or CRC, the MAC verifies that data has not been altered and is therefore authentic. The keyed-hash message authentication code or HMAC is the most commonly implemented MAC in commercial IPsec security gateways. Documented in FIPS 198, it is the only appropriate MAC for use with IPsec. NIST-approved hash functions are used in the calculation of an HMAC along with a secret key known by both parties, hence the name "keyed-hash." The strength of the MAC depends on the hash function used. MACs do not provide nonrepudiation.

When used in combination with the NIST-approved hash function, the MAC is referred to as one of the following: HMAC-SHA-1, HMAC-SHA-256, and so on.

IP Security Review

IPsec operates at the ISO Layer 3 network layer of the TCP/IP protocol stack. Because IPsec operates below the transport and various application layers, it can provide protection for all types of IP packets without the requirement to reengineer the application it is protecting. Therefore, the Virtual Private Networking technology of choice for protecting (confidentiality and integrity,) and authenticating data between two or more sites is IP Security (IPsec).

Host- or client-based IP security is not covered in this chapter. However, we do discuss an alternative to IPsec for host-based VPN at the end of this chapter.

The Internet Engineering Task Force (IETF) has an assortment of request for comments (RFC) on file to proliferate these "standards track" guidelines. The third generation (RFCs 4301-4309) of this suite of RFCs was just released in December of 2005, which makes obsolete the previous standards (RFCs 2401-2412) written in 1998. The original IPsec standards (RFCs 1825-1829) were released in 1995. The changes are too numerous and substantial to list in this text, and you are encouraged to start with a review of section 13 of RFC 4301, which highlights the differences from RFC 2401.

Google "RFC 4301 site:roxen.com" for an easy to read HTML version of the standard.

ICSA Labs and the VPN Consortium have both sponsored interoperability testing over the past year. ICSA just completed a test in March of 2007; specifically, it reviewed IKEv2 implementations. Only one commercial vendor (and none of the "leaders") at the time of this writing has fully implemented the new IPsec standards as outlined in the 4300 Series RFCs.

> **You should be familiar with some of the more important changes introduced in the new standards; however, every vendor today is operating on the old deprecated standards. It may be some time (years) before the vendors are ready with fully baked code based on the new standards.**

Figure 6-1 represents several of the choices in a practical implementation of IPsec using only NIST-approved algorithms, which is what you will most often work with in commercial hardware. The new Authenticated Encryption is also illustrated; however, it will not be available until vendors fully adopt the new standards in their products.

Security Protocols and Modes

IPsec uses two security protocols to provide security services for IP data at the network layer. The Encapsulating Security Payload (ESP) and the Authentication Header (AH) are the two protocols outlined in both old and new versions of the RFCs. ESP provides confidentially (encryption), and integrity (authentication) of IP data. The AH protocol provides integrity only.

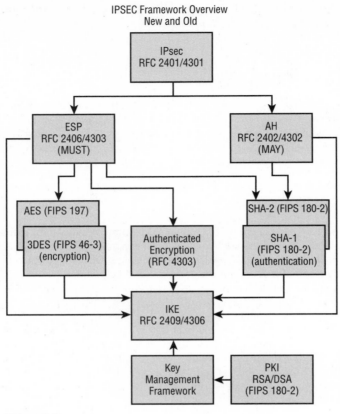

Figure 6-1

Encapsulating Security Payload (ESP)

The ESP version 2 protocol provides confidentiality, authentication, payload integrity, and anti-replay of IP packets. The new version of ESP version 3 provides additional features. ESPv2 is discussed in detail in RFC 2406 (obsolete) and ESPv3 is discussed in RFC 4303 (current.) When implemented, a new ESP header is inserted into the original IPv4 packet, as illustrated in Figure 6-2, after the IP header, and before the payload.

The new RFC 4301 standard specifically states that it is *not recommended* to implement confidentiality without integrity. With confidentiality enabled in ESP, there is the option to enable limited traffic flow security. ESPv3 implements the capability to generate dummy packets during transit across the SA, and a mechanism to identify and discard them at the receiver. In addition, ESPv3 implements variable-length padding up to 255 bytes. This provides the option to hide the length of the original packet to foil crypt-analysis methods. Figure 6-2 illustrates the ESP header based on RFC 2406. Don't expect to capture any ESP packets based on RFC 4303 off the wire anytime soon.

The ESP header includes the following fields:

❑ *Security Parameter Index (SPI)* is a 32-bit value, which uniquely identifies the Security Association (SA) for a particular datagram.

❑ The *sequence number* is a 32-bit value, which is a monotonically increasing counter value. It is used in combination with anti-replay to verify that an ESP packet has not been previously sent. When anti-replay is not configured, the receiver can choose whether to analyze this value.

❑ The *payload data* is a variable length field containing data described in the Next Header field.

❑ The *padding* field provides the ability for block-oriented algorithms to encrypt data in block size units.

❑ The *pad len* field provides the length of the Padding field.

❑ The *next header* field points back to the ESP payload and indicates the type of payload protocol (IP, TCP, UDP, and so on).

❑ The *authentication data* in the ESP protocol does not cover the full IP packet; the authentication provided covers only the ESP header and the encrypted payload.

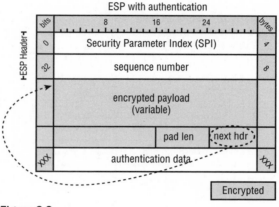

Figure 6-2

As the following list (taken from RFC 4303 Section 7) states, the differences from RFC 2406 are the following:

❑ Confidentiality-only service — now a MAY, not a MUST.

❑ SPI — modified to specify a uniform algorithm for SAD lookup for unicast and multicast SAs, covering a wider range of multicast technologies.

❑ For unicast, the SPI may be used alone to select an SA, or may be combined with the protocol, at the option of the receiver. For multicast SAs, the SPI is combined with the destination address, and optionally the source address, to select an SA.

❑ Extended Sequence Number — added a new option for a 64-bit sequence number for very high-speed communications. Clarified sender and receiver processing requirements for multicast SAs and multi-sender SAs.

❑ Payload data — broadened model to accommodate combined mode algorithms.

❑ Padding for improved traffic flow confidentiality — added requirement to be able to add bytes after the end of the IP Payload, prior to the beginning of the Padding field.

❑ Next Header — added requirement to be able to generate and discard dummy padding packets (Next Header = 59)

- ❏ ICV — broadened model to accommodate combined mode algorithms.
- ❏ Algorithms — Added combined confidentiality mode algorithms.
- ❏ Moved references to mandatory algorithms to a separate document.
- ❏ Inbound and Outbound packet processing — there are now two paths: (1) separate confidentiality and integrity algorithms and (2) combined confidentiality mode algorithms. Because of the addition of combined mode algorithms, the encryption/decryption and integrity sections have been combined for both inbound and outbound packet processing.

Tunnel Mode

ESP in tunnel mode (see Figure 6-3), the preferred method for all site-to-site configurations, encrypts the original IP header, and optionally authenticates. Note that it is always recommended to authenticate regardless if you encrypt the payload or not. It is important to know that your data is your authentic data. In the case of sensitive corporate or government data, encryption is obviously a requirement as well. However, you are strongly discouraged from configuring encryption without authentication for the reason stated previously. The next field indicates the type of payload, which in the case of ESP/Tunnel mode is IP. The next field in the new IP header points to ESP as the payload type.

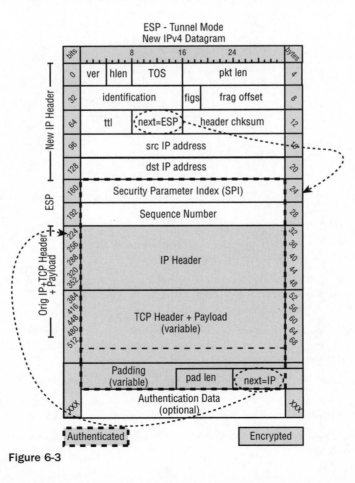

Figure 6-3

Transport Mode

ESP in transport mode looks very similar to ESP in tunnel mode with a few significant differences (see Figure 6-4). The next field in the authenticated portion of the packet points to your transport protocol in use (TCP or UDP), whereas it was simply IP before. In addition, the original IP header remains intact, and the authenticated and encrypted portions of the packet include only the TCP header and the payload.

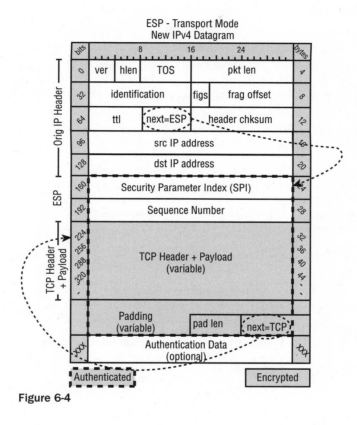

Figure 6-4

Authentication Header

The new version of the Authentication Header has changed only slightly. RFC 4302 highlights the differences from its predecessor documented in RFC 2402. The purpose of AH is to provide data origin authentication and integrity for every immutable field in the IP packet. Some fields are not authenticated because they may change during transit. AH can also provide an anti-replay service.

When configured, although not recommended, AH inserts an AH header into the datagram.

❑ The *Next Header* is an 8-bit field that identifies the next payload type following the AH header. This is key to determining whether transport mode or tunnel mode is used with AH.

❑ The *AH Len or Payload Length* is an 8-bit field, which specifies the length of AH in 32-bit words (4-byte units) minus 2-byte units.

❑ *Reserved* is a 16-bit field, which is reserved for future use.

❑ *Security Parameter Index (SPI)* is a 32-bit value, which uniquely identifies the Security Association (SA) for a particular datagram.

❑ The *Sequence Number* is a 32-bit value, which is a monotonically increasing counter value. It is used in combination with anti-replay to verify that an ESP packet has not been previously sent. When anti-replay is not configured, the receiver can choose whether to analyze this value.

❑ The *Authentication Data* is a variable length field in multiples of 32 bits (4 bytes,) which contains the Integrity Check Value (ICV) for this packet.

The future of AH is certainly in question, because ESP can provide nearly identical services to those that AH can offer. Cryptography experts Schneier and Ferguson suggested in 1999 that AH be eliminated from the IPsec framework to further reduce its complexity. The working group did in fact downgrade the support for AH to a "MAY" support in the new standards. Experts believe that AH will be fully deprecated in future releases of IPsec.

Figure 6-5 represents AH deployments in use today.

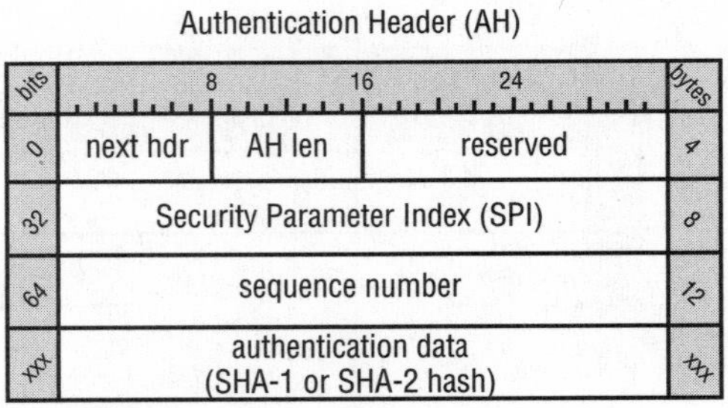

Authentication Header (AH)

Figure 6-5

Tunnel Mode

Similar to ESP in tunnel mode, AH tunnel mode inserts a new IP header. However, there is no option for encryption in AH, thus every possible field that is immutable is authenticated. Any field that may change (mutable) during transit is not authenticated as depicted in Figure 6-6.

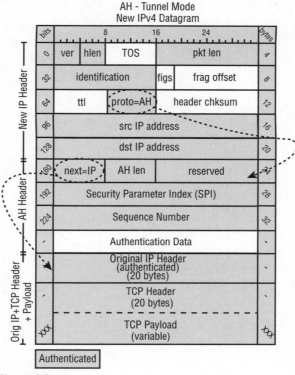

Figure 6-6

Transport Mode

AH in transport mode provides authentication of every immutable field in the packet. The original IP header remains intact with AH transport; however, the proto/next field points to AH, which is the newly inserted AH header. The next field in the AH header points to the transport layer protocol in use (TCP or UDP) (see Figure 6-7).

Key Management with IKE

The Internet Key Exchange (IKE) is the glue that binds all the components of IPsec into a working solution. Yes, manual key is an option; however, we do not cover that option in this text, nor is it a recommended configuration option. The sole purpose of the IKE protocol is to establish a secure channel to exchange secrets, which ultimately results in the establishment of an IPsec Security Association (SA). An SA is a simplex communication channel that either encrypts/authenticates (ESP) or simply authenticates (AH) data passing through it. If both ESP and AH are used, SAs must be established for each protocol in each direction. Thus ESP requires two SAs for each IPsec session, and AH requires two SAs for each IPsec session, resulting in a total of four SAs. IKE uses two phases to kick-start the process. The new RFC for IKEv2 also introduces some new features and removes others. The differences are listed below.

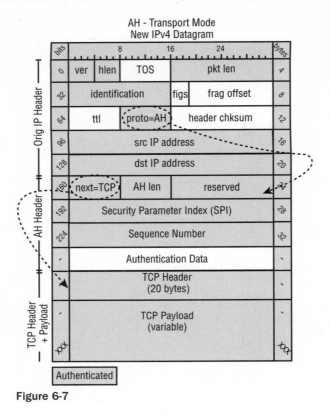

Figure 6-7

The differences between IKEv1 (RFC 2409) and IKEv2 (RFC 4306) are listed as follows (from Appendix A of RFC 4306):

❑ To define the entire IKE protocol in a single document, replacing RFCs 2407, 2408, and 2409 and incorporating subsequent changes to support NAT Traversal, Extensible Authentication, and Remote Address acquisition;

❑ To simplify IKE by replacing the eight different initial exchanges with a single four-message exchange (with changes in authentication mechanisms affecting only a single AUTH payload rather than restructuring the entire exchange) see [PK01];

❑ To remove the Domain of Interpretation (DOI), Situation (SIT), and Labeled Domain Identifier fields, and the Commit and Authentication only bits;

❑ To decrease IKE's latency in the common case by making the initial exchange be 2 round trips (4 messages), and allowing the ability to piggyback setup of a CHILD_SA on that exchange;

❑ To replace the cryptographic syntax for protecting the IKE messages themselves with one based closely on ESP to simplify implementation and security analysis;

❑ To reduce the number of possible error states by making the protocol reliable (all messages are acknowledged) and sequenced. This allows shortening CREATE_CHILD_SA exchanges from 3 messages to 2;

❑ To increase robustness by allowing the responder to not do significant processing until it receives a message proving that the initiator can receive messages at its claimed IP address, and not commit any state to an exchange until the initiator can be cryptographically authenticated;

❑ To fix cryptographic weaknesses such as the problem with symmetries in hashes used for authentication documented by Tero Kivinen;

❑ To specify Traffic Selectors in their own payloads type rather than overloading ID payloads, and making more flexible the Traffic Selectors that may be specified;

❑ To specify required behavior under certain error conditions or when data that is not understood is received, to make it easier to make future revisions that do not break backward compatibility

❑ To simplify and clarify how shared state is maintained in the presence of network failures and Denial of Service attacks; and

❑ To maintain existing syntax and magic numbers to the extent possible to make it likely that implementations of IKEv1 can be enhanced to support IKEv2 with minimum effort.

Negotiations: Phase I

The purpose of the IKEv1 Phase I exchange is to negotiate and establish a secure channel between two security endpoints. This initial SA is routinely called an IKE SA or ISAKMP SA. The IKE SA encrypts and authenticates other IKE exchanges, which results in the establishment of an IPsec SA. An IKE SA is established via one of two modes (not both) to complete the process: main mode or aggressive mode. According to RFC 2409 section 5, main mode MUST be implemented and aggressive mode *should* be implemented.

Google "RFC 2409 site:roxen.com" for more information.

Main Mode

Main mode uses three pairs of message exchanges to initiate an enable an IKE SA.

❑ During the first pair of messages, the endpoints agree on a *protection suite* of parameters. Four options are mandatory during this exchange and are listed later.

❑ The second pair of messages exchange the Diffie-Hellman public information and nonces.

❑ The third pair of messages authenticates the Diffie-Hellman exchange.

A valid protection suite includes four *must-have* options, as follows:

❑ **Encryption Cipher:** Indicates which encryption algorithm is being used to encrypt data. The two most common choices in commercial vendor solutions are TDEA (3DES) and AES, with AES-128 being the recommend choice.

❑ **Integrity Protection Algorithm:** This parameter indicates which keyed-hash algorithms should be used to provide integrity protection. The currently recommended choice is HMAC-SHA-1. When vendors begin implementing IKEv2, more secure options will become available.

❑ **Authentication Method:** There are a few choices for identifying the security endpoints to each other:

❑ **Pre-Share Key:** Just as it sounds, this is a previously agreed-upon key. The implications are somewhat obvious. However, if you are a practitioner who controls both security endpoints, it is possible to leverage a central management solution to easily deploy a preshared key solution.

❑ **Digital Signatures:** As discussed previously, there are two NIST-approved DS algorithms: RSA and DSS.

❑ **Public Key Encryption:** Although not commonly used, public key cryptography can be used to authenticate IPsec peers.

❑ **Diffie-Hellman (DH) Group:** The public-key algorithm Diffie-Hellman is used to generate a shared secret and exchange it securely between endpoints. There are several predefined groups with a key length defined for each group. The authors also present an argument for appropriate group modulus based on the strength of AES and its various key lengths. The generator used for each of these groups is the More Modular Exponential (MODP). The following table illustrates the most commonly used groups, which are labeled 1, 2 and 5. Groups 14–18 are defined in RFC 3526. (Google "RFC 3526" for more information on these new groups.)

Group	Generator	Key
1	MODP	768
2	MODP	1024
5	MODP	1536
14	**MODP**	**2048**
15	**MODP**	**3072**
16	**MODP**	**4096**
17	**MODP**	**6144**
18	**MODP**	**8192**

Aggressive Mode

Aggressive mode reduces the number of messages exchanged for the benefit of expediency.

❑ In the first message, the sender passes the protection suite parameters and the Diffie-Hellman public values and identity.

❑ In the second message, the receiver sends the protection suite parameters, its portion of the Diffie-Hellman exchange, a nonce, its identity, and the authentication payload.

However, with speed comes extra risk. The number of messages from main mode is reduced by half to a total of three messages. The identities of the security endpoints are in the clear during the first message exchange, which should be a cause for concern. Therefore, main mode is recommended over aggressive mode when the option is available.

Negotiations: Phase II

The purpose of Phase II of the IKEv1 process is to establish a secure channel or connection between the security endpoints. This secure connection is called an IPsec Security Association (SA). As discussed previously, IPsec SAs are uni-directional, and therefore it is necessary to establish a pair for each security protocol (ESP or AH) configured to allow full duplex communication between security endpoints. The IPsec SA is established using a single mode known as Quick mode. The Quick mode exchange is completed with three total messages using the previous phase IKE SA to protect the exchange.

- ❑ During the first message, the sender passes keys, nonces, and IPsec SA cryptographic parameters.
- ❑ During the second message, the receiver passes keys, nonces, IPsec SA parameters, and a hash to authenticate.
- ❑ During the third exchange, the initial sender also sends a hash for authentication.

After the final message is validated by the receiver, the IPsec SAs are established. All parameters agreed upon during the exchange are stored in the Security Association Database (SAD).

Security Associations

The goal of IPsec is to protect — encrypt and authenticate or just authenticate — data during transport across an IP network. That goal is satisfied by establishing two or more (in pairs) of IPsec Security Associations (SAs). An IPsec SA is a simplex connection established between two IPsec peers. A bi-directional data flow needs to establish two SA to permit full duplex secure communications between security gateways. Thankfully, IKE does the dirty work for us by automatically establishing an IPsec SA in each direction. One of the most useful tools in your IPsec troubleshooting toolbox is to verify that your IPsec SAs are active.

The IPsec SA is a culmination of the UI suite defined previously, which is also easily verified with vendor-specific commands. In other words, when you define a specific set of cryptographic parameters that match your remote peer, the result is establishment of an SA. RFC 4301 Section 4.1 covers the topic of SA more in-depth.

> If ESP and AH are configured, they each require a pair of Security Associations (SAs).

Security Associations (SA) are stored in the SA Database (SAD), which is referenced each time traffic passes through the security gateway. If an SA is about to expire, a new SA must be established; however, if the SA is not established in a timely manner, the packet must not be forwarded — it should be discarded in accordance with the standards. A Security Association is very specific and unique, and therefore can be identified with the following three parameters, all of which are stored in the SAD:

- ❑ Destination IP address
- ❑ Security Parameter Index (SPI)
- ❑ IPsec security protocol (ESP or AH)

The Security Association Database contains several fields for each established IPsec SA, as follows:

❑ Source IP address

❑ Destination IP address

❑ Security Parameter Index (SPI)

❑ IPsec security protocol (ESP or AH)

❑ Mode (transport or tunnel)

❑ Encryption cipher

❑ MAC algorithm (HMAC-SHA-1)

❑ Keys

❑ Key length

❑ SA lifetime

❑ Sequence number

❑ Anti-replay information

❑ Security policy (which traffic should use these parameters)

Shoring Up the Tunnel

There are several additional features included in the standards that increase the strength of your solution. We discuss a few of these next. It is important to keep your business requirements in mind when considering these options because they may potentially impact performance on some vendor solutions.

Key Lifetime and PFS

This is an age-old question: How much time is enough but not too much? If this question were asked a decade ago, its answer would be drastically different from today's. Nevertheless, the underlying reasoning is still the same. It depends on the cryptographic suite that you implement. When implementing IKEv1, experience shows that a longer lifetime, 86400 seconds or 1 day, is perfectly suitable when implementing with Perfect Forward Secrecy (PFS). Some security practitioners do not fully appreciate the benefit of PFS. The concept of key lifetime does not exist in IKEv2, according to the RFC4306.

PFS is a feature that enables the generation of new keying material without using any prior known derivative of the previous keying material. In other words, if a key becomes compromised during a particular session lifetime, that compromised key cannot be used to compromise newly established key sessions. This is a very important feature to enable and is highly recommended.

Anti-Replay

Anti-replay is an option that prohibits the injection of previously transmitted packets back into an IPsec flow. This prevents attackers from manipulating packets and attempting to retransmit potentially altered datagrams. This option works by keeping track of the sequence numbers.

Traffic Flow Security

There are several features in the new set of standards that incorporate limited traffic flow security when using ESP tunnel mode. These include variable-length padding, which conceals the payload length, and the efficient generation and discard of dummy packets. Tunnel mode also offers the ability to conceal the identities of the source and destination because the original IP header is encrypted.

Best Practice

How does one define "best practice," also known as "industry standard"? Have you ever wondered why the sales guy pitching his products uses the term "industry standard" or "best practice" so authoritatively? It is a term used often in industry. There is no easy answer to this question. In our humble opinion, a "best practice" is just that: an opinion of an individual or group of individuals based on past successful experiences. In some cases, government agencies or interested third parties may author guidelines for how best to do something. NIST is a great example of an organization that develops guides or recommendations. Another example is the Center for Internet Security (Google "CIS"), which develops best practice standards for hardening various networking and OS platforms. Experience shows that simplicity is the key to a successful implementation.

Complexity Trap

Bruce Schneier and Niels Ferguson may very well have coined the term "Complexity Trap" in their 1999 review titled *A Cryptographic Evaluation of IPsec*. With the advent of updated RFCs for each of the components that make up the IPsec suite, some folks may question the validity of this review, which took place nearly a decade ago. If you read the review in detail, you will find that the message is still the same regardless of date and time. The strength and integrity of IPsec suffers from its flexibility. Simply put, there are too many options. It has been our experience and that of others that best practice, if we can safely use that phrase, follows the "keep it simple" philosophy. As an example, we have always recommended and implemented a single defined set of cryptographic parameters with any IPsec solution. Why the option to implement more than one is available in the first place is evident — flexibility — but it is an unnecessary option that potentially allows a less secure suite to be offered and accepted by a remote peer.

Most vendors' IPsec implementations, as described by the RFCs, allow for the configuration of multiple suites. If an organization has a policy defining what is acceptable with regard to securing communications between two or more sites, it begs the question of why would anyone configure an option to permit a weaker protocol. When flexibility takes the front seat in your configurations, you will begin introducing weaknesses in the overall system for any of several reasons, including but not limited to the following:

❑   Increased risk of misconfigurations

❑   Complexity

❑   Implementation defects

❑   Vendor interoperability issues

We do not have enough paper in this book to document and review all the possible combinations of cryptographic parameters (suites) that are possible with IPsec. Let's review the high-level options:

❑ There are currently three different NIST-approved encryption algorithms (AES, Triple DES, and Skipjack).

Only the more common AES and Triple DES (TDEA) ciphers are available in most vendor implementations. Google "NIST Cryptographic Toolkit" for more information on the various NIST-approved algorithms.

❑ There are two IPsec security protocols: ESP and AH.

❑ There are two IPsec operational modes: tunnel mode and transport mode.

❑ There are five hashing/signing algorithms and one MAC algorithm (the HMAC/SHA-1 and HMAC/SHA-2 families).

RFC 3566 introduces support for a newly defined MAC, which uses AES-128 in cipher block chaining mode (CBC) as tag and PRF generation function. It is named AES-XCBC-MAC-96. Google "RFC 3566" for more information.

MD5 was removed from the NIST-approved list in 2005, and NIST strongly discourages its use. MD5 was successfully cracked in 2005 by a Chinese group.

❑ When you put it all together, there are many different permutations for Phase I and Phase II negotiations. Throw in a few more of the following options to keep it flexible, and you have a full-blown mess on your hands:

  ❑ Diffie-Hellman Groups

  ❑ RSA

  ❑ DSA

  ❑ Perfect Forward Secrecy

The IPsec Working Group (now disbanded) recognizes and acknowledges this issue in RFC 4308. The following is an excerpt from this standard:

. . . Implementation experience with IPsec in manual key mode and with IKE has shown that there are so many choices for typical system administrators to make that it is difficult to achieve interoperability without careful pre-agreement. Because of this, the IPsec Working Group agreed that there should be a small number of named suites that cover typical security policies. (RFC 4308)

Unfortunately, the RFC recommends only two predefined user interface (UI) suites, of which neither is appropriate for 2007. VPN-A would benefit greatly from a stronger hash and the NIST recommended cipher AES. VPN-B is not yet implemented in commercial vendor products. The VPN-A suite calls for 3DES and Diffie-Hellman Group 2. Studies demonstrate that AES-128 performs seven to ten times faster than VPN-A in software.

When it comes to business-to-business (B2B) connections, play hardball and use "corporate policy" as your reason for requiring a higher-than-normal set of security suites. In other words, find the highest common factor (not the least common denominator) of cryptographic parameters that your vendors can support that don't adversely impact performance. However, security should never be a trade-off because of the need for performance. Many vendor solutions support gigabit throughput rates with all key lengths in AES.

Google "Juniper Netscreen 5400" for more information on a box that supports gigabit rates.

Implementing IPsec

This section covers several design considerations and several typical configuration scenarios.

Design Considerations

Because of the complexity and various transport technologies in most networks today, implementing IPsec can prove challenging at best. In this section, we review several key items for consideration.

Eliminate the Complexity Trap

Almost every business requirement that demands secure communications over a public or private medium can be satisfied by a single set of cryptographic parameters. This, of course, assumes that all vendor hardware participating in the exchange have a matching set of capabilities and features. Several years ago, this was not necessarily the case with many vendors. Since the inception of and subsequent approval of AES, most if not all vendors have implemented this cipher in hardware or software. The following recommended set of cryptographic parameters is more than adequate to protect *all* nonclassified corporate traffic, and *all* U.S. government organizations protecting "For Official Use Only" (FOUO) traffic.

Most government agencies under the executive branch of the United States government or any contractor providing service to the government must adhere to various public laws and regulations with regard to transmitting FOUO data.

The National Security Agency (NSA) authored a document entitled *CNSS Policy No. 15 Fact Sheet 1* regarding the new Advanced Encryption Standard. (For more information on CNSS and this policy, Google "CNSS Policy 15" for some light reading from the NSA.) In this concise, three-page document, the NSA officially blesses the AES cipher as being cryptographically strong enough to protect U.S. government national security information:

The design and strength of all key lengths of the AES algorithm (i.e., 128, 192 and 256) are sufficient to protect classified information up to the SECRET level. TOP SECRET information will require use of either the 192 or 256 key lengths. The implementation of AES in products intended to protect national security systems and/or information must be reviewed and certified by NSA prior to their acquisition and use. (CNSS Policy No. 15 Fact Sheet 1)

How cool is that? Take note of the last sentence in that quote from the policy. In other words, the security of any system is as secure as its weakest link. We have all heard this many times in our careers, and you are certain to hear it a few more times. With that thought in mind, the NSA clearly states that key management and cipher implementations in hardware, firmware, or software must be reviewed and certified by the NSA prior to acquisition or implementation of any system intended to protect classified national security information using AES. Most successful attacks on cryptographic implementations are based on weak implementations in key exchange and key management or the implementation of the solution in hardware, firmware, or software, not necessarily on the actual algorithm itself.

> **Ponder this: If 128-bit AES is cryptographically strong enough to protect national security information, classified SECRET, what value is there to a nongovernment organization implementing AES 192 or AES 256? All other things being equal (implementation), there is no advantage.**

Recommended VPN suite that will meet and/or exceed most business requirements:

- ❑ Phase I:
    - ❑ Authentication: Pre-shared Key or RSA:DH Group 5
    - ❑ Encryption: AES 128
    - ❑ Integrity HASH : HMAC-SHA1 (If SHA-2 is implemented use SHA512)
    - ❑ Lifetime: 86400 seconds
- ❑ Phase II:
    - ❑ Perfect Forward Secrecy (PFS): Group 5 (or the highest group available)
    - ❑ Protocol: ESP
    - ❑ Encryption: AES 128
    - ❑ Authentication: SHA1/HMAC (If SHA-2 is implemented use SHA512)
    - ❑ Lifetime: 28800 seconds
    - ❑ Options
    - ❑ Enable Anti-Replay

Path MTU Discovery

When implementing protocols that encapsulate or wrap packets with new headers, the result is a larger packet than what you started with. For example, IPsec, depending on the security protocol and mode used, can result in a packet that is roughly 40–60 bytes larger than the original packet. In some cases, the resulting larger packet is marked Do Not Fragment (DF), which means that the network elements across the entire path must honor the DF marked packet. Thus, if a packet arrives at a network element that has a Maximum Transmission Unit (MTU) larger than what is permitted, the network element must discard the packet. The element that drops the packet must return an ICMP Destination Unreachable message with a response code of "fragmentation needed and DF set." One method to resolve this issue is the Path MTU discovery protocol, which uses the concept of the DF bit in a packet to dynamically determine the largest MTU possible. The process ends when the sender determines that the estimate of the MTU is low enough without requiring fragmentation.

Google "RFC 1191 site:roxen.com" for more information.

Some vendors implement proprietary features that dynamically adjust the Maximum Segment Size (MSS). Most of the big commercial vendors have a feature that provides this type of functionality.

NAT Traversal

Network Address Translation may have saved the IPv4 IP space, but it can also be a thorn in our sides when it comes to deploying IPsec. Unfortunately, NAT Traversal is not supported by some commercial vendors, and that can cause some serious issues in your design. Therefore, it is often best to place your IPsec gateway on a public IP facing system. Doing so allows you to mitigate the issues associated with NAT on one end of the tunnel. Not all situations can be easily resolved by implementing NAT Traversal, so it is best to avoid it if possible in your designs and implementations. Client-to-site VPNs are especially susceptible to this issue, which is another strong reason to consider SSL VPN technologies, which can easily pass through any NAT device along the path.

Google "RFC 3947 site:roxen.com" for more information.

Design Scenarios

In this section, we discuss several design scenarios that you may encounter at your new employer's place of business. You may be called upon to understand the difference between a route-based and policy-based VPN, or you may be asked to design a new site-to-site VPN solution that adheres to newly adopted corporate security policy.

Site-to-Site VPN

Site-to-site tunnels are the most common implementation of IPsec. They allow a company to provide secure and inexpensive transport to a remote site via an insecure or untrusted medium. In most cases, that medium is the Internet, which is grossly cheaper in most parts of the world. IPsec site-to-site VPNs are configured in several possible scenarios. The site-to-site VPN, for all intents and purposes, can be viewed as a secure IP circuit — point-to-point — between two sites. It is possible, with some vendor implementations, to deploy point-to-point, point-to-multipoint, or even a fully meshed series of VPN tunnels between all sites.

Each of these scenarios must be considered when reviewing business requirements for site-to-site communications. If all spoke sites communicate only with a central resource or hub location, perhaps a hub and spoke design of point-to-multipoint would be appropriate. However, if a spoke site has a requirement to communicate with other spoke sites, then a hybrid of point-to-multipoint or a full mesh must be deployed. This single requirement can grossly impact the type of hardware you deploy to a branch office. Depending on the number of sites in your network, it can also grossly impact your budget.

Security gateways at each site must agree on a cryptographic suite in order to establish a secure connection between each pair of sites.

Client-to-Site VPN

Client-to-site VPNs using IPsec have been the de facto standard for the past decade. With the advent of SSL/TLS–based VPN solutions, the glory of IPsec VPNs is rapidly fading. All the major vendors, who were the primary players in the IPsec market, have introduced SSL/TLS VPN solutions. The reasons to consider an SSL VPN solution are numerous, and the reasons to stick with an IPsec-based solution are few, according to Gartner and others. Here are a few of each:

❑ Reasons to consider an SSL VPN–based solution:

  ❑ SSL (TCP/443) is ubiquitous and works with NAT. (Rarely blocked anywhere.)

  ❑ There is no client to install and manage.

  ❑ A thin agent is maintained automatically via the SSL VPN appliance.

  ❑ Most major vendor implementations allow the client to roam between networks while maintaining a connection to the VPN: "Roaming."

  ❑ Most vendor implementations include the concept of a Web-based portal to present users with the resources they are allowed to access, and nothing else. Setting up these resources can be easy or challenging, depending on the resource or the vendor.

  ❑ It is a more resilient VPN client than IPsec, which requires a stable network connection.

  ❑ It has granular inspection of endpoint security and the ability to provide various levels of access depending on security posture of endpoint.

❑ Potential drawback to SSL VPN:

  ❑ The easy nature of anywhere access will quickly catch on in your company. Because of the "anywhere" access, folks will find more reasons to check something at work. Translation: The organization may have to purchase more licenses.

Route-Based VPN

Route-based VPNs are the simplest to deploy and require the least number of resources. When traffic enters the security gateway from the local network, the gateway does a route lookup for the destination. If a route exists in the routing table, the traffic is forwarded out the gateway interface where the IPsec tunnel is bound.

Routing is configured on the security gateway to allow traffic to pass across the tunnel. This is a requirement or traffic is dropped into the bit bucket. Depending on the vendor implementation, you can configure dynamic routing (OSPF, RIP, or BGP) or static routing. Static routing is the simplest to deploy in small shops; however, if you are in a large shop, it may be wise to consider a dynamic routing protocol. Maintaining security boundaries is an important consideration for your design, and a Layer 3 implemented security gateway is considered a bump-in-the-wire (BITW), which means that you can't just pass OSPF through a firewall — it won't work nicely. Therefore, protocols such as OSPF and BGP have to be carefully considered in the design.

Years ago, security practitioners would have never dreamed of having a routing protocol on a security gateway. It just didn't make sense at the time. Some of us still feel that way today. A router routes, and a firewall/VPN appliance filters and inspects traffic. Network elements (routers and switches) are now incorporating some of the same features that traditional firewalls appliances have used for years; and vice versa, the firewall is incorporating more networking features. So don't sweat it when the network group asks whether you can run a routing protocol on your box. Defense in Depth, which we discuss throughout the book, speaks to the importance of multiple layers of security.

Policy-Based VPN

Policy-based VPNs require explicitly defined policy in the security gateway before passing traffic through a tunnel. If the tunnel is not yet established, interested traffic is required to initiate the tunnel negotiations. In most vendor implementations, you simply configure an action on the policy to tunnel the traffic. Depending on the size of your environment, implementing policy-based VPNs can consume additional resources. Consider route-based VPNs as an alternative, and apply policy to the egress interface or security zone.

Alternatives to IPsec

We did not discuss the in-depth features and functions of IPsec as a remote access client solution (RAS) because the industry is rapidly moving away from this complex and difficult-to-manage technology in lieu of a greatly more favorable solution. Gartner put it most appropriately in late 2005 when it stated "IPsec dead by 2008." We discuss this option later and in the previous "Client-to-Site VPN" section.

Transport Layer Security (TLS/SSL)

The host-based (client-to-site VPN) replacement killer is none other than the ubiquitous Secure Sockets Layer protocol. Invented by Netscape in 1996, it is often cited as the most widely used security protocol ever. SSL is the key technology enabler that has permitted billions and billions of dollars in transactions. There seems to be no end in sight to the Internet as a means of commerce.

This same technology is now used to "tunnel" legitimate enterprise traffic across the network back to an SSL Proxy appliance. This appliance, depending on the configuration, can then initiate a new connection on your behalf to the internal resource requested. Therefore, clients on the Internet do not communicate directly with the requested business application. Optionally, some vendors provide multiple methods of tunneling data. Common methods include SSL-based proxy as discussed previously, where your source IP is that of the local client machine. In addition, some of the larger vendors provide an IPsec-like feature, which tunnels all traffic, depending on policy, back to the corporate network using ESP, and a hashing algorithm to authenticate the data. Ironically, there still isn't a thick client software package to maintain, because the SSL proxy takes charge of doing that task for you automatically.

Because SSL is a ubiquitous protocol used everywhere throughout the world, it is rarely blocked on service provider firewalls, hotels, hotspots, and so on. Hence, it is literally possible to connect to corporate resources from anywhere in the world from almost any machine without the need for a full-blown security client on the host machine.

Juniper Networks Secure Access (SA) and Aventail's EX family of SSL VPNs are the two leaders in this market, according to Gartner and others.

Internet Protocol V6

Originally known as IPng or IP Next Generation, IPv6 incorporates the concept of IP security (IPsec) directly into the IP stack. IPv6 provides confidentiality, authentication, integrity, and anti-replay features.

The adoption of IPv6 has greatly slowed due to IPv4 features such as Classless Inter-domain Routing (CIDR) and Network Address Translation (NAT). These two features alone have greatly prolonged the use of IPv4 well past its predicted lifetime.

Google "RFC 2460" for more detailed information on the IPv6 protocol. For more information on IPv6 security, take a look at either the old RFC 2401 or the new RFC 4301.

Summary

Various protocols and technologies can offer Virtual Private Networking services. IP Security (IPsec) is extensively used for site-to-site communications over insecure mediums or where protecting data is absolutely critical. The IPsec suite is a complex set of protocols and technologies, which must be well understood by the security practitioner. In this chapter, we reviewed each of the components that make IPsec possible. Symmetric cryptography is the core of IPsec. Without the secret key cipher, we have no security; however, there are many other key components that make the IPsec suite a reality. We discussed the IPsec complexity trap, and more specifically the end result of having so many options to choose from.

There are options to IPsec, with SSL VPN being the king for client-to-site remote access solutions. SSL VPNs offer flexibility well beyond that of any IPsec-based solution. The SSL/TLS protocol is used worldwide for Internet commerce, therefore it is rarely blocked by anyone. This makes SSL/TLS an attractive option for anywhere access to corporate resources. If a pandemic hits the United States, to prevent the spread of disease it will be prudent, if not required, of most employers to make their employees stay home. Those companies that have already planned for this event or other natural disasters are well ahead of the game in their ability to remain productive regardless of where employees are located.

In this chapter and throughout the entire book, we made every effort to direct you to as many resources as possible.

Interview Q&A

The following questions provide an idea of some of the types of questions you should be able to answer.

Q: How many messages are exchanged during Phase I Aggressive mode, and would you recommend it for a site-to-site VPN?

A: Three and no: The identity of the peer is exposed during the reduced number of messages.

Q: What are some issues related to deploying IPsec with ESP across the network?

A: In tunnel mode, ESP adds a new IP and ESP header, which results in a larger packet size. In addition, ESP packets are marked Do Not Fragment (DF) in most vendor implementations. Configuring a Path MTU discovery feature or other vendor-specific feature is required to reduce your MSS to allow successful transmission of full-size packets.

Q: Please explain how you can identify which type of IPsec security protocol and mode are used with only a packet sniffer.

A: The next header field indicates which protocol is next. If TCP, then transport mode is used; if IP, then tunnel mode is used. In the IP header, the Protocol field will indicate what type of protocol is used (ESP IP protocol 50 or AH IP protocol 51).

Q: What protocols are required to pass through the edge of your network to an IPsec appliance running ESP with IKE?

A: ESP is IP Protocol 50, and IKE traditionally operations over UDP Port 500. If NAT Traversal is used, then UDP Port 4500 is traditionally used.

Q: Describe the purpose of a Security Assocation (SA) and what the minimum number are to establish a VPN tunnel with a remote peer using only ESP/tunnel mode.

A: An SA is a uni-directional set of parameters used to establish a secure communication channel with a far end gateway or host. A minimum of two SAs is required to establish bi-directional communication with the far-end peer.

Q: What is the minimum number of parameters needed to uniquely identify a Security Association?

A: Three: SPI, peer IP address, and type of protocol used (ESP or AH).

Q: Please describe some of the resources you have used to evaluate and select an IPsec platform.

A: Depending on the business requirements (and any possible government regulations — FIPS 140-2), I would create a short list of vendors from sources such as Gartner, and Forrester because they review financials and customer support issues that may be difficult to confirm in a lab. Continuing to work against business requirements, I would review the IPsec vendor list from ICSA Labs ("Google ICSA Labs IPsec Certified") if there are interoperability requirements with other vendors or a planned migration. I would reference NIST's Common Criteria Evaluation and Validation Scheme (CCEVS) to reduce my shortlist to a "very" short list. FIPS 140-2 evaluates the vendor's cryptographic implementation for adherence with the standard. Selecting a vendor that meets or exceeds this standard can further reduce your short list. I would also reference the VPN Consortium to review any vendor-specific enhancements or interoperability issues. Finally, I would bring in the top three vendors that meet the stated business requirements, and work with the gear.

Recommended Reading

Practical Cryptography. Bruce Schneier and Niels Ferguson (Wiley. ISBN: 978-0471228943).
Deering, S., and R. Hinden, "Internet Protocol, Version 6 (IPv6) Specification," RFC 2460, Dec. 1998.

Old and new IP Security (IPsec) architecture overview RFCs

[RFC2401] S. Kent and R. Atkinson, "Security Architecture for the Internet Protocol," RFC 2401, Nov. 1998.
[RFC4301] S. Kent and K. Seo, Security Architecture for the Internet Protocol." RFC 4301 (obsoletes RFC 2401), Dec. 2005.

Old and new IP Authentication Header (AH) RFCs

[RFC2402] S. Kent and R. Atkinson, "IP Authentication Header," RFC 2402, Nov. 1998.
[RFC4302] S. Kent, "IP Authentication Header," RFC 4302 (makes RFC 2402 obsolete), Dec. 2005.

Old and new Encapsulating Security Payload (ESP)

[RFC2406] S. Kent and R. Atkinson, "IP Encapsulating Security Payload (ESP)," RFC 2406, Nov. 1998.
[RFC4303] S. Kent, IP Encapsulating Security Payload (ESP)," RFC 4303 (obsoletes RFC 2406), Dec. 2005.

IKE v1 vs IKE v2

[RFC2409] Harkins, D. and D. Carrel, "The Internet Key Exchange (IKE)," RFC 2409, November 1998.
[RFC4306] Kaufman, C., Ed., "Internet Key Exchange (IKEv2) Protocol," RFC 4306, December 2005.
[RFC3526] Kivinen, T. and M. Kojo, "More Modular Exponential (MODP) Diffie-Hellman groups for Internet Key Exchange (IKE)," RFC 3526, May 2003.
[RFC2451] Pereira, R. and R. Adams, "The ESP CBC-Mode Cipher Algorithms," RFC 2451, November 1998.
TCP/IP Illustrated, Volume 1. W. Richard Stevens (Addison-Wesley Professional. ISBN: 978-0201633467).
D. Bleichenbacher, "Chosen Ciphertext Attacks Against Protocols Based on the RSA Encryption Standard PKCS #1," in H. Krawczyk (ed.), *Advances in Cryptology* CRYPTO 1998, LNCS Vol. 1462, Springer-Verlag, 1998, pp. 1–12.
B. Canvel, A. P. Hiltgen, S. Vaudenay, and M. Vuagnoux, "Password Interception in a SSL/TLS Channel," in D. Boneh (ed.), *Advances in Cryptology* CRYPTO 2003, LNCS Vol. 2729, Springer-Verlag, 2003, pp. 583–599.
N. Doraswamy and D. Harkins, *IPsec: the new security standard for the Internet, Intranets and Virtual Private Networks* (Second Edition), Prentice Hall PTR, 2003.
N. Ferguson and B. Schneier, "A cryptographic evaluation of IPsec." Unpublished manuscript, Feb.1999. Available from `http://www.schneier.com/paper-ipsec.html`.
[RFC 3602] S. Frankel, R. Glenn and S. Kelly, "The AES-CBC Cipher Algorithm and Its Use with IPsec," RFC 3602, Sept. 2003.
S. Frankel, K. Kent, R. Lewkowski, A. D. Orebaugh, R. W. Ritchey. and S. R. Sharma, "Guide to IPsec VPNs," NIST Special Publication 800-77, December 2005.
J. Katz and M. Yung, "Unforgeable encryption and chosen ciphertext secure modes of operation." In B. Schneier (ed.), FSE 2000, LNCS Vol. 1978, Springer-Verlag 2001, pp. 284–299.
H. Krawczyk, "The Order of Encryption and Authentication for Protecting Communications (Or: How Secure Is SSL?)", in J. Kilian (ed.), *Advances in Cryptology* CRYPTO 2001, LNCS Vol. 2139, Springer-Verlag 2001, pp. 310–331.
T. Yu, S. Hartman, and K. Raeburn, "The perils of unauthenticated encryption: Kerberos version 4," in Proc. NDSS 2004, The Internet Society, 2004.

7

Knowing IDS/IPS/IDP

You arrive at work around 7:30 a.m. and are immediately met at the door by your Senior Vice President. She wants to know how the corporate network had been hacked the previous night. "Crank-n-Tr00ders" made its mark on your company Intranet page. It also compromised an e-mail server. The intruders accessed an internal message with an attachment containing social security numbers for the entire company. You expected the grilling because you received a late-night call from your network security engineer. You so much want to call the engineer on the carpet for not locking down the network, especially after approving last year's investment of $200K for intrusion detection and prevention (IDP) hardware throughout the company. But you realize that it is as much your fault as his.

Getting to your office, you pull up the reports that your engineer sends you every day on the previous day's attacks. You hardly ever go through them; to you they are noise. But this time, you look at the summary report for the previous month and realize that the source IP of the Trojan had been host scanning your network for well over a month.

The IDP did its job, but somewhere the ball was dropped.

Introduction

The idea of detecting intrusions has been around a while. Harken back to the old-time network engineer's favorite page-turner — "Cuckoo's Egg." This was the account of Cliff Stoll using a dot-matrix printer to record tty traffic of attempts to hack his systems at Lawrence Berkeley National Laboratory (LBL). Well, numerous generations in hardware and software later, the IDS of today comes with intelligence. What does that mean? An IDS detects attacks by comparing traffic to a given set of signatures. Doing this at line rate initially posed a problem; however, most vendors today have overcome this. Arguably, the intrusion-detection system (IDS) takes a major role in most company security architectures. An IDS provides a window into the traffic coming and going from a site. The IDS fits the Defense in Depth model for network protection and is considered a necessary tool in your security toolkit. But as with all tools, you need to know how to use it properly. Most commercial implementations of IDP are as add-ons in their existing capitalized equipment. It was an afterthought to many that IDP systems would be a panacea for the limitations in their firewalls. In reality, they have settled into quiet mediocrity — fulfilling a simple, reactive forensics capability and providing a place to troubleshoot unwanted traffic. In spite of differing philosophies, IDP systems are a reality in most of today's networks. And in your interviews, you have to be prepared to answer questions about IDP systems. The following sections are divided into the actual interview questions that we have either researched or been asked ourselves. Consider yourself prepared.

Questions

The remainder of the chapter is in a question-and-answer format. The questions are drawn from real interviews that we have conducted ourselves or have been asked ourselves in interviews. The answers are written so that you are comfortable with the subject. We recommend that you still do some background research to familiarize yourself with the subject in question. For multi-part questions, break down the question into pieces and address each part. Because we believe that a picture does tell a better story, we recommend using a whiteboard for all answers. Most technical interviewers are right-brained, anyway.

Explain the Types of IDS and IDP Systems and Provide Some Examples of Each.

This is always a good start to the IDP portion of the interview because it gets immediately to the heart of the IDS/IDP debate. Network security hardware and software vendors have confused many network professionals with markets and submarkets of intrusion detection. Originally, there was just "intrusion detection." The systems (also called sensors) were either network-based, also known as a *network IDS* (NIDS), or host-based, also known as a *host IDS* (HIDS). The early systems simply tapped into the network at switches with monitored/mirrored ports.

The term IDS is now considered a first-generation term. Today, many vendors distinguish detection from prevention. *Detection* means passive monitoring, whereas *prevention* means active monitoring. With the introduction of the term *prevention* came the introduction of new acronyms — NIPS (Network IPS) and HIPS (Host IPS). Vendors like to call detection *reactive* and prevention *proactive*. The IPS devices have the ability to detect as well as prevent attacks using a response mechanism — if in a tap/span configuration — or blocking mechanism — if using an inline configuration (as explained later in this chapter).

IPS is more of a second-generation term. Many equate an IDS to a burglar alarm. Network sensors detect an intrusion much the same way a door or window sensor detects unwanted entry. The home sensors alert the alarm company or home siren to the intruder. An IPS is a way to prevent attacks from penetrating the network. Some vendors and even NIST have gone so far as to use the acronym IDP (Intrusion Detection and Prevention) to include both the IDS and IPS functionality. Throughout this chapter, we continue to use IDP to represent both IDS and IPS systems.

What Is Deep Inspection and What Is the Benefit?

Deep inspection (DI) is another vendor favorite. Most vendors' IDS/IPS product lines support Layer 3 through 7 inspection. Deep inspection is just another way of saying that the device does more than just stateful inspection of Layer 4 sessions. DI is the analysis of packets at higher layers using patterns in traffic such as excess fragments as well as string patterns in application transactions. Just remember that vendors will apply whatever terminology is most advantageous to them.

What Are the Different Modes That a Sensor Can Operate In?

Inline and passive are the two main modes of a sensor. *Inline* mode means that the sensor is directly in the path of the traffic being monitored. The traffic comes in one port and leaves another port. This configuration allows the sensor to block unwanted traffic.

A *passive* sensor is usually "spanned" off a monitor port off a network switch. The monitor port gets a copy of the actual network traffic to process. A passive sensor is only "listening" to traffic. It is usually deployed at key choke points in a network. Typically it is placed above a firewall to detect all attacks as well as below the firewall to detect what made it through. Most deployments include sensors to monitor each demilitarized zone (DMZ). Passive sensors may also use a network tap to monitor traffic. As the name implies, a network tap physically taps into the network media — whether fiber, wireless, or copper. Although not as prevalent, taps are used by many organizations when switch performance is an issue.

McAfee's IntruShield Modes

McAfee's latest IntruShield line of IPS products can work three different modes, as follows.

❑ Span mode is used when the sensor configuration allows for sending TCP resets to an attack.

❑ Tap mode is used when any response the sensor may make will use another interface as a source to update a firewall access list or send a TCP reset to the offending session.

❑ Inline mode is used when attacks can be blocked on the device.

Open source Snort v2.6 also has multiple modes of operation that include inline and passive.

What Are the Layers of the OSI Reference Model and Where Do IDP Systems Operate?

The purpose of this question is to probe your grasp of networking fundamentals and how an IDP system fits into the mix. You should be able to spout off the OSI layers and TCP/IP layers without hesitation. Refer to Figure 7-1 if you do not remember.

Most IDP systems can detect attacks and perform stateful protocol analysis at Layers 3 and above. Maintaining state information is one key for today's sophisticated attacks. Also key is the ability to handle IP fragmentation, TCP segmentation, protocol (or RFC) ambiguity, content matching and quoting, as well as application layer fragmentation such as RPC record fragmentation.

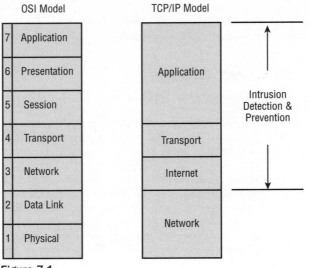

Figure 7-1

The best reference for understanding protocols and primitives between model layers, whether it's the OSI model or the TCP/IP model, is TCP/IP Illustrated, Volume 1: The Protocols *(Addison-Wesley, ISBN 978-0201633467) by W. Richard Stevens.*

How Does an IDS/IDP System Detect Attacks?

Intentionally open-ended, this question is a probe to see whether you know the basic detection methods employed in IDP systems. Be prepared to go into depth on signature matching.

There are two basic methods that IDS/IPS systems employ to detect and act on traffic. *Rules-based* or *signature matching* uses "signatures" or content patterns that match a given definition. For instance, the signature for the IIS command execution vulnerability is "cmd.exe". This is the same model used by virus scanners. As long as signatures are updated, new attacks are detected. More sophisticated IDP systems may employ stateful rules in addition to signature matching. With these rules, an IDP is capable of making sense out of two seemingly benign events — for instance, a TCP host scan followed by unsuccessful SSH login attempts. This is interesting if the source has an external IP address.

The second method uses "normal" traffic patterns as a baseline and then runs comparisons against this baseline to detect any deviations or anomalies. This is *anomaly detection*. Normal traffic is usually defined in terms of specific ports/protocols/services and source-destination pair traffic patterns. These patterns are usually deterministic and populated through a "learning" period.

For more information on signature matching and anomaly detection, Google "signature matching site:sans.org."

What Are Some of the Problems with an IDP System?

This is another great, open-ended question to get you talking. You have to be aware of some of the known problems with IDP systems. One of the major ones is the problem of missing new attacks, also known as "zero-day" attacks. Sure, an IDP receives periodic updates from the vendor, but how can you be proactive with that type of solution? Attack signatures are morphed numerous times before there is a public update available. The vendor response to this question is that "anomaly detection" will be the proactive mechanism of detection. But you know that these IDP systems depend on an accurate baseline of data to define "normal" behavior. As all programmers are aware, garbage in equates to garbage out: If your baseline was normalized with garbage, your system will make comparisons that are garbage. Another major problem is performance. Many early IDP systems had problems with handling detection at line rate. As signature databases grow, so does the processing requirement of the IDP system.

A good response to this question is to admit that an IDP has these faults but is only a tool for the engineer to use. Make the interviewer aware that you know the problems and that you are prepared to learn that organization's network in depth. Mention experience at writing your own signatures and where you have had success adapting to new attacks.

What Is a False Positive? What Is a False Negative?

No IDP solution is 100 percent accurate, so you need to know how to customize or tune them. Much as when you set off your own car alarm, an IDP is known to have the same problem. This is called a *false positive*. In other words, an IDP identifies normal traffic as malicious. An example of this is the use of nonstandard TCP or UDP ports. Many attack signatures are based on not only the content of a packet but also the port used. If an application is using a port known to be a threat, it may pop up as a malicious attack. You would have to modify your IDP policy to not trigger this as an attack. Conversely, if the IDP fails to trigger on malicious activity, you have a *false negative*.

What Are Some of the Challenges You Have Faced When Looking into IDP Systems?

This question is a great soapbox opportunity for you. The challenges you faced are probably similar to the ones the prospective company faces. Here are the top five challenges:

❑ **Right people:** Finding the right people is an obvious benefit. This is why they are looking at you as a candidate. Bring up information on building a team. Put yourself in the interviewer's position and imagine what you would expect.

❑ **Regulatory drivers:** With regulations such as Sarbanes-Oxley and HIPAA, companies have a responsibility to protect customer data as well as employee data. Companies also need to know whether and when their customer data was compromised.

❑ **Right policy:** Determining a good working policy and limiting false positives is a challenge either the company faces today or you will face when you land the job. Reference your experience with tuning. Mention your experience with customizing IDP policy and the consequences it had, such as the time you enabled all attack signatures in your policy to catch all events — shooting the incidence of false positives through the roof. Mention how you have spent time and resources to analyze false positives and how there was a greater chance to become immune to true attacks.

❑ **Product concerns:** Whether the organization has an existing IDP or relies on you to bring one in, determining the right IDP for an organization is a challenge. Mention experience with the product lifecycle. Recall experience drawing up system requirements, product selection, and budgeting. The real purpose of the IDS is to give network administrators a view into their network. It gives them a sense of what traffic is coming and going. But as with many security products, it also gives a false sense of security. Investments in the initial deployment of IDP equipment are made, but little is done to sustain the operation.

❑ **Incident response:** Companies frequently grapple with how to respond to a network incident. Bring up your expertise in establishing incident response procedures. Mention that it is critical to have an established response that is agreed to by upper management. Note how you will review the procedure and look to improve it on a periodic basis.

What Can You Tell Me About Different Attack Categories?

The interviewer is looking for the major categories of attacks. Most vendors organize attacks into various categories regardless of severity. When an attack is detected from a signature match or from the anomaly engine, it is generally categorized. Take McAfee IntruShield, for example. Major attack categories include: reconnaissance, volume denial of service (DoS), exploits, and policy violation. If you reference these, you can then answer any follow-up questions as to a specific type of attack. Here are examples of each category.

The *reconnaissance category* includes network traffic that may be benign but not desired based on specific protocol behavior. Threats include brute force, isolated probes, host scans and sweeps, port scans and sweeps, and fingerprinting. Many of these threats are used in correlation analysis. Examples include TCP/UDP host sweeps, TCP SYN host sweeps, and TCP ACK host sweeps.

> *For more information on reconnaissance attacks, Google "intrusion reconnaissance attack site:sans.org."*

> *For more information on TCP SYN attacks, Google "SYN site:securitydocs.com."*

The *volume Denial of Service (DoS) category*, to include Distributed (DDoS), includes traffic patterns that potentially affect network service. Threats include attempts to disable a host, network device, or application; also included are threats that could affect performance. Examples include TCP control segment anomalies and high ICMP/UDP/TCP RST packet volume.

Exploits are all other malicious activities with specific attention to the actual content of packets. Threats include buffer overflows, viruses, and worms as well as threats involving file privileges and modification through root authorization attempts. Examples include the Back Orifice Trojan, ASP IIS buffer overflow, and the MyDoom worm.

Policy violations are attacks that are detected with higher-layer content matching but may violate the company policy. This includes access to sensitive content, installation of illegal applications, and so on. Examples include P2P traffic such as BitTorrent, Kazaa, and eDonkey; Instant Messaging traffic such as AIM; and adware such as SaveNow and Hotbar.

For more information on DoS attacks, Google "DoS attack site:sans.org" and "Policy violations site:securitydocs.com."

When Would a TCP Host Sweep Be Considered an Attack?

TCP host sweeps do not usually mean malicious activity. They are established TCP connections from a given source IP address going to multiple destination IP addresses in your network. Usually, a sweep is triggered by the anomaly engine where thresholds are defined and crossed. But what needs to be analyzed is the source IP address involved in other malicious activity. Mention that you would have to view a packet log and compare this traffic with legitimate traffic in order to definitively identify this as a false positive attack.

What Is the Difference between a Worm and a Trojan Horse?

This is an entry-level question of definitions. A Trojan horse is a malicious application disguised as a legitimate application. After being installed, it enables a remote user to compromise a system. Usually transferred via Web downloads or e-mail, the compromise is made after a user installs or executes the application. A worm differs from a Trojan horse in that it replicates itself. This autonomous behavior allows worms to quickly propagate and infect peer hosts. Trojan horses and worms are typically spread through e-mail attachments.

For more information on bots, Google "worms site:securitydocs.com."

What Can You Tell Me about the Back Orifice Trojan Horse Exploit?

This question probes to see how well you know some of the popular exploits. The Back Orifice (BO) Trojan communicates via encrypted UDP packets instead of TCP packets. What is interesting about BO is that it can attach to another Windows executable that runs after installing the original. BO can also use browser plug-ins that can change the size of an executable. After being installed, BO will open ports 31337 and 31338.

For more information on the BO Trojan, Google "back orifice site:hackfix.org."

What Can You Tell Me about Bot Exploits?

This is another question to see how well you know network traffic and whether certain traffic can be exploited. "Bots" is a term that is short for Web robots. They are programs whose function is to capture information covertly and then report back via another connection. Examples include the capture of personal information such as browsing behavior and the capture of keystrokes. Originally intended for marketing purposes, these applications can now be a mechanism for malicious activity — especially denial of service attacks. Bots usually communicate using Internet Relay Chat (IRC) or IM (Yahoo, Google, AOL, and so on). Some bots may set up a backdoor to allow remote command execution on a server.

Typically, site administrators will block this type of traffic (IRC, IM, and the like) coming in and scan servers for the actual programs when traffic is detected as originating internally.

For more information on bots, Google "bots site:securitydocs.com."

What Can You Tell Me about Buffer Overflow Exploits?

Buffer overflows are a popular exploit and easy to execute. Basically, a buffer overflow occurs when an attempt is made to exceed a normal data storage boundary. After the boundary is exceeded, the extra data can overwrite the adjacent memory space, potentially copying over other variables used in the application. The result of a buffer overflow can range from a system crash to garbled output. Many system vulnerabilities are the result of poor programming of open-source applications. Adept users can look through the code and find the weaknesses in memory allocation. They can then send formed input to trigger a malicious event. An IDP will detect a buffer overflow event when the malicious packets are matched for a specific server application.

For more information on buffer overflows, Google "buffer overflow site:securitydocs.com."

Explain Event Correlation.

Event correlation is the ability to take seemingly disparate, unrelated events and, when analyzed together, make up a concerted attack. Most IDP devices support summarization and can be integrated into an event correlation system. These niche event correlation products are known as security information management (SIM) products. The benefit of event correlation is simplification of events and also the ability to digest large quantities of information (such as error logs). Normalizing and summarizing allows staff to review and analyze more attacks in a given time period. Also, staff can take multiple events and perform trend analysis.

For more information on general event correlation, Google "event correlation site:securitydocs.com" and "event correlation site:sans.org."

Demonstrate How Well You Know the Wireshark (a.k.a. Ethereal) Analyzer and Use It to Decompose an Attack.

The interviewer may provide you with output similar to Figure 7-2. The purpose of this question is to see how well you know the latest analytical tools to identify some of the latest application triggers and demonstrate how to decompose a packet. In this snapshot, you have a packet from a Bit-Torrent session in which the application is pinging peers. The triggers for Bit-Torrent are UDP payload strings of "2:id20:" and "4:ping."

For more information on the WireShark/Ethereal network analyzer, Google "wireshark site:wireshark.com."

For more information on the Bit-Torrent protocol, Google "bittorrent faq site:dessent.net."

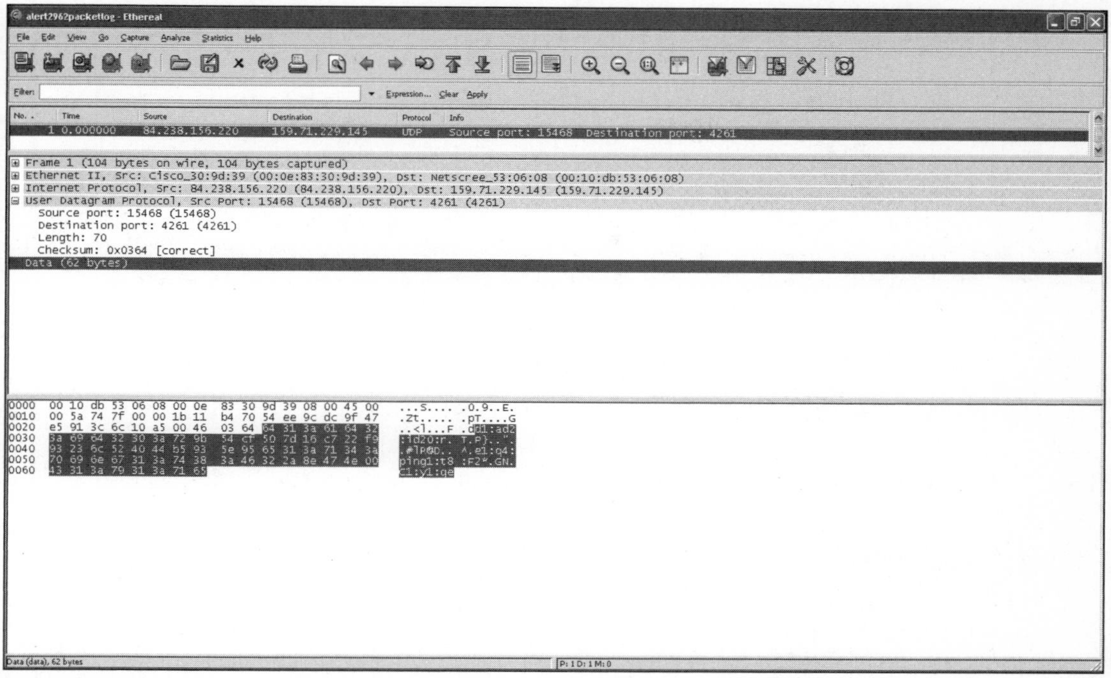

Figure 7-2

What Intrusion Detection and Prevention Products Do You Have Experience With?

The interviewer wants to hear your response to actual product lines and get an idea of your experience with those products. Interviewers want to know that your experience is relevant and that you know the products that are available today. They also want to hear that you know the difference between products and where they fit in your network. Vendors with large product lines (Cisco, Juniper, and so on) have more to gain from applying security measures in all their products. Because of how ubiquitous Cisco is in the networking sector, many businesses choose to go with a vendor they know and use them as a single vendor for routing, switching, remote access, and now IDS.

The following sections provide some great places to find out more product-specific information. Also included are some of the adjunct tools that are used for analysis, reporting, and so on.

❑ **NIDS/NIPS**

   ❑ Cisco: Cisco Intrusion Prevention System Solution

      Google "intrusion prevention system site:cisco.com"

   ❑ Juniper: Juniper Networks Intrusion Detection and Prevention Solutions

      Google "intrusion prevention system site:juniper.net"

❏ McAfee: McAfee Network Intrusion Prevention

Google "intrusion prevention system site:mcafee.com"

❏ Snort: Intrusion Detection and Prevention System (Open Source)

www.snort.org

❏ ISS: Proventia Network Intrusion Prevention System

Google "intrusion prevention system site:iss.net"

❏ **HIDS/HIPS**

❏ Cisco: Cisco Security Agent

Google "cisco security agent site:cisco.com"

❏ ISS: Proventia Desktop

Google "proventia desktop site:iss.net"

❏ McAfee: McAfee Host Intrusion Prevention

Google "host intrusion site:mcafee.com"

❏ **Tools**

❏ WireShark (a.k.a. Ethereal): Network Protocol Analyzer

www.wireshark.com/

❏ Tcpdump: Network Protocol Analyzer

www.tcpdump.org/

Where Is the Proper Place to Deploy an IPS? Mention the Pros and Cons of Your Choice(s).

This question is best in front of a whiteboard. The answer is not all that clear, either. The key is to focus on which assets the organization wishes to protect and from where. In general, you want to use your IDP to reinforce the overall security policy. Interviewers may provide a diagram similar to Figure 7-3. Your IDP should not only monitor and block malicious traffic but also be used to document attacks for later prosecution. Your IDP should be a means to check your border router and firewall rules to assure that you are blocking traffic correctly. A good model today is one in which you have multiple modes of operation and an immediate response to an attack.

Shown in Figure 7-4, the correct locations would be inline above the firewall with spanned ports on each DMZ and one on the inside of the firewall. Be sure to add a caveat. A good final response to the interviewer would be that in your experience, the best place for an IDP is the place where you could look at the logs most frequently.

Placing an IDP in front of the firewall, you will know what attacks are hitting you, but you will have a lot of data to analyze. In addition to that, the use of NAT on your firewall will make tracking inside addresses difficult. Placing the IDP behind the firewall, the attacks detected are the ones that made it through your firewall, and you will have a significantly lower number of attacks to analyze. However, in this configuration, you will not have all the information available for trends, which could lead to a false sense of security.

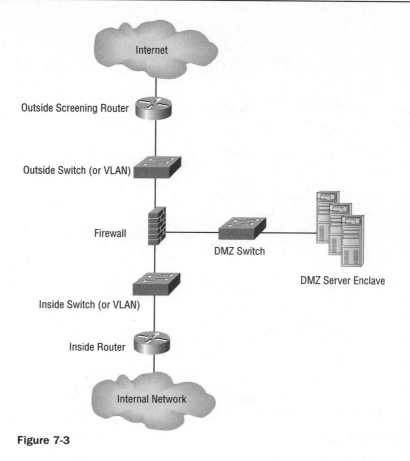

Figure 7-3

How Well Do You Know Snort Rules?

This question will determine whether you can identify an outside request for a Web page update. This is a common method for Web page defacement and it uses the HTTP PUT command.

```
alert tcp $EXTERNAL_NET any -> $MY_NET $HTTP_PORTS (msg:"LOCAL Put attempt";
flow:to_server,established; tag:session,50,packets; pcre:"/^PUT /A"; sid:3000001;
rev:1;)
```

How Well Do You Know Snort Configurations?

This question establishes how well you know the SnortSam firewall agent. This rule sends a command to the firewall to block the source IP address for two minutes after the detection of an nmap xmas scan.

```
$MY_NET any (msg:"SCAN nmap XMAS"; flow:stateless; flags:FPU,12;
reference:arachnids,30; classtype:attempted-recon; sid:1228; rev:7; fwsam: src, 2
minutes;)
```

For more information on Snort, Google "snort rules site:snort.org."

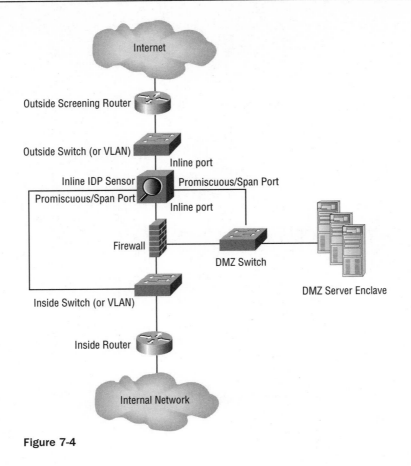

Figure 7-4

What Questions Do You Want to Ask Me?

Always a way to end an interview, but you want to take advantage of the opportunity to ask the interviewer questions. Here are some you have to ask regarding IDP systems.

❑   Where is your company in its IDS lifecycle? Was it an early adopter?

❑   How confident are you of an IDP's effectiveness?

Recommended Reading

General and Network-Based IDP Resources

An Introduction to Intrusion Detection Systems, `www.securityfocus.com/infocus/1520`

Comparison of Firewall, Intrusion Prevention and Antivirus Technologies (Google "intrusion+prevention site:juniper.net")

Evaluating Intrusion Prevention Systems (Google "intrusion+prevention site:cioupdate.com")

Intrusion Detection System Frequently Asked Questions (Google "idfaq site:sans.org")

Intrusion Detection: Implementation and Operational Issues (Google "intrusion detection site:af.mil")

Intrusion Prevention Systems (Google "intrusion detection site:checkpoint.com")

Intrusion Prevention Systems (IPS) (Google "intrusion prevention site:securecomputing.com")

Intrusion Prevention Systems (IPS) (Google "intrusion prevention site:ittoolbox.com")

Intrusion Prevention Systems: the Next Step in the Evolution of IDS (Google "intrusion prevention site:securityfocus.com")

Recommendations for Deploying an Intrusion-Detection System (Google "intrusion detection site:techtarget.com")

SANS Glossary of Terms Used in Security and Intrusion Detection (Google "intrusion detection glossary site:sans.org")

State of the Practice of Intrusion Detection Technologies (Google "intrusion detection site:cmu.edu")

The Evolution of Intrusion Detection Systems (Google "evolution site:securityfocus.com")

Wireless IDP Resources

Wireless IDSes Defend Your Airspace(Google "airspace site:eweek.com")

Wireless Intrusion Detection and Response (Google "wireless intrusion site:gatech.edu")

Wireless Intrusion Detection Systems (Google "wireless intrusion site:securityfocus.com")

Wireless Intrusion Detection Systems: GIAC Security Essentials (Google "wireless intrusion detection systems site:sans.org")

Anomaly Detection Resources

Anomaly Detection Can Prevent Network Attacks (Google "anomaly detection site:techworld.com")

Anomaly Detection in IP Networks (Google "anomaly detection site:gatech.edu")

Design and Implementation of an Anomaly Detection System: an Empirical Approach (Google "anomaly detection site:ntop.org")

IDS: Signature Versus Anomaly Detection (Google "anomaly detection site:techtarget.com")

Packet vs Flow-Based Anomaly Detection (Google "anomaly detection site:esphion.com")

The State of Anomaly Detection (Google "anomaly detection site:securityfocus.com")

A Design for Building an IPS Using Open Source Products (Google "design for building an IPS site:sans.org")

Host-Based IDP Resources

Host-Based IDS vs Network-Based IDS (Google "host-based site:windowsecurity.com")

Host-Based IDSs Add to Security Policy (Google "host-based IDS site:networkworld.com")

Host-Based Intrusion Detection Systems (Google "host-based IDS site:uva.nl")

What Is Host-Based Intrusion Detection? (Google "host-based site:sans.org")

Everything You Ever Wanted to Know about Wireless but Were Afraid They'd Ask

Wireless networking, especially as it relates to IT Security, used to be a niche that a few specialists concerned themselves with. Wireless networking and the security implications of adding a Wireless Local Area Network (WLAN) to an organization's infrastructure just wasn't that common. That was then; this is now. Wireless networking is everywhere, and if you go to a job interview for an IT Security position, you will deal with wireless networking in one way or another.

Your prospective employer may have a large, enterprise-wide wireless network for which you will need to provide security support. Perhaps that company has a small wireless network composed largely of consumer-grade equipment. You need to be aware of the security implications of both of these types of wireless networks, but what if the company has a policy that prohibits wireless? Does this mean that you don't need to concern yourself with wireless for your interview? Almost certainly not. Wireless clients can be just as dangerous, if not more so, to an organization's security posture. Failure to understand this could quite possibly cost you a legitimate shot at the job you covet.

Understanding the concepts in this chapter will allow you to be prepared for questions that prospective employers may ask you about wireless networking and, more specifically, the security implications of wireless networks. First, you will learn the fundamentals and history of wireless security. Next, you will gain an understanding of the different Wireless Local Area Network (WLAN) cards and the chipsets that they use. Linux has become the operating system of choice for many wireless security tasks, and you need to understand the differences in the drivers that are available to you. No discussion of wireless security is complete without a discussion of encryption. This chapter presents you with the different types of encryption available for wireless networks.

Whether you are interviewing for an offensive (penetration testing, vulnerability assessment, and so on) position or a defensive (network security, intrusion detection, and so on) position, you need to familiarize yourself with the products that are on the market and designed specifically for wireless security. You also need to be aware of rogue access points and how you can either use them to your advantage or determine that one has been deployed in your environment. Finally, no discussion of security concepts can be complete without standards, so you will need to familiarize yourself with both 802.11i and the National Institute of Standards and Technology (NIST) 800-97.

The Fundamentals

There are two fundamental concepts that you should have a good grip on when preparing for the wireless portion of your interview: the nomenclature of 802.11 wireless networking and the history of wireless security. Without understanding these two concepts, you are unlikely to be able to intelligently answer questions about more advanced topics.

What Do All These Letters Mean?

The Institute of Electrical and Electronics Engineers (IEEE) 802.11 standard is the wireless networking standard developed by the IEEE. You should be familiar with five over-the-air modulation techniques when preparing for your interview:

- ❑ 802.11a
- ❑ 802.11b
- ❑ 802.11g
- ❑ 802.11i
- ❑ 802.11n

The 802.11 refers to the original 802.11 standard, and the letter following it (a, b, g, i, or n) refers to an amendment of that standard.

802.11a

802.11a refers to wireless networks that operate in the 5 GHz frequency range. 802.11a networks have a maximum data rate of 54 Megabits per second (Mbit/s). This speed was faster than the original 802.11 networks that operated in the 2.4 GHz range; generally, less interference occurred on the 5 GHz band than on the 2.4 GHz band. 802.11a networks have a range of approximately 100 feet. 802.11a supports only Wired Equivalent Privacy (WEP) encryption.

802.11b

802.11b was the first wireless networking standard to gain consumer popularity. 802.11b networks operate in the 2.4 GHz frequency range and have a maximum data rate of 11 Mbit/s; however, vendors have released proprietary extensions to increase the maximum throughput of 802.11b. To take advantage of these speed increases, a given vendor's equipment must be utilized on both the server (access point) and client (WLAN card) side. 802.11b originally supported WEP encryption, but most 802.11b firmware can be flashed to support WiFi Protected Access (WPA) security. Twelve channels are available to 802.11b networks in the United States. Europe, Asia, and some other regions also support channels 13 and 14.

802.11g

802.11g also operates in the 2.4 GHz range, on the same channels as 802.11b. The primary difference between 802.11g and 802.11b is the maximum throughput that can be achieved. 802.11g networks have a maximum throughput of 54 Mbit/s. Most 802.11g devices readily support both WEP and WPA.

802.11i

802.11i is sometimes referred to as WPA2. 802.11b and g devices that support WPA still rely on the flawed RC4 encryption algorithm. 802.11i (WPA2) requires the use of the Advanced Encryption Standard (AES), a much more secure algorithm. Both the access point and the client must support WPA2 for this to work. Many 802.11g device firmwares can be flashed to support WPA2. 802.11i is covered extensively in the National Institute of Standards and Technology (NIST) Special Publication 800-97, available at http://csrc.nist.gov/publications/drafts/8 (http://www.wi-fi.org/)00-78-1/draft-SP_ 800-78-1-070306.pdf). WPA2 compliance is granted by the WiFi Alliance (http://www.wi-fi.org).

802.11n

802.11n is the next-generation standard being developed by the IEEE. 802.11n is expected to support speeds up to 540 Mbit/s and can operate in both the 2.4 GHz and 5 GHz frequency ranges. The range of 802.11n devices will be significantly smaller than previous standards — approximately only 160 feet. 802.11n is still in the approval stages, with ratification not expected until 2008.

You can find more information on the 802.11 standard at the IEEE 802.11 working group Web page (www.ieee802.org/11).

IEEE and the WiFi Alliance

Some confusion exists about the difference in standards for wireless networks. This confusion comes about mainly because the 802.11 specifications and the WiFi labels that are placed on packaging are often used interchangeably. The reality is that the Institute of Electrical and Electronics Engineers (IEEE) writes the standards for 802.11 specifications. The IEEE determines what is required for a device to be labeled 802.11g, 802.11i, and so on. The WiFi Alliance, on the other hand, is a nonprofit organization consisting of more than 300 members. These members verify the interoperability of wireless devices and certify them as WPA, WPA2, and so on. Most wireless devices that you see have a WiFi Alliance logo (shown in Figure 8-1) on them to show that they have been certified by the WiFi Alliance.

Figure 8-1

A Brief History of Wireless Security

The first encryption standard for wireless networking was Wired Equivalent Privacy (WEP), based on the RC4 encryption algorithm. WEP was initially available in two strengths: 40 bit and 108 bit. These are commonly referred to as 64 bit and 128 bit because of the 24-bit header that WEP uses. Later, 256-bit WEP became available but was never widely deployed. As wireless networks started to gain popularity, three researchers, Scott Fluhrer, Itsik Mantin, and Adi Shamir, released a paper called "Weaknesses in the Key

Scheduling Algorithm of RC4" (http://www.drizzle.com/~aboba/IEEE/rc4_ksaproc.pdf). This paper explained that WEP used a number of weak initialization vectors (IVs) and that if an attacker captured enough of them, the WEP key could be broken. This type of attack is commonly referred to as an FMS attack. FMS refers to the first letter of the last name of the paper's three authors. Shortly after the FMS paper was released, tools such as WEPCrack and AirSnort were released, which automated the FMS attacks. Although these attacks were possible, a large number of packets had to be captured in order to collect enough weak IVs to crack WEP. This requirement led many security professionals to refer to FMS attacks as possible but largely theoretical.

In response to the weaknesses in WEP, new security mechanisms were developed. Most notable of these were Cisco's proprietary Lightweight Extensible Authentication Protocol (LEAP) and WiFi Protected Access (WPA). WPA was specifically developed to replace WEP and was available in two flavors: WPA-PSK (Pre-Shared Key) and WPA-RADIUS. A major drawback of WPA was (and, outside of Windows environments, still is) that it was difficult to implement and deploy due to poor driver support. WPA and LEAP did, however, provide a secure alternative to WEP — for a while.

In March of 2003, Joshua Wright disclosed that LEAP was vulnerable to a dictionary attack wherein an attacker could capture LEAP traffic and, using a strong wordlist, break LEAP. Although this was the first public disclosure of the problem with LEAP, it has since come to light that Cisco was aware of this vulnerability prior to Wright's disclosure. A short while later, Wright released the ASLEAP tool that automated attacks against LEAP. About a year after Wright's initial disclosure, Cisco released EAP-FAST as a replacement for LEAP.

Unfortunately, the hits just kept coming for wireless security. In November of 2003, Robert Moskowitz of ISCA Labs disclosed that WPA-PSK suffered from a similar vulnerability as that of LEAP and that it was also vulnerable to dictionary attacks. He released a paper entitled "Weaknesses in Passphrase Choice in WPA Interface" that explained the problem. Luckily, this vulnerability applied only to passphrases that were shorter than 21 characters. About one year later, Joshua Wright released his CoWPAtty tool. CoWPAtty automated the dictionary attack process against WPA-PSK.

Until this point, the attacks against WEP were still very difficult to implement because of the large amount of traffic that had to be captured to successfully crack a WEP key. In 2004, the largely theoretical vulnerability of WEP became much more realistic when h1kari of Dachboden Labs released a paper detailing a more effective way to crack WEP based on a technique called *chopping*. Chopping attacks take a WEP packet and remove, or chop off, the last byte, breaking the CRC/ICV. If the last byte is 0, the last four bytes are xor'ed with a specific value to make a valid CRC and then the packet is retransmitted to the network. The use of chopping effectively ended the need to capture weak IVs; with it, only unique IVs were required. This technique significantly sped the process up. In 2004, tools such as Aircrack and weplab were released to automate this process, effectively ending any realistic hope that organizations could have of deploying WEP securely.

As we have moved forward from 2004, strides have been taken to secure wireless networks. WPA2 has been introduced. WPA2 requires the use of the Advanced Encryption Standard (AES) and has no known vulnerabilities. Additionally, security-specific wireless products have been released to help deploy wireless networks in a safe manner. These tools are discussed later in this chapter.

Wireless Cards and Chipsets

Many different wireless cards are available to security professionals. For the most part, however, these cards all use one of five chipsets. During your interview, you may be asked which chipset different cards use as well as the advantages and disadvantages of the different chipsets for security professionals. One of the best card comparisons can be found at `http://seattlewireless.net/HardwareComparison`.

Prism (2, 2.5, and 3)

The Prism chipset is one of the more popular, both with end users and security professionals. For your interview, it is important to know the reason that this chipset, although 802.11b only, is still one of the most popular choices of security professionals. The Prism chipset is extremely versatile. In fact, cards based on the Prism chipset can operate to some extent with three different Linux drivers: hermes, wlan-ng, and hostap. Prism-based cards are also very versatile, working in Linux, Windows, Apple OS X, and BSD variants.

Many wireless cards use the Prism chipset. The most popular for security professionals is the Senao 2511 because of its dual antenna jacks and 200 mw power output, as well as extensive Linux support.

Hermes

The Hermes chipset is another 802.11b chipset that is still very popular with security professionals. Of all the chipsets, Hermes-based cards have the most feature-rich compatibility with the largest number of WLAN discovery tools. For instance, Hermes cards are the only cards fully supported by NetStumbler. Fully supported means that in addition to WLAN discovery, you also get accurate Signal to Noise Ratio (SNR) data. The most popular Hermes-based card is the Orinoco Classic Gold. Several different companies, including Lucent and Proxim, have manufactured this card. Additionally, the Dell TrueMobile 1150 is a rebranded Orinoco card.

Atheros

Atheros chipsets provide support for 802.11a, 802.11b, and 802.11g, sometimes referred to as 802.11 a/b/g. Atheros-based cards work well in Windows using official drivers. Linux users have to use the open source community–developed Multiband Atheros Driver for WiFi (MADWIFI) driver.

Broadcom

Broadcom chipsets are common in many commercial cards, most notably the Dell TrueMobile 1300 and 1400 cards. These cards work well with Windows; however, Broadcom has not released the reference driver to the open source community. Linux users therefore are required to use a wrapper program such as Linuxant's DriverLoader (a commercial program) or the open source NDISWrapper with these cards. Wrapper programs translate the NDIS driver's calls to the NT kernel into native Linux calls. This method works for basic wireless functionality, but because many of the advanced features of the card can't be implemented, Broadcom cards are generally not a top choice for security professionals.

Aironet

Aironet chipsets are found primarily in cards manufactured by Cisco Systems, such as the Aironet 340 and Aironet 350. These are 802.11b-only cards. Aironet chipsets provide full support for Windows, Linux, Apple OS X, and BSD variants. Cards based on the Aironet chipset were very popular prior to the availability of the Senao 2511.

Intel

Intel chipsets have become more popular in recent years with the user community. Intel chipsets come in four main varieties: the PRO Wireless 2100; PRO Wireless 2200BG; PRO Wireless 2915 ABG; and PRO Wireless 3945 ABG. These cards perform well in Windows. Because most of the Intel-based cards on the market are Mini-PCI and do not allow the operator to attach an external antenna without hardware modifications, the Intel-based cards are not an extremely popular choice for security professionals.

Wireless Drivers for Linux

By now, you have probably noticed that in our discussion of the different chipsets, Linux compatibility is almost always a factor. We include this topic because Linux-based programs, in general, provide much more wireless functionality to security professionals. This is because of Linux support for rfmon, or monitor mode, which allows you to detect access points that are not broadcasting the SSID in the broadcast beacon frame. To obtain the same functionality in Windows, you have to purchase expensive commercial products.

Hermes

The Hermes drivers (hermes, orinoco, orinoco_cs, and so on) are easily compiled into the Linux kernel or built as modules. In the past, additional kernel patches were required to get these drivers to function in monitor mode. This is no longer the case because monitor mode can now be built right into the 2.6 kernel. The Hermes drivers work well with tools such as Kismet.

MADWIFI

The MADWIFI driver is an open source–developed Linux driver that supports the Atheros chipset. MADWIFI is an acronym for Multiband Atheros Driver for WiFi. As of 2005, Atheros has provided the MADWIFI developers with a code base so that advanced features can be integrated into the driver. Kismet has full support for the MADWIFI driver in 802.11a, b, and g, making it a very versatile driver for security professionals to use. The lack of a legal 802.11 a/b/g card with external antenna connectors in the United States has possibly hindered MADWIFI and Atheros from gaining a stronger foothold in the security community.

IPW Variants

Intel cards such as the PRO Wireless 2100, 2200 BG, and 2915 now have Linux support using the Intel-sponsored IPW suite of drivers (ipw2100, ipw2200, ipw2915, and ipw3945). These drivers are available at http://ipw2100.sourceforge.net/. The ipw2100 drivers are fully functional in Linux and include rfmon and noise levels. Other variants of the IPW suite of drivers support rfmon, but they do not report noise levels, or they report them inaccurately.

Wlan-ng

The wlan-ng drivers (www.linux-wlan.com) were initially released in 1999 to provide Linux support for Prism-based cards. Through the years, the wlan-ng drivers have been maintained and developed by the open source community and continue to provide excellent support for Prism-based cards, including support for rfmon and noise levels. The biggest drawback of the wlan-ng drivers is the lack of ability to enter master mode.

HostAP

Perhaps we have saved the best for last. The HostAP drivers have become the de facto choice for most security professionals who use Linux for wireless activities. HostAP drivers support rfmon and accurate noise levels, as do other drivers. In contrast to other Linux drivers, HostAP has support for master mode. This allows a user to turn a Prism-based card into an access point, which is invaluable for attacks against the client, setting up rogue access points, and performing man-in-the-middle attacks. Additionally, the HostAP drivers can be used with virtually every Linux wireless security program, including attack tools such as the Aircrack suite.

The HostAP drivers also have full support for the WPA supplicant, allowing Linux connections to WPA-enabled access points. Additionally, the HostAP drivers now have support for 802.11i. Overall, the HostAP driver is easily the most robust wireless driver available for Linux, and full support for all HostAP functionality is now available in the Linux kernel, either built in or as a module.

WLAN Detection (WarDriving)

Regardless of the information security position you are pursuing, you will almost certainly be asked about WLAN detection or WarDriving. WarDriving is the act of detecting wireless access points and clients while in motion. WarDriving itself does not involve connecting or associating with the networks that are found.

You may be asked about several aspects of WarDriving during your interview process. It is important to know about the tools of WarDriving, the benefits of each, and the drawbacks. You should also be prepared to answer questions regarding access points versus clients. Finally, you should be prepared to explain how the data you collect during a WarDrive can be used, either by an attacker or a penetration tester, to compromise a network.

WarDriving Tools

As WarDriving has become more popular, the number of tools that are available to security professionals has increased exponentially. In most interview situations, you only really need to understand the most popular tools for Windows, Linux, and OS X.

NetStumbler for Windows

NetStumbler (www.stumbler.net) is easily the most popular WLAN discovery tool used on Windows systems, probably because NetStumbler is free yet feature rich. Using NetStumbler has two primary benefits. First, it is easy to install and almost no post-installation configuration is required. Second, NetStumbler provides a highly useful and easy-to-understand SNR graph. It is therefore beneficial for direction finding and tracking down specific access points or clients.

Unfortunately, with ease of installation and use come feature limitations. The biggest drawback to using NetStumbler is that it can detect only active access points. Active access points are those that are broadcasting the SSID in the beacon frame. Because many organizations have their wireless networks operating as cloaked (sometimes referred to as stealth mode), meaning that the broadcast beacon does not contain the SSID of the network, NetStumbler is unable to detect them. Additionally, NetStumbler fully supports only cards based on the Hermes chipset. Other cards may work but the results are not consistent.

Kismet for Linux

Kismet (`www.kismetwireless.net`) is by far the most used WarDriving tool for the Linux operating system. In fact, it is probably the most used WarDriving tool available. Kismet is a passive discovery tool. This means that in order for the program to work, the WLAN card must be placed in rfmon, or monitor, mode. Then the card detects 802.11 traffic and identifies the existence of an access point or client. In order for Kismet to detect a wireless network, the SSID does not need to be broadcast. Another major benefit of Kismet is the large number of chipsets and cards that it supports. Almost every major chipset is supported to some degree by Kismet, with most offering full features such as SNR information.

In the past, the major drawback to Kismet was being able to successfully configure the Linux kernel and the WLAN driver to support monitor mode. This is not much of a problem anymore because kernel and driver patching is rarely necessary and this functionality can now be configured directly in the kernel. The biggest drawback to Kismet now is the configuration process. The default `kismet.conf` file allows Kismet to function with only slight modifications. To maximize the effectiveness of Kismet, though, users are required to do some significant and frequent tweaking of the `kismet.conf`. Additionally, the non-graphical user interface can be off-putting and in some cases difficult to decipher. Finally, Kismet does not always accurately report the encryption in use correctly, particularly when WPA or WPA2 is used. These drawbacks are certainly a small price to pay for the power and functionality of a tool such as Kismet, which is totally free.

Kismac for OS X

Apple users are not out of luck when it comes to WLAN discovery tools. In fact, Kismac is probably the single most complete WLAN auditing tool available today. Kismac provides the ability to use either active or passive mode and provides support for a large number of cards in both. Active mode support for the built-in Airport and Airport Extreme cards is available, as are Broadcom chipset–based cards. The passive mode support for Kismac is nearly as impressive as the support for Kismet. Airport and Airport Extreme are both supported, as are Atheros-based cards, Cisco Aironet-based cards, Prism 2, 2.5, and 3, and PrismGT cards. Kismac even includes passive mode support for many USB WLAN adapters. Kismac's graphical interface is easy to use and navigate, and provides a broad spectrum of information about each device that is discovered, including SNR data and the type of encryption in use. The other major benefit of Kismac is that, in contrast to its Windows and Linux counterparts, Kismac has built-in support for performing many of the active attacks against wireless networks such as disassociation, ARP spoofing, WEP cracking, packet injection, and WPA passphrase cracking.

The biggest disadvantage to Kismac is the obvious requirement for Apple hardware, which is far less common than systems capable of running Windows and Linux. Also, the mapping capabilities built in to Kismac are difficult to use and very difficult to customize for your customer's needs. If you are interviewing at an organization that uses Apple equipment already, your understanding that Kismac is superior in many ways to NetStumbler and Kismet, and your ability to discuss its many advantages as well as the few drawbacks to its use, will demonstrate your suitability for the position to your prospective employers.

Handheld Devices

Although not nearly as important as laptop-based WarDriving tools, you may be asked about WarDriving with handheld devices. As long as you can effectively convey that WLAN discovery tools can be used with handheld devices running both Windows Mobile and Linux, you will likely have provided all the information necessary.

MiniStumbler is the Windows Mobile version of NetStumbler and can be used with Hewlett Packard iPaqs and other devices running Windows Mobile. You should also know that MiniStumbler produces the log files in the same format as NetStumbler and that these files can be seamlessly imported between the two programs. MiniStumbler possesses the same functionality as NetStumbler.

There is also a port of Kismet for handheld devices such as the Sharp Zaurus that use ARM processors. The ARM port of Kismet provides the same functionality as the regular Linux version of Kismet.

Access Points Versus Clients

Just being aware of the tools used for WarDriving will probably get you through a few cursory questions during your interview, but you likely will be asked some questions that require you to demonstrate an understanding of the data produced by these tools. One of the easiest ways to demonstrate your understanding here is to explain how you can differentiate an access point from a wireless client and what this means to you when analyzing the data.

Access Points

To determine whether a particular found network is an access point or a client, you need to first take a look at the Kismet main panel, shown in Figure 8-2.

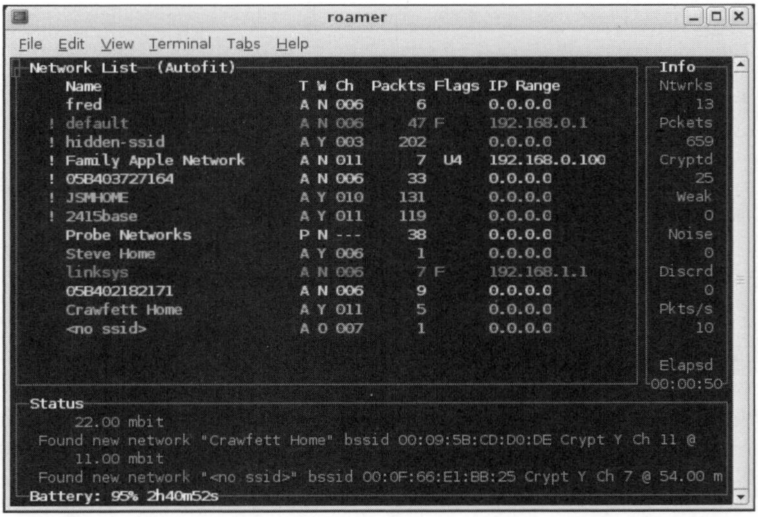

Figure 8-2

As a general rule, most of the networks in the network list will be access points; however, it is difficult or impossible to be sure without looking at the network details, as shown in Figure 8-3.

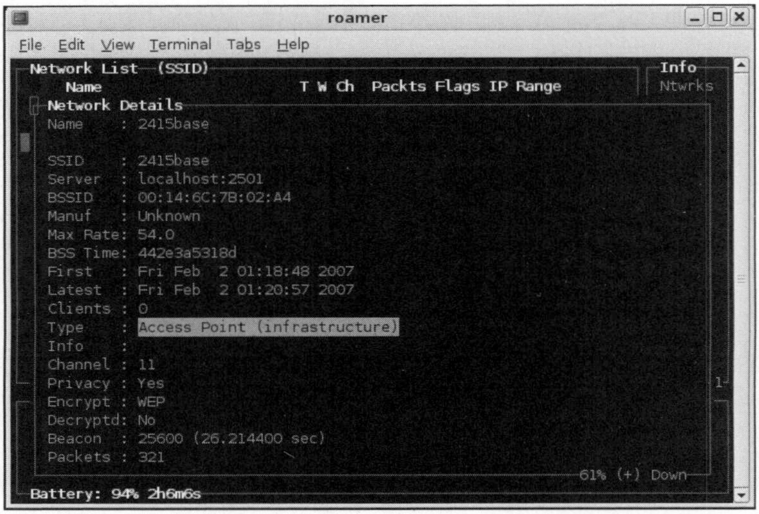

Figure 8-3

In the Type field for an access point, you will see "Access Point (infrastructure)," denoting that the network is an actual access point. If you know your organization's SSID, you can easily verify that the BSSID (MAC Address) of each access point broadcasting the SSID actually belongs to your organization.

Clients

Although finding access points is very important, you should also be able to explain the process for determining whether clients are broadcasting in your client's vicinity. Again, go to the Kismet main panel. Clients will display in Kismet in one of three ways. First, the network name that the client is trying to find may be displayed. Second, the network may appear as "Data Networks." Finally, if the client is trying to probe for available networks, it may show as "Probe Networks." Both Data Networks and Probe Networks are visible in Figure 8-4.

Just as when checking for access points, you may need to go to the Network Details to determine whether it is indeed a client, as shown in Figure 8-5.

If the network you are investigating is a client, the Type field will show "Probe Request (searching client)." During your interview, you may be asked why you should care about probing clients. If you are responsible for maintaining the security of a network, you want to ensure that only authorized wireless activity is taking place. You can do so by ensuring that all the access points in the building are indeed authorized, as discussed in the previous section. You also want to ensure that no clients are attempting to connect to an access point that doesn't belong to that organization, such as a home network or local wireless hotspot. Although a probing client may seem relatively benign, the next section helps you explain why it can be one of the most dangerous threats to your organization's network.

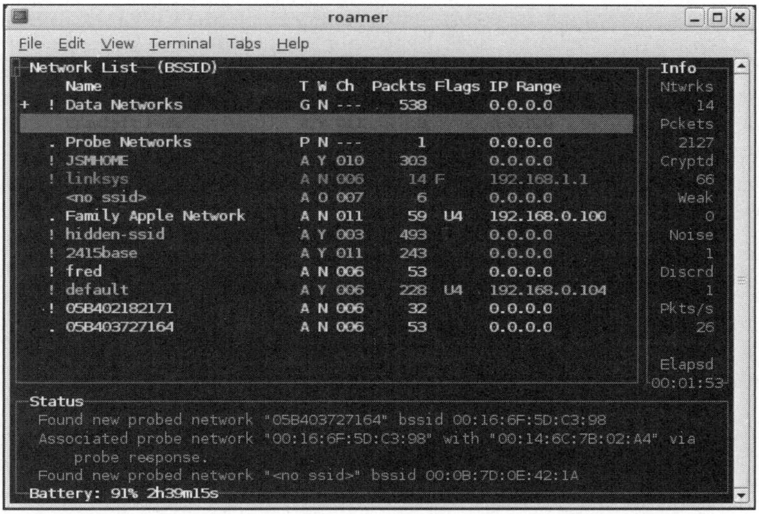

Figure 8-4

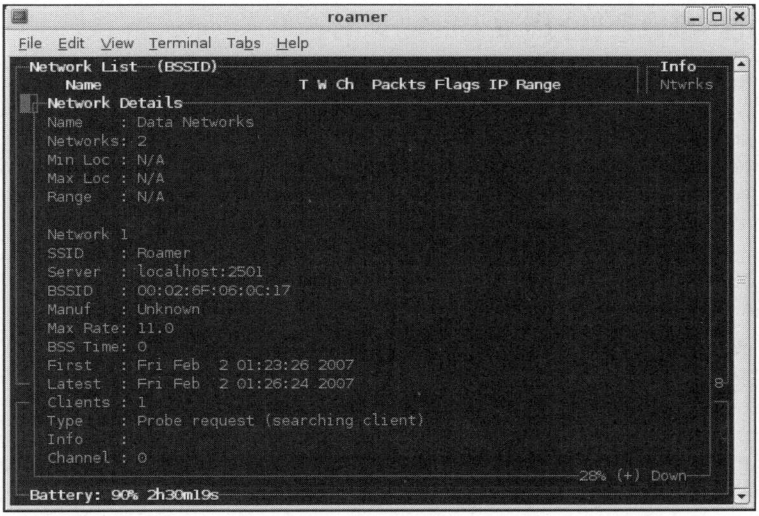

Figure 8-5

Using WarDrive Data to Compromise Networks

Whether you are interviewing for a penetration testing job or a position in which you will be responsible for maintaining the security of a network, you will probably be asked how an attacker can use the data gained during a WarDrive to compromise a network. Again, an attacker has two ways to accomplish this: using a probing client or using an insecure access point.

Organizations have a tendency to consider their wireless network as the only point of wireless vulnerability on their network. This belief couldn't be further from the truth. Many attackers will eschew an organization's actual wireless network because there is more likelihood of monitoring and detecting wireless intrusion. If an attacker can identify a client card in a laptop that is attempting to connect to a home network or local hotspot, the attacker can easily set up a rogue access point with the SSID that the client is attempting to connect to. The probing card will associate with this access point and then the attacker can use the laptop, which is probably connected to the organization's internal network, as a jumping-off point to begin probing or attacking the internal resources.

Attackers can also use the data they obtain during a WarDrive to identify the organization's authorized wireless network. All the popular WLAN detection tools provide information about the method of encryption in use, if any. If the attacker discovers that the WLAN is either open (not using any encryption or backend VPN) or configured using a known vulnerable form of encryption, such as WEP or WPA-PSK with a short passphrase, the attacker can try to gain access to the WLAN. If no encryption is in use, gaining access is trivial for an attacker. Simply configuring his or her client card with the SSID of the target WLAN will force the client to associate with the network. The attacker can then request an IP address from the DHCP server and begin the process of infiltrating the network. Both WEP and WPA-PSK have vulnerabilities that attackers can use to gain access to the WLAN. These vulnerabilities are discussed in detail in the next section.

Wireless Security

The 802.11 standard was not developed with security in mind. In fact, it was designed in the exact opposite way: to be open and allow for ease of connection and expansion. This design makes setting up and configuring both managed and ad hoc networks easy. Unfortunately, it also means that security mechanisms for wireless networks were developed mostly as an afterthought. You should have an understanding of both the encryption mechanisms in place for wireless networking and some of the security-centric products that have come to market in recent years.

Wired Equivalent Privacy (WEP)

WEP was the first encryption standard for wireless networks. WEP can be deployed in three strengths: 64, 128, and 256 bit. WEP is based on the RC4 encryption algorithm. As wireless networks gained popularity, a vulnerability in the key scheduling algorithm of RC4 was discovered wherein a subset of the initialization vectors (IVs) used by WEP were determined to be weak. By collecting enough of these weak IVs, an attacker could determine the WEP key and potentially compromise the wireless network. Many vendors issued firmware updates for their wireless equipment that reduced the number of weak IVs that were generated. These updates, coupled with the amount of time it took to gather enough weak IVs to crack the key, greatly reduced the effectiveness of attacks against WEP.

Security researchers discovered another way to attack WEP, called *chopping*. As explained previously, chopping involves taking a WEP packet and removing, or chopping off, the last byte, which breaks the CRC/ICV. If the last byte is 0, the last four bytes are xor'ed with a specific value to make a valid CRC and then the packet is retransmitted to the network. This attack effectively ended the need for weak IVs to be collected in order to crack WEP. Using chopping methods, only unique IVs needed to be collected. The amount of time involved in data collection was significantly reduced. Despite these vulnerabilities, WEP is still the most used form of wireless encryption deployed worldwide. These numbers are slightly misleading, though, because the majority of WEP networks are deployed in home WLANs. Corporate and government WLANs rarely use WEP now and have migrated to a more secure form of encryption.

WiFi Protected Access (WPA)

In response to the problems with WEP, the WiFi Alliance released WiFi Protected Access (WPA). WPA was initially released in two forms: Pre-Shared Key (WPA-PSK) and in conjunction with RADIUS. WPA uses Temporal Key Integrity Protocol (TKIP) to hash the IVs with the WPA key to create the RC4 key that is transmitted. Initially, this appeared to be the fix to the problems with wireless security; however, as vulnerabilities were discovered in WPA when deployed using the Pre-Shared Key, it became apparent that further attention had to be paid to wireless security, and WPA2 was developed to address these issues.

WPA-PSK

WPA with a Pre-Shared Key is the easiest way to deploy WPA on a wireless network. WPA-PSK is sometimes referred to as WPA Personal because it was designed for use primarily in home networks or smaller corporate environments. To use WPA-PSK, a passphrase is set on the access point, and any client that wants to connect to it must transmit the passphrase. WPA-PSK works well unless the passphrase is shorter than 21 characters. If the passphrase is shorter than 21 characters, it can be guessed using a dictionary attack. The disclosure of this vulnerability led many experts to believe that wireless could never be deployed securely, and the WiFi Alliance went back to work to develop yet another security mechanism for wireless networks.

WPA-RADIUS

WPA can also be used in conjunction with a backend RADIUS server to perform authentication. This mechanism is sometimes referred to as WPA Enterprise because it was designed to be used in large environments in which distributing the PSK to each individual might not be feasible. This mechanism removes the requirement of a Pre-Shared Key and instead uses WPA to transmit authentication information to the RADIUS server. WPA-RADIUS relies on an Extensible Authentication Protocol (EAP). EAP-TLS was initially certified by the WiFi Alliance for use with WPA-RADIUS; however, five additional EAPs have now been certified:

- ❑ EAP-TLS/MSCHAPv2
- ❑ PEAPv0/EAP-MSCHAPv2
- ❑ PEAPv1/EAP-GTC
- ❑ EAP-SIM
- ❑ EAP-LEAP

Currently, no known weaknesses are associated with WPA-RADIUS.

WPA2

WPA2, sometimes called 802.11i, requires the use of the Advanced Encryption Standard (AES) instead of TKIP but operates in the same way as WPA. WPA2 can also be deployed with either a PSK or by using a RADIUS server. No WPA2 vulnerabilities have been discovered to date. WPA2 is covered extensively in NIST Special Publication 800-97, available at http://csrc.nist.gov/publications/drafts/800-78-1/draft-SP_800-78-1-070306.pdf.

Extensible Authentication Protocol (EAP)

In contrast to other security mechanisms, EAP isn't an encryption standard per se but rather is an authentication framework that is most commonly, but not always, used in WLANs. There are many different types of EAPs, some of which are vendor proprietary, such as the Lightweight Extensible Authentication Protocol (LEAP) from Cisco. EAP is defined by the IETF RFC 3748 (`http://tools .ietf.org/html/rfc3748`). Although some problems occurred in early wireless implementations, most EAP types deployed on wireless networks today are considered secure.

Wireless Intrusion Detection Systems (IDS)

As wireless security has evolved, wireless-specific security products have become available. The most widely deployed type of wireless security product is the wireless IDS. Just as with a wired IDS, a wireless IDS primarily uses pattern matching technology (or signatures) to identify potentially malicious activity. The wireless IDS passively monitors all wireless traffic within range and matches malicious activity to the signature set configured in the IDS. The engineer who receives the alert must then determine what to do about the alert. A decision may be made to continue monitoring to further determine the nature of the attack or to drop, or blacklist, the attacker. Additionally, most modern wireless IDS products have the ability to provide a general location of the attacker, which allows the person monitoring the IDS to track down the system where the possible attack is originating and investigate it further. Some of the most common signatures a wireless IDS looks for are MAC address cloning or spoofing, man-in-the-middle attacks, rogue access points and clients, ARP packet injection, and disassociation floods.

In their earliest stages, wireless IDS products were not extremely effective, having only a small subset of possible attack signatures. As they have evolved and competition between vendors has ramped up, wireless IDS products have become very effective. AirDefense and AirMagnet produce add-on wireless IDS products that can be purchased regardless of the hardware in place and added to the existing wireless network. Cisco and Aruba networks have chosen to take a different path and include wireless IDS capability in their security-centric wireless-security products.

Just as with any security product, the effectiveness of the wireless IDS is heavily reliant on the ability of the people who use them. A good engineer who can configure and tweak the IDS to the specific environment is crucial. Additionally, having well-trained, knowledgeable personnel to monitor the alerts is required.

Rogue Wireless Devices

During your interview, you may be asked about rogue wireless devices. Rogue devices can take two forms: rogue access points and rogue clients. It is important to familiarize yourself with both and to understand the difference. Additionally, you should be able to relay to a perspective employer how to detect rogue devices and how an attacker can deploy a rogue access point on his or her network.

What Is a Rogue Access Point?

A rogue access point is a wireless device operating as an access point on a network without permission or knowledge of the network administrators. A rogue access point is much more likely to be connected to the internal, wired network than to the wireless network. A common misconception about rogue access points is that they are always malicious. To the contrary, most rogue access points are placed on the network by a legitimate, authorized user in order to make some portion of their daily work easier or more efficient. An example is a researcher connecting an access point to a network segment in his research lab that is firewalled off from the rest of the network. He wouldn't do this so that an outsider could connect to the network and steal or modify his research data. In all likelihood, he would do this so that he could access his research data from a different segment of the network, such as his office, while preparing a report on his findings or a similar, seemingly benign task.

The same can be said of an employee who wants to create his own small network in his office or cubicle. He is, in all likelihood, attempting to improve his productivity, but unwittingly exposes internal resources to anyone within range of the access point. Doing so obviously exposes internal resources to greater risk because these rogue access points aren't managed by the IT staff and likely aren't configured with the security of the network in mind, but rather are configured to facilitate ease of use.

Of course, not all rogue access points are placed by employees looking to improve their productivity. A malicious insider can place an access point on the network in order to more easily remove sensitive or proprietary data from the network without going through the organization's monitoring process.

Finally, in rare instances, an attacker who is able to gain access to a facility may place an access point on the internal network so that he or she can return later and use that access point as an initial launching pad for attacks against internal resources, either to steal data or to further compromise the network and establish a foothold on the internal, wired network that can be used even if the rogue access point is discovered and removed.

What Is a Rogue Client?

A rogue client is a wireless client card, such as a built-in wireless card in a laptop that is probing for an access point either in an area where wireless networking is prohibited or for an access point in a different geographical location. This situation is most commonly seen when employees have corporate laptops with built-in wireless cards that they use either at home or at a wireless hotspot. Although rogue clients are almost always unintentional, that fact doesn't reduce their potential impact on an organization.

A likely scenario involving a compromise that results from a rogue client device is that of an employee who connects to a hotel network while traveling. Most hotel networks do not require encryption, and authentication, if required, occurs after the client has associated successfully with the access point. When the employee returns to his or her office, the wireless card will attempt to associate with the last access point it was connected to. Because that access point doesn't exist within range of the corporate facility, the client will continually send out probe requests for the last SSID it was associated with.

An attacker who discovers these probes can then set up a rogue access point using the SSID that the client is attempting to connect to. When associated, the attacker can use this connection as a launching point for attacks against that particular laptop, and eventually to launch attacks against internal resources on the corporate network.

Fortunately, this type of attack can be proactively stopped. Security policy settings can be set at the Domain Controller that disables wireless clients when the system they are in authenticates to the domain.

How Do You Detect a Rogue Wireless Device?

Detecting rogue access points has become much easier with advances in wireless IDS technology. A good wireless IDS product can identify the location of any wireless device that becomes active in your facility. Of course, enough sensors must be deployed to provide complete coverage of the facility. Additionally, unless a thorough and up-to-date list of authorized wireless devices is maintained, identifying a rogue device when it becomes active on your network is difficult if not impossible.

Obviously, not all organizations can deploy a comprehensive wireless IDS, so you will need to have an understanding of the size of the organization you are interviewing with and be prepared to explain how to detect rogue access points without the benefit of an expensive, well-deployed wireless IDS. In situations in which a wireless IDS is not deployed, a complete list of authorized wireless devices still needs to be maintained. Tools such as Kismet that operate passively can be deployed at minimal cost and monitored for probing clients as well as active access points. After you have identified an access point that is not authorized, or a client probing in your environment, old-fashioned manual direction finding will allow you to track the device so that you can evaluate and react to the situation.

How Can You Become a Rogue Access Point?

Whether you are interviewing for a penetration test position or a position in which you will be required to maintain the security of a network, you need to be able to describe the process that an attacker uses to become a rogue access point. This does not mean plugging an access point in to the network. Rather, this process relates to using a laptop equipped with a Prism 2–based card and the HostAP drivers to effectively become an access point. You accomplish this very simply using the `iwconfig` command:

```
iwconfig <interface> essid <network_name> mode master
ifconfig <interface> <IP Address>
ifconfig <interface> up
```

At this point, your laptop is effectively functioning as an access point. The options available to you at this point are plentiful. You can begin a man-in-the-middle attack by configuring a DHCP server and, using a second card, forward traffic to through the legitimate network. You can simply attack the system that associated with your laptop and then, after it is compromised, use it as a launching point to attack other systems on the network.

If you discover that a client that is connected to the wired network is attempting to associate with a home WLAN or hotspot, you simply configure your card with the SSID of the network that the client is attempting to connect to in master mode. The card will associate with your system, and you can use that system to hop into the wired network.

Summary

If you are being interviewed for any information security position, you will almost certainly be questioned about wireless networking to some degree. You need to be able to effectively demonstrate that you have a basic understanding of the fundamentals of wireless networking, such as the differences between 802.11 a, b, g, and i. You should also be able to explain how and why wireless security has evolved over time.

An ability to explain the different cards, chipset, and drivers used by wireless devices is also important. You should be able to explain why a security professional would prefer to use Linux with a Prism 2 card and the HostAP drivers. You need to effectively explain the difference between active and passive WLAN discovery and which cards, chipsets, drivers, and operating systems allow you to enter monitor mode. You should also be familiar with the different security and encryption protocols used in wireless networks and the benefits and drawbacks of each. Be prepared to explain when WEP ceased to be a viable option and why. Be prepared to explain the difference between WPA and WPA2. Finally, you need to be able to explain how rouge wireless devices can be used by attackers to compromise networks, both wireless and wired.

The concepts outlined in this chapter are by no means comprehensive. Entire books have been devoted to wireless security, and the concepts presented here are just a subset of these topics. Understanding the topics presented in this chapter, however, will allow you to be prepared for the most common topics that you are likely to be faced with during an interview for an IT Security position.

Interview Q&A

Q: If my wireless network doesn't have a lot of traffic, is it okay to use WEP because the IVs required to crack the WEP key won't be generated?

A: No. Automated tools are available that allow attackers to capture an ARP packet and reinject it to the access point very rapidly. This generates a significant amount of traffic and allows the attacker to capture enough unique initialization vectors to quickly crack the key.

Q: What is the difference between active and passive WLAN detection?

A: Active WLAN detection requires that the SSID be broadcast in the beacon frame. Passive WLAN detection listens to all traffic in range of the device and determines what WLANs are in range.

Q: Briefly describe the process involved in cracking WEP.

A: To efficiently crack a WEP key, you first need to obtain an Address Resolution Protocol (ARP) packet from the access point you want to attack. You can obtain this packet using a tool such as Void11 (`www.wlsec.net/void11`) to send deauthentication packets to the clients associated with that access point. When the clients reassociate to the access point, ARP packets will be generated and can be captured. After you have captured a valid ARP packet, you can use a tool such as Aireplay, a part of the Aircrack suite (`http://freshmeat.net/projects/aircrack/`), to inject the ARP packet back into the network. This injection process will cause a large number of initialization vectors to be generated. You can capture this traffic with any pcap format sniffer. Ethereal, Airodump, and Kismet all support pcap format. After you have captured between 500,000 and 1 million unique initialization vectors, you can then crack the WEP key using Aircrack or other, similar tools. Most of these tools are available for free on the Internet.

Q: How many types of Extensible Authentication Protocols (EAPs) are supported by WPA/WPA2 and what are they?

A: There are six fully supported EAP types for WPA/WPA2: EAP-TLS; EAP-TLS/MSCHAPv2; PEAPv0/EAP-MSCHAPv2; PEAPv1/EAP-GTC; EAP-SIM;and EAP-LEAP.

Q: What is the primary difference between 802.11g and 802.11a?

A: 802.11g operates in the 2.4 GHz frequency range, as do 802.11b and 802.11i, whereas 802.11a operates in the 5 GHz frequency range.

Q: What is the difference between the HostAP drivers and the wlan-ng drivers for Linux?

A: Both of these drivers work with a variety of cards; however, only the HostAP drivers allow you to place your card in monitor mode.

Q: Who determines the wireless standards?

A: The IEEE develops and determines the wireless standards (802.11a, b, g, and so on). The WiFi Alliance, the group that owns the WiFi trademark, then certifies the interoperability of these devices.

Q: What tools do you use to WarDrive?

A: Depending on the operating system in use, Kismet for Linux or Kismac for OS X provide the greatest level of functionality for detecting and identifying WLANs. NetStumbler is available for Windows but supports only active WLAN detection and identification, whereas the Linux and OS X tools both support passive WLAN detection and identification.

Q: What is the minimum passphrase length that should be used for WPA-PSK?

A: Because WPA-PSK with a short passphrase is vulnerable to a dictionary attack, and automated tools are available to facilitate this process, a WPA-PSK passphrase should be at least 21 characters long.

Q: Our organization doesn't have a wireless network, so is it even important for our security engineers to understand wireless security?

A: Yes. Even though wireless networking isn't allowed at your site, it is important that the security staff understand that laptops with wireless cards (authorized or unauthorized) pose a threat to the network and know how to identify them and react accordingly. Additionally, the staff should be able to identify rogue access points and the potential impact they can have on the security of the network.

Recommended Reading

Wardriving & Wireless Penetration Testing by Chris Hurley, Russ Rogers, Frank Thornton, and Daniel Connelly (Syngress Publishing. ISBN: 159749111X)

Infosec Career Hacking: Sell Your Skillz, Not Your Soul by Aaron W. Bayles, Chris Hurley, Johnny Long, and Ed Brindley (Syngress Publishing. ISBN: 1597490113)

Real 802.11 Security: Wi-Fi Protected Access and 802.11i by Jon Edney and William A. Arbaugh (Addison-Wesley. ISBN: 0321136209)

NIST Special Publication 800-48 (`http://csrc.nist.gov/publications/nistpubs/800-48/NIST_SP_800-48.pdf`)

Proxim's Guide to Wireless Network Security (`http://www.proxim.com/learn/library/whitepapers/wireless_security.pdf`)

9

Finding Your Posture

The security posture of an organization or company is an aggregation of many factors that provide protection. In the information security realm, those factors include the measuring of managerial, operational, and technical controls to ensure adequate confidentiality, integrity, and availability of information, as defined by the needs of the organization. Assessing the security posture is a fundamental requirement for risk management. Without knowing what the security posture is, the organization cannot perform adequate risk management.

In this chapter, we want to address the "what and how" of a security posture. Although there are complete college curriculums and commercial training courses focused on information security, they do not always boil the issues down to the basics. This chapter provides a quick review of the high points so that you can focus your efforts. We hope that you find this chapter useful, but you should not take it as the final word on what you should know. Working in the information security industry means that you will need to continually expand your knowledge. To understand the security posture, you should have a basic understanding of where the security posture comes from, and why. The following sections provide a quick overview of significant changes in the history of security.

History of Information Security

Since the early days of the Roman Empire, people have understood that it was necessary to provide protection for written correspondence (confidentiality) and to detect whether the writing was tampered with (integrity). Julius Caesar is credited with the development of the Caesar cipher, around 50 B.C., to prevent his messages from being read by his enemies.

The evolution of information security is not much different from the way past societies secured themselves from attack. In Europe, for example, there was a time when castles fortified cities and protected them from assault. Little protection existed outside these castle walls. For commerce to flourish, kingdoms emerged to provide greater protection over larger areas, thereby creating empires. These governments provided the centralized law and security needed for global trade. During these times, commerce prospered, clearly illustrating how security and commerce are tied closely together.

By World War II, the techniques and technology of information protection had advanced significantly. Major techniques introduced for information protection include, but are not limited to, the formalized classification of data based on sensitivity and background checks for personnel prior to the granting of access to sensitive data. Most significant was the introduction of automation, such as the German Enigma machine used to encode and decode communications. Rapid advancements in telecommunications and computer hardware and software have continued ever since and will continue into the future.

Modern Information Security

The growth of electronic data processing and the Internet since World War II have created the need for better methods of protecting the information that is stored, processed, and transmitted by computers, personal data assistants (PDA), and many other electronic devices. Academic disciplines of computer security, information security, and information assurance have emerged along with professional organizations such as the International Information Systems Security Certification Consortium (ISC2) and the Information Systems Security Association (ISSA; www.issa.org/). The goal of these academic and professional organizations is to provide better methods and standards for ensuring the reliability and security of information.

The growth of the Internet has significantly affected the growth in legislation to criminalize actions that have a negative impact on public or private information systems. The following is a partial listing of European, United Kingdom, and American laws and regulations that have a direct effect on the standards for data processing, transmission, and storage of information. These legislative actions provide most of the basis for compliance in information security. Chapter 4 of this book provides an in-depth look at each of these, but we have also included a brief overview here to keep you on track:

- ❑ United Kingdom and European Union legislation

  - ❑ The UK's Data Protection Act 1998 makes provisions for regulating the processing of information relating to individuals, including the obtaining, holding, and use or disclosure of such information.

  - ❑ The European Union Data Protection Directive (EUDPD) requires that all EU members adopt national regulations to standardize the protection of data privacy for citizens throughout the EU. More information is available at www.opsi.gov.uk (search "Data Protection Act").

  - ❑ Various EU Data Retention laws require Internet service providers and phone companies to keep data on every electronic message sent and phone call made for between six months and two years.

- ❑ United States legislation

  - ❑ The Family Educational Rights and Privacy Act (FERPA) protects the privacy of student education records. The law applies to all schools that receive funds under an applicable program of the U.S. Department of Education. Generally, schools must have written permission from the parent or eligible student in order to release any information from a student's education record. More information is available at www.ed.gov (search "FERPA").

  - ❑ The Health Insurance Portability and Accountability Act (HIPAA) requires the adoption of national standards for electronic health care transactions and national identifiers for providers, health insurance plans, and employers. HIPPA requires health care providers, insurance providers, and employers to safeguard the security and privacy of health data. More information is available at www.cms.hhs.gov (search "HIPAA").

❏ Gramm-Leach-Bliley Act of 1999 (GLBA), also known as the Financial Services Modernization Act of 1999, protects the privacy and security of private financial information that financial institutions collect, hold, and process. More information is available at www.senate.gov (search "GLBA").

❏ Sarbanes-Oxley Act of 2002 (SOX), Section 404, requires publicly traded companies to assess the effectiveness of their internal controls for financial reporting in annual reports they submit at the end of each fiscal year. Chief Information Officers (CIOs) are responsible for the security, accuracy, and reliability of the systems that manage and report the financial data. This act also requires publicly traded companies to engage independent auditors who must attest to, and report on, the validity of their assessments. More information is available at www.sec.gov (search "Sarbanes-Oxley Act").

❏ The Federal Information Security Management Act of 2002 (FISMA) provides the government-wide requirements for information security, superseding the Government Information Security Reform Act and the Computer Security Act. Federal agencies are responsible for providing information security protection of information collected or maintained by or on behalf of the organization and information systems used or operated by or on behalf of the organization. NIST has been tasked to develop standards and guidelines, including minimum requirements, for providing adequate information security for all organization operations and assets. One thing to note is that these standards and guidelines do not apply to national security systems. More information is available at www.nist.gov (search "FISMA").

❏ Department of Defense (DoD) Information Assurance Certification and Accreditation Process (DIACAP) establishes the DoD information assurance (IA) certification and accreditation (C&A) process for authorizing the operation of DoD classified and unclassified information systems consistent with the Federal Information Security Management Act (FISMA), DoD Directive (DoDD) 8500.1, and DoDD 8100.1. DIACAP also provides visibility and control of the implementation of information assurance (IA) capabilities and services, the C&A process, and accreditation decisions authorizing the operation of DoD information systems, to include core enterprise services (CES) and Web services–enabled software systems and applications. More information is available through a Goggle search for "DIACAP."

❏ Payment Card Industry Data Security Standard (PCI DSS) establishes comprehensive requirements for enhancing payment account data security. It was developed by the founding payment brands of the PCI Security Standards Council, including American Express, Discover Financial Services, JCB, MasterCard Worldwide, and Visa International to help facilitate the broad adoption of consistent data security measures on a global basis. The PCI DSS is a multifaceted security standard that includes requirements for security management, policies, procedures, network architecture, software design, and other critical protective measures. More information is available at https://www.pcisecuritystandards.org/.

❏ State Security Breach Notification Laws (California and many others) require businesses, nonprofits, and state institutions to notify consumers when unencrypted "personal information" may have been compromised, lost, or stolen.

Security Objectives

Information security, or cyber security, is analogous to physical security in the world around us. We can understand how locked doors and windows, along with alarms, can be used to make lives more secure. Information security can be compared to these physical security approaches. Information security is intended to make our Internet presence or cyber world more secure. Passwords function like door locks to keep intruders out, and intrusion detection methods serve as alarms to warn us of unauthorized entry. It all depends on the perspective of the individual viewing what you are doing. As with anything that we translate from the physical world to the cyber world, we must define our terminology and the business needs before the cyber version can work to protect us. Most businesses understand that the default installation of a computer operating system alone is not adequate protection by itself.

If you are new to information security, you will soon learn that there is much more to it than keeping the "evil" hackers out of your systems. Information security has three objectives: confidentiality, integrity, and availability. Protecting the information that is processed, transmitted, or stored on your computer and network is equivalent to ensuring that the information is kept secret, not changed without permission, and ready to use when you need it.

The three objectives of confidentiality, integrity, and availability can never be completely separated. The definitions and solutions can overlap among the three. That is not a problem. As the information security professional, you are responsible for understanding how the three objectives fit within the business and assisting with meeting the business objectives. Most of this will come from understanding the customers and their business goals.

Business goals will vary from industry to industry, and sometimes even among businesses within an industry. For example, if you look at the differences in business goals between a hospital and a bank, you will see that while confidentiality, integrity, and availability are needed in both, each has another objective that overlap with two of the original three objectives.

The hospital needs to add authorization or authentication. This authentication is a combination of confidentiality and integrity. *Authentication* is the process of proving that only those verified and authorized can make changes to data.

The bank needs to add nonrepudiation, which is a combination of integrity and availability. Simply defined, *non-repudiation* is the process of proving that the individual who sent data, or information, is who he or she claimed to be and that the recipient cannot legally dispute the receipt of the data, or information.

Nonrepudiation can become an issue for businesses that focus on the processes and not the information. It is the information that we need to make the business run, not the applications or systems that process, transmit, or store that information. We just need to keep the end goal in mind: Computer systems must do what we want, when we want, and do so safely and securely, because they are business tools, not business owners.

The first objective of security is confidentiality. Simply defined, *confidentiality* is protecting information from unauthorized exposure. To accomplish this requires knowing what data we are protecting and who should have access to it. It requires that we provide protection controls for the data while it is stored in the computer and while it is being transmitted between computers. We need to know the applications or programs that we use to process the information, and we need to control the use of those applications. Your job in information security is to evaluate, implement, and maintain those controls. In effect, you are determining the security posture of an organization.

There are few places to find out what needs to be protected. Two sources are published by the National Institute of Technology (NIST): Federal Information Processing Standards Publication (FIPS PUB) 199 and 200. There is also the National Security Agency (NSA) Information Assurance Training and Rating Program (IATRP). For more information on the FIPS PUB, go to www.nist.gov *and search "FIPS." You can find additional information about the IATRP at* www.iatrp.com.

Since the original Privacy Act of 1974 (which can be found at www.usdoj.gov; search "Privacy Act 1974"), confidentiality has taken on an expanded meaning in the form of privacy controls.

The Privacy Act of 1974 is intended to balance the individual's rights from unwarranted invasion of privacy by the government with the government's need to maintain information about individuals.

For some industries, such as health care and finance, privacy is now a regulatory issue. U.S. companies operating in one state are now governed by the privacy legislation of other states if they have employees or customers in any of those other states. Public demand for privacy is forcing companies to formulate and implement clear privacy policies and procedures to prevent customers from leaving because of loss in confidence and to prevent significant regulatory fines.

The second objective of information security is integrity. Simply defined, *integrity* is protecting the information stored in the computer system from unauthorized modification. Both confidentiality and availability contribute to integrity. Preventing unauthorized exposure and ensuring that those who have a legitimate and authorized need to the information are able to get it are fairly basic ways to help maintain the integrity of the information.

But many integrity failures happen despite adequate controls. These failures can occur because the people we trust are not always trustworthy. There are legitimate business needs to extend levels of trust to people about whom we know little or nothing, such as temporary workers, third-party business partners, or consultants. Integrity controls have to go beyond the simple "who" definitions and handle the "what" conditions. When people have been granted access, what operations can they perform on our computer systems? This question requires us to define the constraints of access within the computer system and adds to the complexity of computer systems.

The need for information integrity ties computer security closely to two related business needs — business continuity planning and disaster recovery. Information will eventually be damaged by hardware failure, software failure, human errors, or security control failures. Recovery processes are a necessary part of any business plan.

The third objective of security is availability. Simply defined, *availability* means ensuring that information is accessible by those who need it, when they need it. Availability can be a broad topic addressing issues such as fault tolerance to protect against denial of service and access control to ensure that data is available to those authorized to access it. Most computer systems can distinguish at least between two classes of users: privileged users or system administrators, and normal or end users.

Authorization or access should extend beyond discriminating between system administrators and end users. In a well-secured computer system, all users should be assigned roles based on their job description. The computer system should determine exactly what each user is allowed to do based on those roles. This *role-based access control* (RBAC) can be use to limit the modification of security controls even for system administrators or privileged users.

In the modern world, availability has, like confidentiality, taken on an expanded meaning. One of the most common security problems for Internet accessing systems or applications is the *denial of service* (DOS) attack. This is a focused attempt by an attacker to make a computer system and its data unavailable. This type of attack is commonly done in one of two ways. First, the attacker may try to damage, disable, or take control of the target computer system or some network component on which the computer system depends and render the system inaccessible to users. Second, the attacker may simply send so many messages to the target system that it cannot possibly process them all. Commonly called *flooding*, it results in authorized users finding that the service is unavailable when it's needed. You have probably read about the attempts to take down the Internet DNS servers through this type of attack.

Determining the Security Posture

When it comes to determining the actual security posture of an organization, there are several options. All the methods reviewed here are intended to provide the management of an organization with enough information to perform risk management. The most comprehensive is the risk assessment. A true risk assessment contains all the other types of assessments that are done. However, if an organization does not want to perform a risk assessment but instead wants to complete a less comprehensive assessment, such as a vulnerability assessment, that is not a bad thing. The reasons for doing a less comprehensive assessment will vary among organizations and is a management decision. Each of the other assessments should fit the current business need of an organization, therefore serving as feeders to the risk-management process.

The underlying premise of risk management is that every organization exists to provide value for its stakeholders. All organizations face uncertainty, and the challenge for management is to determine how much uncertainty (risk) is acceptable as managers work to increase the value for stakeholders. Uncertainty presents both risk and opportunity, with the potential to decrease or increase the stakeholder value. Risk management is a key tool that enables management to effectively deal with uncertainty and the associated risk.

Risk Assessments

Risk assessment from a project, program, or process view involves a three-step process that always includes the following:

- ❑   Identification of risk
- ❑   Measurement of risk
- ❑   Risk management

Risk identification is key to risk assessment because risk cannot be measured, prioritized, or managed until it has been identified. The three main approaches to risk identification are as follows:

- ❑   **Exposure analysis**: Identification of risks that could affect assets.
- ❑   **Environmental analysis**: Identification of risks that could affect operations.
- ❑   **Threat scenarios**: Specialized risk identification of frauds and disasters.

Exposure analysis is best for processes that depend heavily on assets for goal achievement. This approach takes into consideration the size, type, portability, and location of assets. These assets include the following: physical assets such as plant and equipment; financial assets such as cash and investments; human assets (including the knowledge and experience of the staff); and intangible assets such as information and reputation.

Environmental analysis is used to explore risks that could affect the accomplishment of objectives by considering risks arising from various states of the environment, such as physical environment, economic environment, government regulation, competition, customers, technology, and so on.

Threat scenarios are mostly used for dealing with fraud or security issues. Examples of threats could be errors, delays, omissions, or fraud.

Defining and Measuring Risks

Risk assessments start with managers defining the risks to the processes and programs for their particular organization. Therefore, risk assessment starts with managers answering questions such as the following:

- ❑ How do we define success? Then, what must we do to succeed?
- ❑ What could happen to cause failure to meet objectives?
- ❑ Where is our greatest exposure?
- ❑ On what information do we rely most? Then, what would happen if that information were not correct or available?
- ❑ Where are we most vulnerable?
- ❑ What is our greatest asset? Then, how do we protect this asset?

Risks consist of both external and internal risks. External risks arise from activities outside the control of the organization. Technological developments, changing public expectations, legislative directives, and economic changes all have the potential for creating external risks in an organization. Internal risks arise from activities the organization controls. An example is disruption of a critical computer system or telephone system, which would cause obvious operational problems.

Based upon management's identification of different risks to its organization, consideration must be given to the likelihood that these risks can occur, and if so, the significance or impact that such risks would have on the organization. After management has identified key risks to its organization, it is responsible for monitoring and controlling these risks.

More important than the specific method used to identify risks is management's careful consideration of factors unique to its own organization. However, managers must document their risk-assessment process. One method is to use a simple Risk Self-Assessment and Control Activities Worksheet, such as the NIST SP 800.26 (found at www.nist.gov; search for "Special Publications") to ascertain that control activities are present to manage risk. This method uses subjective measures to measure the likelihood that risks will be realized and the significance or impact that they would have on the organization.

Another method for measuring risk is the use of observable risk factors for measuring a specific risk or class of risks. Using risk factors for measuring risk is useful when an organization's subelements share much in common, such as local branch offices of banks, state parks, local branches of medical facilities, and so on. The completion of a systematic risk assessment will reveal areas within an organization that comprise the highest risk and therefore deserve the most attention by management to ensure that control activities are adequate to manage risk. Generally, the more that a risk factor is present, the higher the risk and more costly the consequence. This approach requires the establishment of risk factors that can be evaluated by each division so that it can provide a quantitative measurement of risk. Although the following is not a comprehensive list, examples of risk factors may include the following:

❑ Human Resources/Employee Turnover

❑ Information Technology — Security and Integrity

❑ Level of Centralization

❑ Regulatory Oversight

❑ Contractual Relationships

❑ Consumer Impact

❑ Complexity of Business Processes

❑ Extent of Audit Coverage

Each organization must decide on the risk factors that it will use in its evaluation. After all organization areas are evaluated, the scores from the questionnaires can be entered into a worksheet to tally the results. The higher scores indicate areas that should receive additional reviews to determine that proper control activities are adequate to manage the risk. The use of a subjective versus the more objective measurement tool depends on the specific risk identified. It is very common for both methods to be used during an overall organization risk assessment.

Approaches to Risk Assessment

The risk-assessment process is one area that sees a lot of different approaches, and no assessment method that includes both organizational and technical review of the applicable management, operational, and technical controls is consistently applied by all organizations. In fact, the subject of what is a risk assessment and how to do it can be confusing and even mind numbing. This situation has created a growing interest in using a consistent, repeatable process. Currently, two methodologies meet the needs of a risk assessment: the Information Assessment Methodology (IAM) and Information Evaluation Methodology (IEM). Both of these methodologies are derived from merging the National Security Agency (NSA) processes with commercial practices to create a best-of-breed approach.

The IAM is a detailed and systematic way of examining cyber vulnerabilities and was developed by experienced NSA and commercial INFOSEC assessors. NSA is providing the IAM to assist both INFOSEC assessment suppliers and consumers requiring assessments. The IAM was originally created by the PDD-63 requirement for vulnerability assessments of automated information systems that support the U.S. infrastructure. In addition to assisting the governmental and private sectors, an important result of supplying baseline standards for INFOSEC assessments is fostering a commitment to improve organizations' security posture.

The INFOSEC Evaluation Methodology (IEM) is a hands-on methodology for conducting evaluations of customer networks using common technical evaluation tools. Students can expect to learn an easily repeatable methodology that provides all customers a road map for addressing their security concerns and increasing their security posture. This course is a follow-on course to IAM.

You can find more information about the IAM and IEM at www.iatrp.com.

Although these two approaches are good, you also should be aware of other approaches that can be tailored to risk assessments. When you understand how each works, you can choose the approach that meets customers' needs.

❑   International Standards Organization (ISO) *27001:2005 Information technology - Security techniques - Information security management systems - Requirements* is an international standard designed to provide a process model for an organizational security program. The model is implemented based on the needs, objectives, security requirements, size, and structure of an organization. This approach requires a long-term commitment by the organization to develop the processes needed for implementation. After it is implemented, ISO 27001 allows for scaling to meet changes in the organization. You can find more information searching the Internet for "ISO 27001."

❑   *ISO 17799:2005 Information technology - Security techniques - Code of practice for information security management* establishes the guidelines and principles for starting, implementing, maintaining, and improving an organization's information security management. Each of the controls and control objects is intended to be implemented to meet the requirements that are identified by a risk assessment. One of the benefits of using this ISO derives from its use as a practical guideline for developing tailored organizational security standards and an effective security program. You can find more information by searching the Internet for "ISO 17799."

❑   Operationally Critical Threat, Asset, and Vulnerability Evaluation (OCTAVE) is an approach for managing information security risks. OCTAVE is focused on organizational risk, strategic, and practice-related issues. Using this approach, an organization makes decisions based on the risks to confidentiality, integrity, and availability of critical information and those related assets. All the aspects of risk are used in the decision making that allows the organization to match the best mitigation strategy to the organizational security risks. You can find more information by searching the Internet for "OCTAVE."

❑   Federal Information Technology Security Assessment Framework (FITSAF) provides an approach for federal agencies to determine how they are currently meeting existing policy and establish goals or targets for improvement. This approach is fairly technology based and designed for assessing security controls for identified major applications, general support systems, and mission-critical systems. The biggest advantage to using this approach is that it will address the requirements identified by the Office of Management and Budget (OMB) and the guidelines provided by the National Institute of Standards and Technology (NIST). You can find more information by searching the Internet for "FITSAF."

❑   Information Systems Security Assessment Framework (ISSAF) is fairly new in the information security industry, with the first draft version 0.2 being released in April 2006. It was developed as a structured framework that breaks down the assessment into various domains while providing specific evaluation and testing criteria for each domain. The overall framework is intentionally large and is based on the assumption that it is easier to delete sections that do not apply than to try to develop new ones. This is a good approach to keep an eye on as it develops. You can find more information by searching the Internet for "ISSAF."

❑   The Security Officers Management and Analysis Project (SOMAP.org) has developed both the Open Information Security Risk Management Handbook (Handbook) and the Open Information Security Risk Assessment Guide (Guide). The Handbook provides details of how to manage the risk assessment workflow, whereas the Guide provides information on two risk-analysis methodologies, both qualitative and quantitative. SOMAP.org recommends using the Security Officers Best Friend (SOBF) tool to implement the Guide. You can find more information at www.somap.org.

Vulnerability Assessments

Vulnerability assessments usually consist of using tools, scanners, scripts, and manual checks of the components of a system. These assessments scan systems and services on the system devices and simulate common intrusion or attack scenarios. In essence, it answers the question, "What can an attacker see and exploit on the system?"

A vulnerability scan begins by "discovering" all the active devices on the network. This action is followed by a port scan, which identifies ports that may have exploitable services active. The process also checks operating systems for unauthorized modifications and known problems that should have been fixed by patches. Next, the assessor analyzes the data and generates a report detailing potential vulnerabilities and fixes.

If you are doing this work, you should provide the customer with a written document that contains an overview of the system or network as it is currently configured. You should also include in this document recommendations for all vulnerabilities, unnecessary open ports, ineffective passwords, and missing critical system or security patches.

The bottom line is that vulnerability assessments are a systematic examination of an information system (IS) or application to determine the adequacy of security controls, identify security deficiencies, and provide enough information to predict the effectiveness of the proposed security controls.

Threat Assessments

A threat assessment is a formal description and evaluation of threats to an IS that processes, transmits, or stores information. A comprehensive security plan requires broad definitions of threats so that a range of exposures can be considered. Through the analysis, the focus on threats should be narrowed to target threats that are deemed the most applicable or likely to occur.

A threat assessment begins by compiling data on past security incidents, including incidents at a particular location, within the organization, and within the industry. For a complete threat assessment, you should do the following:

❑ Determine whether patterns of criminal behavior exist and define their nature.

❑ Review loss records, safety records, and legal judgments involving the organization.

❑ Consult the company's legal counsel and examine any past court settlements to identify exposures with an implication for security.

❑ Conduct interviews with management, insurance underwriters, and even local emergency management authorities to identify applicable threats.

❑ Review criminal data and compare crime rates for the nation, state, metropolitan statistical area, and municipality.

❑ Identify threats unique to the location and the organization.

❑ Consider threat scenarios that may not have occurred yet but are applicable because of the nature of the business and because of political and social issues.

A threat assessment is a qualitative analysis, although some quantitative techniques are used. It is important to emphasize that any assessment, including a threat assessment, is a snapshot in time. As circumstances change, so does the threat environment. Consequently, the assessment must be updated to ensure that the security program is consistent with the needs of the time.

Each threat can be categorized as probable (expect the event to occur), possible (circumstances are conducive for an event), or unlikely (you do not anticipate the event to occur). The severity of each issue can also be categorized as high (a disastrous event), moderate (a survivable event), or low (relatively inconsequential).

The success of an attack depends on more than the exploitation of a single vulnerability. Multiple enabling events, as well as planning and technical knowledge (at both the system and application levels) are usually required. Therefore, an expanded form of threat assessment is required, not only to identify potential threats but also to understand their likelihood of occurring.

Two elements are required for a threat to exist. First, the threat must be capable of occurring. Second, exploiting that capability must be possible. In terms of information security, doing so requires access, either logical or physical. When both of these elements exist, they create a threat enabler.

Identifying threat enablers is a critical step in the threat assessment process. Properly applying this process will expose a large number of potential threats. Many will never be exploited; others require significant investment by the attacker. Further analysis is required to refine the likelihood of a threat's actually occurring. This analysis is critical because resources to mitigate or prevent threats are limited and should be applied where they will be most effective.

In this threat-assessment model, enablers are further prioritized using an intelligence-based process to detect the presence of specific indicators of potential activity. A prerequisite of indicators is intent or motive. Intent and motive also help to qualify the potential effort, skill, and the expense an attacker is willing to incur to attack the system.

Indicators are specific actions on the part of individuals, groups, or organizations. An example of open-source indicators is the communication of specific threat enablers in Usenet news groups. The method used to exploit vulnerabilities could be published on a Web site. Another example is to test methods of exploiting vulnerabilities or simply to demonstrate the feasibility of the threat. If indicators are present, they create a greater potential that the enablers will be exploited, and more effort should be placed into safeguards or investigation of suspicious activity.

The final prioritization of threats takes place when indications exist of targeting against a specific information asset. When this targeting occurs, threats can be categorized as either potential (that is, the attack has not actually taken place) or active (an attack has been attempted or in some other way demonstrated to be feasible). In considering implementation of security controls, these threats, if applicable to the information assets of an organization, should receive the highest effort and priority.

Audits

You may see the phrase "penetration test" or "vulnerability scan" used interchangeably with the phrase "computer security audit." They don't mean the same thing. A penetration test (also known as a pen-test) is an external attempt to look for security vulnerabilities in the Internet-facing resources, such as a firewall or Web server. Penetration testers may be looking at only one service on a network resource or at the entire Internet presence. They usually operate from outside the firewall with minimal inside information in order to provide a more realistic simulation of how attackers would attack the site.

On the other hand, a computer security audit is a systematic, measurable technical and organizational assessment of how the organization's security policy is employed at a specific site. Such an audit is normally conducted to meet some security-compliance requirement. Computer-security auditors work with the full knowledge of the organization, at times with considerable inside information, in order to understand the resources that are being audited.

Security audits should not take place in a vacuum. Security audits are part of the ongoing process of defining and maintaining effective security policies. Audits are not just conference room activities; they can involve anyone who uses any computer resources throughout the organization. Given the dynamic nature of computer configurations and information storage, some managers may actually wonder whether any way truly exists to check the security controls. Security audits provide such a process — a fair and measurable way to examine what the security posture really is.

Security auditors perform their work though various personal interviews, vulnerability scans, examination of operating system settings, analyses of network shares, and historical data. They are concerned primarily with how security policies are actually being implemented.

Self-Assessments

Self-assessments involve the process of evaluating one's own organizational security and are usually an internal process. Self-assessments provide a method for any organization to determine the current status of its information security programs and establish a target for security improvement. The NIST SP 800-26 self-assessment guide mentioned earlier in this chapter uses an extensive questionnaire containing specific control objectives and techniques against which an unclassified system or group of interconnected systems can be tested and measured. The control objectives and techniques are extracted directly from long-standing requirements found in statute, policy, and guidance on security. The NIST self-assessment questionnaire can be used for the following purposes:

❑ Agency managers who know their agency's systems and security controls can quickly gain a general understanding of needed security improvements for a system (a major application or general support system), group of interconnected systems, or the entire agency.

❑ The security of an agency's system can be thoroughly evaluated using the questionnaire as a guide. The results of such a thorough review produce a reliable measure of security effectiveness and may be used to

  ❑ Fulfill reporting requirements

  ❑ Prepare for audits

  ❑ Identify resources

❑ The results of the questionnaire can assist in fulfilling budget requests as outlined in Office of Management and Budget (OMB) Circular A-11, "Preparing and Submitting Budget Estimates."

Prioritizing the Vulnerabilities

No matter which assessment is performed, the result will be findings, or vulnerabilities, that need to be addressed by the organization. There are two kinds of findings: organizational and technical. Organizational findings are usually identified by deficiencies in policies and procedures. Organizational findings may also include vulnerabilities of a technical nature found through documentation review or system demonstrations. Technical findings are normally identified via the technical evaluation process using tools or scripts or are found during manual console reviews. But let's take this a bit deeper to define exactly what is a vulnerability.

You might think that this would be an easy question to answer, but in fact it turns out not to be. You can look up both "security" and "vulnerability" in a dictionary and probably achieve a reasonable understanding of the definitions. Doing so would lead you to conclude that a security vulnerability is anything that offers a potential avenue of attack, or threat vector, against a system. Such threats would include viruses, incorrectly configured systems, passwords written on sticky note pads, and so on. Although these situations do increase the risk to a system, this description is a little more generalized than what is used in the security community.

Most security professionals usually accept that a security vulnerability is a security exposure that results from a discovered product flaw — a flaw that the product's maker should have mitigated against. This flaw makes it difficult to impossible to prevent an attacker from escalating privileges on the system, controlling its operation, or compromising data processed, stored, or transmitted on it.

Although most tools and scanners used to identify vulnerabilities give you a starting point as to the severity of impact (high, medium, or low), you still need to understand the business impact of the vulnerability. This understanding can then change the severity of impact. All these tools are based on the use of Common Vulnerabilities and Exposures (CVE) and CVE candidates, commonly called CANs.

The Mitre Web page defines the Common Vulnerabilities and Exposures (CVE) as the following: "A list of standardized names for vulnerabilities and other information security exposures — CVE aims to standardize the names for all publicly known vulnerabilities and security exposures."

Further, the Mitre Web site states that the CVE is "a Dictionary, NOT a Database — The goal of CVE is to make it easier to share data across separate vulnerability databases and security tools. While CVE may make it easier to search for information in other databases, CVE should not be considered as a vulnerability database on its own merit."

The issue that we have seen is that the CVE process does not assist in identification of the impact value to an organization. Though such was never the intended function of the CVE, having an initial or recommended impact value would be nice. That is where the National Institute of Standards and Technology stepped up to help the community. You can find more information about the CVE at www.cve.mitre.org/.

The National Institute of Standards and Technology (NIST) developed ICAT. Although the ICAT name does not currently officially stand for anything, the ICAT project was initially intended as a database of Internet attacks used by malicious hackers, and ICAT was its acronym. As the project changed its focus to a searchable database of all system findings, what ICAT stood for became obsolete but the name ICAT was kept. ICAT is a searchable index of information on computer vulnerabilities. It provides a search capability at a fine granularity and links users to vulnerability and patch information.

One of the nice things aspects of using the search capabilities of the ICAT is the simple process of inputting the CVE or CAN number and getting more information than is available in the CVE dictionary. ICAT allows for searching by vendor, product, version, keyword, or severity. The ICAT databases is a filterable search engine that enables you to quickly locate a particular finding in the database and identify the initial or recommend severity level by NIST.

As with any input tool used in developing and implementing the reporting portion of any assessment report, the ICAT is not meant as the last or only word in what the severity level of a particular finding is. ICAT is a starting point; your expertise combined with the customer's input will determine the final severity level for each finding. You can find more information on the ICAT at www.nist.gov (search for "ICAT").

Developing a Mitigation Roadmap

After you have identified a finding or security exposure, you need to fully identify three pieces of information. Each finding needs to have a name, discussion of why it is a finding, and mitigation strategy or options. Each finding needs to be traceable to a specific business requirement, or goal, that it will directly impact. So with every finding you identify, you need to map the finding to the organizational information that will be impacted and the impact attributes that will be compromised.

The discussion accompanying the finding concerns the justification for why an organization should care about fixing that finding. Justifications should address both the threat that can exploit the finding and its possible impact on the customer or organization for whom you are performing the work. The customer does not always understand why a finding should be given the importance you have assigned it. The justification provides management with enough information to make good risk management decisions.

Consider a finding that you have identified, such as the lack of adequate auditing on a critical server. The administrator of that server might not agree that a particular level of auditing needs to take place and might feel what is already being done is adequate. Yes, you can point to security industry standards that require auditing, but does the management know those standards? Probably not. So you will need to provide this information to allow a manager to listen to the administrator's point of view and make a good risk-management decision.

Resource Allocation for the Roadmap

One common issue that may need to be addressed in any security roadmap involves resource requirements. The term "resources" refers to all the tangible inputs that are required to implement the security roadmap for the organization. Normally, the two basic resources all companies have are time and money. All other resources can be derived from these two (especially the money) and include tools, equipment, employee labor, contactors, and so on. When you prioritize the findings for the security roadmap, the most common issues that customers ask you to address are pricing, scheduling, operational impact, and ease of implementation. Although most of these items cross boundaries with each other or can directly affect each other, they can be addressed independently.

❑ **Pricing** goes beyond the cost of buying new equipment or software. Pricing can be a derivative of other factors, such as the cost of training, man-hour requirements for testing, loss of income due to down time during implementation, and so on. The easy part is if the customer wants to address only the purchase price and training. Those aspects are easily determined. Harder to determine are income loss due to down time and man-hours for implementation.

❑ **Scheduling** involves determining when a finding can be fixed and when it should be fixed. Some findings can be mitigated with a patch or upgrade that will require the system to be offline to reboot it. Some will require only that the affected system service be restarted. The issue is, when is a good time to do this — during scheduled maintenance window or immediately? Based on the severity of the impact to the organization, you might need to provide a recommendation stating how soon the organization needs to implement the mitigation strategy.

❏ **Operational impact** is normally thought of as a function of the changes the organization will be required to make. This impact can be as simple as a few more steps for authentication or it can be more significant, for example, changing the way users access information. Consider the impact to the organization if you implement a significant change in information access. The users will need to be trained on the new access procedures. How will this training affect normal day-to-day operations? Will the users easily accept the learning curve or will they try to find a workaround to let them do business as usual?

❏ **Ease of implementation** is a factor based on the experience or expertise of the implementer. Some fixes that are based on patch management can readily be implemented, and the average administrator has the skills and expertise to do the job. But what if you perform a significant upgrade of the operating system? Every new version of an operating system comes with a learning curve that equals the relative difficulty for implementing recommendations. A high level of difficulty may require expert-level implementation, and that may need to be contracted out. Moderate levels of difficulty may require an average administrator's level of expertise (say, an administrator with a background of one to two years with that application or operating system). Low levels of difficulty may require only an entry-level administrator's level of expertise with less than one year's experience.

Vulnerability Management

Patch and vulnerability management is a security practice designed to proactively prevent the exploitation of IT vulnerabilities that exist within an organization. The expected result is to reduce the time and money spent dealing with vulnerabilities and exploitation of those vulnerabilities. Proactively managing vulnerabilities of systems will reduce or eliminate the potential for exploitation and involve considerably less time and effort than responding after exploitation has occurred.

Patch Management Is a Start

Patches are additional pieces of code developed to address problems (commonly called "bugs") in software. Patches enable additional functionality or address security flaws within a program. Vulnerabilities are flaws that can be exploited by a malicious entity to gain greater access or privileges than it is authorized to have on a computer system. Not all vulnerabilities have related patches, and system administrators must be aware not only of applicable vulnerabilities and available patches but also other methods of remediation (for example, device or network configuration changes, employee training) that can limit the exposure of systems to vulnerabilities.

Timely patching of security issues is generally recognized as critical to maintaining the operational availability, confidentiality, and integrity of any system. However, failure to keep operating system and application software patched is one of the most common issues identified by security and IT professionals. New patches are released almost on a daily basis, and it is often difficult for even experienced system administrators to keep abreast of all the new patches and ensure proper deployment in a timely manner. Most major attacks in the past few years have targeted known vulnerabilities for which patches existed before the outbreaks. Indeed, the moment a patch is released, attackers have been known to reverse engineer the patch, measurable in days or even hours, identify the vulnerability, and develop and release exploit code. The time immediately after the release of a patch is a particularly vulnerable time for most organizations because of the time lag in obtaining, testing, and deploying a patch.

It's true that patching is the way to mitigate many well-known vulnerabilities. However, many other vulnerabilities cannot be fixed by simply updating to the latest product version. Product updates require tweaking and reconfiguring various system parameters and may introduce new vulnerabilities. Vulnerability management was born of a need to intelligently prioritize and fix discovered vulnerabilities, whether by patching or other means.

So if you are busy every Tuesday implementing the latest Microsoft patches, but you're not doing anything to eliminate other nonpatch-related vulnerabilities during the other days of the month, you are not managing your vulnerabilities adequately.

Vulnerability management alone does not fix vulnerabilities. Patch and configuration management can assist in doing so, and antivirus software seeks to block or eliminate identified malware. Simply stated, vulnerability management helps managers understand network assets, identify weaknesses, measure security control effectiveness, enforce policy, and assess the success of remediation efforts.

Tracking Progress

Tracking the progress of vulnerability management or trending the organizational security posture can be shown to the customer as a simple numeric value or as a complicated scorecard. Although many theoretical approaches to trending security postures or developing security metrics exist, none gives a process for implementation within the organization. A simple Internet search on "security metrics" will provide you with plenty of reading to develop your own process, but none of these approaches is easy to understand without previous experience in developing metrics. One source is a community Web site for security practitioners called securitymetrics.org (www.securitymetrics.org). This site is intended to provide a repository and sandbox for exploring and developing security metrics.

The most effective method for tracking the vulnerability management of an organization or trending the organizational security posture comes from the National Security Agency (NSA) Information Assurance and Training Program (IATRP) (www.iatrp.com). This process, taught in the INFOSEC Evaluation Methodology (IEM), creates the INFOSEC Posture Rating (IPR). The process allows for the development of vulnerability metrics and the ability of management to measure the effectiveness of the security program in vulnerability management. The end result of the IPR is a numeric value that will show customers where their security posture is. This is also useful when you have parent/child relationships in an organization. More information on the IPR can be found by attending the IEM courses or by reading *Network Security Evaluation Using the NSA IEM* (Syngress, ISBN 1-597490-35-0).

A more complicated method is to use a scorecard approach. The best scorecard approach is from the federal government. The Office of Management and Budget (OMB) creates a quarterly executive branch management scorecard on federal agencies to show the progress each agency is making on implementing the President's Management Agenda (PMA). Although the approach that each federal agency has taken to implement the PMA has been different, the results have always been reported in the scorecard. To improve and standardize the federal agencies' approaches to the meeting the PMA, NIST has introduced a draft publication for public review (NIST SP 800-80, Guide for Developing Performance Metrics for Information Security (www.nist.gov; search "special publications"). More information on the OMB score card and the PMA can be found at www.whitehouse.gov (search "PMA").

Cost Avoidance versus Return on Investment

Security has been and will continue to be an overhead expense for all organizations, as are payroll and other administrative tasks that are required to keep an organization running. The question that seems to pop up every few months in the security industry is, What is the value of all the security work that takes place within an organization? Organizations want to see what the Return on Investment (ROI) is for the security budget that is currently used or expected to be used in the future. Establishing an RIO is a very difficult task. After all, if the security team is doing its job, the organization will likely not see a measurable impact from security problems.

Although several projects are under way to determine what the ROI on security is, none of them has effectively or simply defined what the ROI is for security. You can find more information on this subject by performing a simple Internet search on "Security ROI." The best approach is not trying to determine the ROI for security, but rather to determine the benefit of cost avoidance provided by the security work accomplished, and what ROI that can provide.

Determining the benefit of cost avoidance is based on a simplified formula for Annual Loss Expectancy (ALE). Simply stated, how much loss can be expected from a single security incident each year? When you have the ALE from an possible security incident, how much can mitigation of the incident save the organization? The three factors that need to be defined to determine the ALE are as follows: the cost of the incident, the probability of occurrence, and the percentage of resultant mitigation, which can be mathematically expressed as

Incident Cost × (Probability × Mitigation) = Annual Loss Expectance

Consider the impact of worms and viruses over that last few years. To give an overly simplified example of how calculating such an impact works, we consider a virus outbreak for an organization. We assume that for your organization, a single virus infection costs one million dollars in resources to clean and restore operations. We also assume that the organization has historical evidence to show that the probability of a virus infection is 35 percent per year. If you installed up-to-date antivirus software at an annual cost of $75,000 for annual licensing, and did so prior to the virus or worm outbreak in the organization, you can expect to have mitigated about 50 percent of the chance of the security incident's happening. The resultant calculation would then be as follows:

Incident Cost × (Probability × Mitigation) = Annual Loss Expectance

$1,000,000 × (0.35 × 0.5) = $1,000,000 × 0.175 = $175,000

Based on the ALE of $175,000 for a virus outbreak within the organization, we can determine a simple ROI for the security mitigation of installation of antivirus software. With the previously defined value of $75,000 annually for the software license, we can show the organization a security ROI of $100,000 by implementing this mitigation strategy because the cost of mitigation is less than the cost of the loss.

Many other factors could be defined by each organization to tailor the cost of mitigation to fit its business model; this example was simplified to get you thinking about how security ROI could be determined for management.

Summary

The security posture of an organization or company is an aggregation of many factors to provide protection. Determining that security posture is a fundamental requirement in risk management. Risk management is a business need and function, but it is also directly influenced by compliance issues generated by many legislative actions.

Information security has three objectives: confidentiality, integrity, and availability. Each of these objectives can be measured through assessment activities. Assessment activities are feeders to the risk management process. The most comprehensive assessment activity is the risk assessment, but vulnerability assessments, threat assessments, self-assessments, and audits all have their appropriate uses.

The output of any assessment activity is the reporting in detail of identified findings. Those findings must be traceable to the business function or business impact that a successful exploitation would result in. Each of the findings is then prioritized using input, if available, from the CVE database. The result of the prioritization is the roadmap to improving the security posture.

The roadmap must include the resource requirements for fixing the findings as well as a means to track progress. The NSA IPR was given as the best method for tracking the progress of vulnerability management. Vulnerability management includes, but is not limited to, patch management. Simply stated, vulnerability management helps managers understand network assets, identify weaknesses, measure security control effectiveness, enforce policy, and assess the success of patching efforts.

Although information security and identification of the security posture does not provide a Return on Investment (ROI), it does provide cost avoidance. We hope that this chapter was informative, but it does not provide all-encompassing answers on the particulars for any area covered. It is meant to provide a foundation for you to build on through study and application.

Interview Q&A

Q: Why should we care about what our security posture is?

A: The short answer is liability and risk management. Companies that are taking an active risk-management approach will reduce the likelihood of failure to meet regulatory compliance. Knowing what your security posture is can assist management in effectively assigning resources to achieve business and security goals.

Q: I'm looking at working with the federal government; what should I read?

A: The Federal Information Security Management Act of 2002 (FISMA) and the related documents that are discussed in the FISMA document.

Q: My company currently supports the DITSCAP process. Why was that not covered in this chapter?

A: DITSCAP has been superceded by DIACAP. The transition process is fully explained on the DITSCAP Web site (go to http://iase.disa.mil and click DIACAP).

Q: Can you use more security objectives than confidentiality, integrity, and availability?

A: Yes, but doing so is customer specific. Some customers may want authentication or nonrepudiation. Authentication is the process of determining whether someone or something is who or what he, she, or it claims to be. Nonrepudiation is the ability to ensure that the sender of a communication cannot deny the authenticity of his or her signature on a document or the sending of a message that he or she originated. Other security objectives used depend upon the customer.

Q: How does a risk assessment differ from a self-assessment?

A: Risk assessments are normally conducted by an independent group that cannot be influenced by organizational politics. Self-assessments can be any of the assessments discussed in this chapter but are conducted by internal staffing.

Q: What is the validity of PDD-63? I was under the impression that PDD-63 expired when President Clinton left office.

A: That is correct. PDD-63 expired when Clinton left office, but President G. W. Bush signed PDD-1 as an interim stopgap measure to prevent the intent of PDD-63 from dying. The current authority for Critical Infrastructure Protection is HSPD-7.

Q: Can I use something like the DISA IAVA system instead of CVE?

A: Yes, the requirement is to use an industry standard. IAVA is a DOD industry standard, whereas CVE is a security industry standard. It is important to pick the appropriate standard for your customer and stick with it.

Q: If CVEs comprise a dictionary of vulnerabilities and ICAT is a database of vulnerabilities, which should I use?

A: We recommend that you use the ICAT. ICAT provides much more information than CVE and includes all the CVEs.

Q: Why is it important to provide a justification discussion for every finding?

A: The discussion portion of every finding is important to ensure that management has enough information to make good risk-management decisions. Consider that a report is delivered 30 days after the conclusion of the assessment. Management may not have time for the next week or two to start implementing the vulnerability management. What is the chance that the managers will remember what you told them in the out-briefing? They probably won't remember exactly what you explain and will have to rely on their favorite administrator to fill in the gaps. If the administrator does not want to do the remediation for a particular finding, he or she will try to shift the management opinion. So you need to provide enough information to make good risk-management decisions.

Q: I have never seen the IPR before. Is it truly useful?

A: Yes. At the end of the out-briefing, the customer wants to know how his or her company is doing. For years, the answer has always come as a personal opinion on the assessor's part. The IPR shows how the customer is doing without much opinion playing a part.

Recommended Reading

UK Data Protection Act 1998: www.opsi.gov.uk (search "Data Protection Act").

Family Educational Rights and Privacy Act (FERPA): www.ed.gov (search "FERPA").

Health Insurance Portability and Accountability Act (HIPAA): www.cms.hhs.gov (search "HIPAA").

Gramm-Leach-Bliley Act of 1999 (GLBA): www.senate.gov (search "GLBA").

Sarbanes-Oxley Act of 2002 (SOX), Section 404: www.sec.gov (search "Sarbanes-Oxley Act").

Federal Information Security Management Act of 2002 (FISMA): www.nist.gov (search: "FISMA").

Department of Defense (DOD) Information Assurance Certification and Accreditation Process (DIACAP) (Google "DIACAP").

Payment Card Industry Data Security Standard (PCI DSS): https://www.pcisecuritystandards.org.

Various NIST Special Publications on Information Security: www.nist.gov (Search "Special Publications").

10

Tools

We have all heard the phrase, "There is more than one way to skin a cat." When it comes to technology in the information security profession, you have plenty of choices. To be a successful security professional, you must be proficient with multiple tools. During the interview, you may need to be able to explain what tool you would choose for a task and why. Because choosing the correct tool depends on several factors, and no single tool can do it all, your answer should reflect your familiarity with both how the tools work and which situations call for particular tools. For most tasks, relying on only one tool is unwise; you can lessen the possibility of false positives and false negatives by using at least two tools.

Our discussion of all the tools mentioned in this chapter assumes the use of the most usual network architecture — TCP/IP over Ethernet. Some of these tools work in other network environments as well. Read the tool's documentation to verify that your network architecture is supported.

For the purpose of this book, we have divided the discussion of the tools into categories. These categories, presented in the following list, represent different areas of expertise a security professional should have. They are *based* on the National Security Agency's (NSA) INFOSEC Evaluation Methodology (IEM).

- ❑ **Enumeration, Port Scanning, and Banner Grabbing.** These tools are used to enumerate what service and version of service is listening on each machine attached to the network.

- ❑ **SNMP Scanning.** Here we are looking at the configuration of the network, both network and host devices.

- ❑ **Wireless Enumeration.** With the increase in wireless (802.11) networks, understanding how to scan for them becomes more important.

- ❑ **Vulnerability Scanning.** After we know what is attached to the network, it is important to understand how to test for vulnerabilities.

- ❑ **Host Evaluation.** Not all vulnerabilities are network based. Many are host-based attacks. This category of tools concerns testing the machine from the console.

❑ **Password Compliance Testing.** The idea is not to crack the password but to verify whether users are complying with corporate password policies.

❑ **Application Scanning.** Not all vulnerabilities pertain to a network or operating system. Many applications have security vulnerabilities that need to be checked.

❑ **Network Sniffing.** How do you know whether nefarious traffic is occurring on your network? You must sniff the network to understand the traffic patterns of the company.

❑ **Penetration Testing.** When explicitly requested, these tools help to actually break into sites.

❑ **Learning.** How do you learn to use these security tools? By using them. You do not want to do this training on your company's production network.

Enumeration, Port Scanning, and Banner Grabbing

These tools are used to enumerate what is on the network, starting with what IP addresses you can communicate with, and listing what ports are listening on each IP. Banner grabbing helps to determine what applications, and what versions of those applications, are running on the listening ports. Ports between 1 and 1024 are the "well-known" ports. The list of common services and the port is maintained by the Internet Assigned Numbers Authority (www.iana.org/).

SuperScan

Web site: www.foundstone.com/

OSes: Windows

SuperScan is a freeware tool from Foundstone. This is a graphical tool that runs on Microsoft Windows operating systems. SuperScan is very fast and can be used for enumeration, port scanning, and banner grabbing. SuperScan can produce a nice HTML report.

Foundstone notes that Windows XP Service Pack 2 limits access to raw ports. Foundstone advises that users run net stop SharedAccess before running SuperScan. SuperScan does require Administrator privileges to run.

Nmap

Web site: www.nmap.org/

OSes: Windows, UNIX, OS X

Nmap is an open source tool that can be used for enumeration, port scanning, banner grabbing, and versioning. Nmap has a built-in fingerprint database of many operating systems and applications. With this database, you know with a fair amount of accuracy what type and version of software is listening on a port, along with the underlying operating system. With every new version of Nmap, the number of servers and operating systems that Nmap can accurately fingerprint grows. Although the fingerprinting in Nmap is very accurate, you still must confirm the output (as is true with findings from all automated tools).

Nmap is a command-line tool. Graphical front ends for both Windows and XWindows are available, but they are limited and do not give access to the full power of Nmap. The NmapFE has a nice feature that will give you the command line produced with the options chosen within the GUI.

One of the cool things about Nmap is the Perl module Nmap::Scanner. You can download the module from `http://nmap-scanner.sourceforge.net/`. This module enables you to easily build scripts to help automate your scan and the output that is generated. With some clever scripting, you can also incorporate other tools with the Nmap module.

Another tool that uses Nmap is PBNJ (`http://pbnj.sourceforge.net/`). With this tool, you can use the Nmap ability to scan your network and use Perl's database capabilities to keep tabs on your network.

The following is a quick example that will scan the host 192.168.1.5, even if the host does not respond to the `ping` command, returning what ports are open, the probable version of server responding on each port, and the probable operating system. The `-P0` option tells Nmap to scan even if `ping` does not respond.

```
nmap -sV -O -P0 192.168.1.5
```

SNMP Scanning

The Simple Network Management Protocol (SNMP) is a very useful method for managing and monitoring equipment attached to the network, not just network equipment. SNMP uses "community strings" to manage access and authorize read-only versus read/write access. Most SNMP servers come configured with the default community strings of public (read-only) and private (read/write). Because of the information available from SNMP servers, it is imperative the community strings be changed.

When using SNMP scanning tools, you first want to scan for the default public and private community strings. You very likely will find many systems with the default settings; printers and VOIP phones are the common culprits. After you scan using the default, it is good to scan with the proper strings. SNMP servers should be configured to allow only a few privileged machines to access the service.

SNScan

Web site: `www.foundstone.com/`

OSes: Windows

SNScan, by Foundstone, is a Windows-based SNMP detection utility that can quickly and accurately identify SNMP-enabled devices on a network. This is a very simple tool to use. The only gotcha is the process to input addresses to scan. You must enter your target into the appropriate box and then press the corresponding arrow to move the address to the target list. All SuperScan does is enumerate which IP addresses answer to which community string. This tool looks only at the six primary SNMP UDP ports: 161, 162, 193, 199, 391, and 1993. Although SNScan is limited, there still is value in knowing which machines are or are not following your company SNMP policy.

Net-SNMP

Web site: `http://net-snmp.sourceforge.net/`

OSes: Windows, UNIX, OS X

Net-SNMP is a suite of applications used to implement SNMP. These tools work on most operating systems. You can find binaries for most UNIX, Mac, and Windows operating systems. The functionality may not be the same on all operating systems. The tool `snmpget` downloads the SNMP information from a single machine. The tool `snmpwalk` traverses multiple machines. For those new to SNMP or needing refreshers, the Tutorial documentation section is the best starting point.

The following is a quick example that connects with version 3 of SNMP to the host 192.168.1.5 using the community string ABCincRO. The output will be in ASCII text.

```
snmpwalk -c ABCincRO -Oa -v3 192.168.1.5 system
```

SolarWinds

Web site: `www.solarwinds.net/`

OSes: Windows

The company SolarWinds offers many commercial applications. The SolarWinds Toolset contains many useful tools for network, system, and security administrators. For SNMP scanning, the tool `IP Network Browser` is what you are looking for. This basic tool is available in all of SolarWinds toolkit offerings and is a nice, fast SNMP scan tool. It allows you to input multiple targets as well as multiple community strings. As the scan progresses, you can instantly see the results and drill down as each host is finished.

When using SolarWinds' Network Browser, you can download the entire configuration from your Cisco equipment. In case your IOS configuration does not set the encryption properly for all passwords, they are easy to decrypt. With one of the features of Network Browser, you can quickly decrypt these passwords by clicking the Decrypt Passwords button.

Along with offering a 30-day evaluation version of the Engineer's Toolkit, SolarWinds also offers some free tools. With the proliferation of variable subnet masks (CIDR blocks) the complexity of network addressing has increased. The Subnet Calculator is a great tool for computing subnets. SolarWinds also offers a TFTP server.

Wireless Enumeration

Many companies claim not to have wireless (802.11) networks. However, many wireless networks were brought into the corporate world by employees connecting rogue access points to the corporate network. So, even if the company states that it has no wireless networks, it is always best to scan for them.

If not properly configured, a machine might be connected to both a wireless network and the corporate network, becoming a gateway between the two networks. To account for this, wireless enumeration looks for multiple things:

❑ Are wireless access points connected to the corporate network?

❑ Are wireless access points masquerading as a corporate access point?

❑ Are access points within reach of the corporate environment that are configured with common service-set-identifiers (SSIDs) that roaming laptops might automatically connect to?

There are two types of wireless scanners: passive and active. The passive scanners do not broadcast anything and only listen to the airwaves. With an active scanner, the wireless card does broadcast some information.

Many wireless enumeration tools allow you to connect to a GPS device. With the GPS data, you can map both the location and footprint associated with each access point.

Kismet

Web site: www.kismetwireless.net/

OSes: Windows, UNIX, OS X

The Kismet Web site has this to say about this tool: "Kismet identifies networks by passively collecting packets and detecting standard named networks, detecting (and given time, decloaking) hidden networks, and inferring the presence of nonbeaconing networks via data traffic."

Kismet has hooks for connecting GPS receivers. This gives you a decent ability to map relative locations of access points. You can then combine an aerial photo of the area with the color-coded footprint for a decent picture of the wireless footprint.

Kismet has sound feedback for each of the different findings; this makes a lot of noise! Learn to use the "m" key to mute the sounds. (However, the sounds do have meaning behind them and can be a lot of fun.)

KisMAC

Web site: http://kismac.de/

OSes: OS X

If you are a Mac person, this may be the tool for you because it is written specifically for Apple computers. KisMAC started off as an OS X "Kismet-like" implementation of a passive wireless scanner. It is based on a graphical interface.

AirMagnet

Web site: www.airmagnet.com

OSes: Windows

AirMagnet offers many products geared to 802.11 wireless-network administration. The Survey tools are most beneficial for planning and tuning your wireless infrastructure. You can input a CAD drawing of your office space and use the Survey tool to find the best location for your access points. You can use the same tool to map the wireless footprint of your current access points. The Survey tools will work in multi-floor facilities with the CAD input.

They also offer some analyzing tools that can be used either on a laptop or handheld. These tools are most beneficial for monitoring and troubleshooting issues.

The Enterprise tools are for protecting your network. These tools allow you to combine wireless monitoring with the wired environment. By training the tools about your approved wireless devices, the tools can monitor for rogue devices and shut them down. For a corporation with multiple locations, the Enterprise suite is a good protection tool.

Vulnerability Scanning

Vulnerability scanners scan only for well-known vulnerabilities. Vulnerabilities are not threats; be careful not to confuse the two. Vulnerabilities are the mechanisms a threat may use to compromise the CIA of the critical data.

Each vulnerability scanner has a database of its known vulnerabilities. By default, it scans for IP addresses that will respond to a `ping` and then looks for the open ports on those addresses. For each port, the scan tool knows what the common services are. For each common service that runs on that port, it will start scanning for known vulnerabilities.

You should not run these tools in the default state. You should always configure them based on the known variables of the network being scanned. By properly configuring these tools, you can lessen the amount of time they take to run. By using tools that are designed for enumeration and feeding that output into the scan configuration, you can reduce the time required to enumerate the network. Turning off AIX scans in a Microsoft Windows–only shop will lower the number of tests required per machine.

Nessus

Web site: `www.tenablesecurity.com/`

OSes: Windows, UNIX, OS X

Nessus is the current leader in vulnerability scanners. Nessus version 2 scanner engine is 100 percent GPL code. It still uses the Tenable vulnerability database (to which Tenable owns the copyright). Version 3 of the Nessus vulnerability database is a hybrid between free and commercial. You may download the version 3 binaries for free and then choose the version of database that is appropriate for your needs.

The actual Nessus application is free. The vulnerability database is a hybrid free and commercial application. The free version of the database is seven days behind the commercial version. To have access to the free version, you still must register your Nessus installation with Tenable. Version 3 binaries are available for UNIX, Windows, and Macintosh.

For scanning large networks, you can deploy Nessus daemons around the network. These distributed nodes can be controlled centrally with Security Center. Distributed scanning can help mitigate choke points on the network.

Saint

Web site: `www.saintcorporation.com/`

OSes: Linux, Solaris, FreeBSD, OS X

The Saint tools have been around for more than 10 years. The tools started as a free source application and over time became a commercial application. These tools are very efficient and effective. The interface is your Web browser. You can create nice reports with the SaintWriter tool, which is integrated into the Saint software.

IBM Internet Scanner Software (ISS)

Web site: www.iss.net/

OSes: Windows

Internet Scanner Software started as a free tool in 1992. The company Internet Security Systems started in 1994, and after commercializing the tool, the company grew into a billion-dollar corporation, which IBM recently bought. Internet Security Systems offers many security tools, ranging from intrusion prevention to vulnerability management. The IBM Internet Scanner Software (ISS) can identify more than 1,300 types of systems. After ISS identifies the network devices, it then runs vulnerability scans against each device.

eEye Retina Network Security Scanner

Web site: www.eeye.com/

OSes: Windows

eEye is a well-known security company that specializes in finding vulnerabilities. Its vulnerability-scanning tool is built around its database of vulnerabilities. eEye's Retina Network Security Scanner is a fast, efficient scan tool. Retina is specified as being able to scan an entire class C network in less than 15 minutes.

Host Evaluation

Host evaluations need to be run on each machine. These tools are looking for operating system and application common configuration deficiencies. Each of these tools returns results based on the programmers' opinions. You cannot use these tools to compare machines between organizations. Host-based evaluations are very important because the configuration of the operating system and applications is the last technological layer of defense.

CIS Scripts

Web site: www.cisecurity.com

OSes: Windows, UNIX, OS X

The group Center for Internet Security (CIS) is a nonprofit enterprise whose mission is helping businesses improve their security posture. The benchmark tools help with the configuration of many varieties of operating systems. These tools are accepted by the U.S. government for compliance testing. By using these tools to harden your operating systems, you mitigate many avenues of attack.

Pay special attention to the Terms of Use (TOU). They are rather restrictive concerning who is allowed to use and distribute the benchmarks. Fees are involved with using the benchmarks for commercial work. U.S. government agencies may use the benchmark tools within the agency.

Bastille

Web site: `www.bastille-linux.org/`

OSes: Linux, HP-UX, OS X

The Bastille program helps organizations lock down their operating systems. You can also use Bastille to assess the current posture of the system. The `-assess` option helps you manually step through the evaluation.

In the default state, Bastille will interact with the system administrator. After asking numerous questions, the tool creates a policy. Only then will the policy be applied to the system. Bastille prides itself on working with the system administrator and allows the administrator to determine what the security posture of the system will be.

MBSA

Web site: `www.microsoft.com/`

OSes: Windows

The Microsoft Baseline Security Analyzer is the Microsoft tool for assessing Windows. The MBSA will tell you whether you have the critical patches installed, and in the correct order. The MBSA scans more than just the operating system; other checks include Microsoft Office, Internet Information Services (IIS), Automatic Updates, and other aspects of the system The default configuration requires the ability to download an updated CAB file from Microsoft. You can configure MBSA to use a local file. Having a local WSUS server is the best way to have offline scanning.

Password Compliance Testing

Password compliance testing is not about how fast I can crack your password. All passwords are crackable. It may take 10 years, but the password can be cracked. The idea is to test whether users are complying with corporate policies and procedures.

There are three type of password-cracking tools: dictionary, brute force, and hybrid. The dictionary tool uses a list of dictionary words and tries each word against each password. The brute force starts with "a," followed by "b," "aa," "ab," and so on to "zzzzzzzzzz," continuing the pattern. A hybrid uses a combination of the two. The introduction of rainbow tables (a list containing the hash for each brute-force string) has drastically decreased the amount of time required to crack passwords by eliminating the need to encrypt each attempt and just requires comparing the already encrypted password against the hash database.

John the Ripper

Web site: www.openwall.com/

OSes: Windows, UNIX, OS X

John the Ripper is an open source password-cracking tool. The commercially supported version is called John the Ripper Pro, which is distributed as a binary package only. The open source version requires compiling; some prebuilt binaries are available. John the Ripper can handle multiple types of password files and encryption schemes. When running this tool, do not forget to remove the john.pot file from the directory or you may get mixed results.

A quick example:

```
john -wordlist=French-wordlist.txt shadow
```

Cain & Able

Web site: www.oxid.it/

OSes: Windows

Cain & Able is a multifaceted application that can do more than just password recovery. This is a very powerful tool that takes time to master. With Cain & Able, you can either sniff the network or use local files for cracking passwords or network keys. It does contain ARP poisoning capabilities to allow for sniffing on switched networks.

This tool can do other things, such as analyze the SSH1 and HTTPS protocols. You can use Cain & Able for man-in-the-middle attacks.

NGSSQL Crack

Web site: www.nextgenss.com/

OSes: Windows

You have more than just login passwords to worry about. Weak or default passwords in databases pose significant security exposures for corporations. NGSSQL Crack is a tool for Microsoft SQL Server that allows you to quickly scan the database for weak passwords.

Application Scanning

Most organizations have applications that are considered critical. More and more of these applications use the desktop browser connecting to a Web server. These Web server applications may connect to one or more database servers. The N-Tier applications can be difficult to test for security vulnerabilities. Some of these vulnerabilities can be found with network vulnerability scanners. For a better scan, a tool designed for the specific type of server is required.

WebInspect

Web site: www.spidynamics.com/

OSes: Windows

SPI Dynamics is focused solely on Web application security and offers a suite of Web application security products. The company's Assessment Management Platform (AMP) is used to consolidate its tools in a central application server.

The WebInspect product is a fast and accurate scanning tool. It has been re-architected to handle newer services that are being offered (sometimes called Web 2.0). It supports complicated sites using JavaScript, Flash, Web services, SOAP, or AJAX. With WebInspect, you can scan more than one system at a time.

Wikto

Web site: www.sensepost.com/research/

OSes: Windows

Wikto is not a Web application scanner. It tries to find interesting directories and files on a Web site. Wikto requires that you have Microsoft Windows .NET framework installed. You should configure Wikto to mirror the Web site you are evaluating; doing so speeds up the scans. You can use the Googler tab to use Google for finding interesting items without touching the actual Web site, but this approach is not as thorough as the mirror tool.

The Wikto tab is based on the Nikto tool written by CIRT (www.cirt.net/). Nikto is a command-line Perl script that looks for vulnerabilities in Web servers. Wikto uses the Nikto database but does not use Nikto itself.

Suru

Web site: www.sensepost.com/research/

OSes: Windows

The author of Wikto stated that his tool is "a lame chicken pecking away at the dirt" at BlackHat 2006, during the talk about Sensepost's new tool Suru. Suru is a man-in-the-middle tool and sits between the Web browser and Web server. This positioning allows the user to fuzz the data being sent to the Web server.

Suru does have some of the basics from the Wikto tool, but Suru has more built-in smarts. As a user works through the application, Suru learns more about the application to help with the analysis.

AppDetectivePro

Web site: www.appsecinc.com/

OSes: Windows

Application Security, Inc. (AppSecInc) is a provider of database security solutions. AppDetectivePro is a network-based vulnerability scanner for databases. It can scan a good variety of database types ranging from MySQL to IBM DB2 on a mainframe. AppDetectivePro can be used to find and inventory all the database applications in the enterprise.

NGSSquirreL

Web site: www.nextgenss.com/

OSes: Windows

Next Generation Security Software Ltd. (NGSSoftware) is a European-based business founded in 2001. NGSSoftware specializes in security consulting, research, and products. NGSSoftware's database-scanning tool is known as NGSSquirreL, which can be found for multiple versions of database servers. The NGSSquirreL applications are specific to the database server being scanned.

OraScan

Web site: www.nextgenss.com/

OSes: Windows

OraScan is another vulnerability-scanning tool from NGSSoftware. This tool can fully audit Oracle Web applications from the Web site through the backend database server. This multilayered approach gives you a complete view of the application.

Network Sniffing

Knowing exactly what type of traffic is traversing your network is the only way to find nefarious traffic. It is also the only way to accurately trend network bandwidth utilization. Network sniffing enables you to watch for unencrypted authentications, thus grabbing usernames and passwords.

Network sniffing works best in nonswitched networks. Switches limit the amount of traffic that is seen on your port. If you can connect to a span port on the switch, you should have access to all traffic on that switch. Pay attention to the amount of traffic that will be sent to the port and how much traffic your operating system's network stack can handle.

Network sniffing with wireless adapters is not the same as with wired adapters. When the wireless cards are sniffing in promiscuous mode, they behave differently from when they are in normal connected mode. Make sure that you read your sniffer's documentation about dealing with wireless networks.

You must be careful when sniffing the network. There may be sensitive or private information that needs protection.

Tcpdump

Web site: www.tcpdump.org/

OSes: UNIX, OS X

The tcpdump tool is a great, quick way to look at packets flowing through your network stack. This is a command-line–only tool. The output can be tough to parse until you learn to craft a capture filter that meets your needs. Most network analyzing tools can read files generated by tcpdump.

The tcpdump tool relies on the pcap library, as do most capture tools. The capture filter syntax is set by the pcap library. The filters are case sensitive.

The following is a quick example that will use the eth0 interface and filter out only packets to or from 192.168.1.5 and that are ICMP:

```
tcpdump -i eth0 host 192.168.1.5 and ip proto ICMP
```

Snoop

Built into Solaris

OSes: Solaris

Snoop comes with the Sun Solaris operating system. Snoop is very similar to tcpdump. When you work in a heterogeneous environment, be careful of the command-line options. An example is specifying the interface. In tcpdump, you use the -i option. In snoop, you use the -d option.

The following is a quick example that uses the hme0 interface and filters out only packets to or from 192.168.1.5 and that are ICMP.

```
snoop -d hme host 192.168.1.5 and icmp
```

WinDump

Web site: www.winpcap.org/windump

OSes: Windows

WinDump is the Microsoft Windows version of tcpdump. It requires you to install WinPcap. The command-line options are completely compatible with tcpdump.

Here's a quick example that lists the available network interfaces:

```
windump.exe -D
```

Wireshark

Web site: www.wireshark.org/

OSes: Windows, UNIX, OS X

Wireshark is the new name for the Ethereal network protocol analyzer (same code base, same developers). The name change happened because the original author changed jobs and the previous company owned the copyright to the Ethereal name.

Wireshark is a graphical interface to network sniffing and is a free software application. You can use Wireshark to capture network packets or use another tool to capture the packets. By using the libpcap library, Wireshark can read many other analyzers' dump files.

Pay special attention to the different filters. The display and capture filters are different. The capture filters are limited to what the libpcap filter understands. The tcpdump documentation contains the filter syntax for libpcap.

The Wireshark page offers many different capture files that you can download. These files provide a great way to learn about different protocols and how to analyze network traffic.

Penetration Testing

The normal daily work of the security professional does not include doing penetration testing. The tools in this category are primarily used for penetration testing. These tools can be very useful when you're testing new applications or servers being introduced to your environment.

Penetration testing can be detrimental to the network and hosts being evaluated.

Ettercap

Web site: ettercap.sourceforge.net/

OSes: Windows, UNIX, OS X

Ettercap bills itself as a suite for man-in-the-middle attacks because it allows you to ARP-poison the network, forcing all traffic to be sent to you first. Ettercap then sends the packet to the host that you specify or the correct destination host. This action severely hampers the network throughput and should be noticed by the users of the network because all network use slows to a crawl.

Do not believe network engineers who tell you that a switched network eliminates the ability to sniff the network. Port security will not protect a network from ARP poisoning. Some operating systems are adding more security to the ARP table, but even those will not completely stop Ettercap's ARP poisoning ability.

The Ettercap interface can be command line, curses, or graphical. Ettercap has many operating modes with different features. You can do everything from passively watching the network to actively changing the packets being sent between two hosts.

The authors do not support any binary releases of Ettercap. In order to submit a bug, you must compile the source code yourself.

BiDiBLAH

Web site: www.sensepost.com/

OSes: Windows

Much of the security process is boring and repetitive. SensePost wrote BiDiBLAH with the intention of reducing the mistakes and omissions that happen when you do boring tasks. By harnessing the power of Google, BiDiBLAH helps find the external presence of the target, your company, or client. This leads into querying DNS to further your knowledge of the target. It can do enumeration and banner grabbing and then feed into Nessus.

BiDiBLAH runs on Microsoft Windows with .NET. BiDiBLAH does come with a Google API key, but if you use this key, you may be limited to the number of Google queries the tool can perform. To use the full power of BiDiBLAH, you need your own Google API key. The final piece requires you to install your own Nessus server. BiDiBLAH contains hooks to connect to Nessus but not the application itself.

Metasploit

Web site: www.metasploit.com/

OSes: UNIX, OS X, Windows with Cygwin

The Metasploit Framework is a tool for penetration testing. When you're doing penetration testing, custom payloads are extremely beneficial. The Framework separates exploits and payloads, allowing for the creation of custom payloads. Metasploit can be used for more than just penetration testing. Read the documentation on all the different modules.

Metasploit can be used either from the command line or with a Web browser. If you use the Web interface, by default the system listens only on localhost on port 55555. Using the option -a aaa.bbb.ccc.ddd allows you the bind to a specified IP address. Use 0.0.0.0 to indicate all IPs on this host. Use the option -p num to change the default port.

Metasploit supports Microsoft Windows only with Cygwin.

Core Impact

Web site: www.coresecurity.com/

OSes: Windows

Core Security Technologies has been in the security business since 1996. Core Impact is its penetration testing tool. This graphical tool requires Microsoft Windows.

Core Security uses a six-step approach to penetration testing, and Core Impact is designed to follow this six-step methodology. Steps one through four deal with information gathering, exploitation, and privilege escalation. The final two steps are cleanup and report generation.

The cleanup phase is important. Core Impact installs a small agent that runs within the target system's memory.

The native format for reports is Crystal Reports. Business Objects' (www.businessobjects.com) Crystal Reports is a very common business-reporting tool that allows for vast flexibility. You also have the option for generating reports with HTML, PDF, and Microsoft Word.

Canvas

Web site: www.immunitysec.com/

OSes: Windows, UNIX, OS X, other platforms that support Python

Immunity's Canvas uses Python and PyGTK. By doing so, Immunity can support Canvas on multiple platforms, including certain mobile devices. Canvas is a graphic penetration testing tool. The tool has a slide bar on the bottom that allows you to choose the level of chattiness. Do you want to be stealthy or do you want to make a lot of noise announcing your presence?

The tool has plenty of power. The autohack tool will try all the hack tools to automatically penetrate a system. This module is very loud and leaves many fingerprints on the target system.

Canvas can install connect-back services to help when a system is behind ACLs or Firewalls. Canvas also allows you to install a back door on the system to allow for future connection from the Canvas tool.

One very nice feature is the status window, which allows you to basically watch the tool in action. Each step is logged.

Learning

How do you learn to use the applications? The knowledge you can gain from reading books and articles is not equal to actually using the applications. If you can afford to have a complete test network, you are probably rich enough to not be required to work. For the rest of us, an alternative must be found.

Virtualization is the answer. Applications that create virtual machines enable you to have multiple "machines" running on one piece of physical hardware. With proper configuration, you can run tests in a "machine" that destroys the operating system. Close the virtualized machine and copy the old "hard drive" over the trashed one, and you are back to where you started. Very nice when learning.

The network speed from a virtual machine is degraded because of the extra layers required to reach the physical wire. This slowdown causes some security tools to not perform well within a virtual machine.

VMWare

Web site: www.vmware.com/

OSes: Windows, UNIX

VMWare has been around for 10 years. It is an x86 emulation/virtualization application that offers multiple versions of its tool to everyone for free. There are also commercial versions that offer more functionality and support. The VMWare Player is an application that allows you to run virtual machines that are created by others. Many software vendors, along with network citizens, have created "machines" that anyone can download and use.

One of the first free machines offered — the "Browser Appliance" — was created by VMWare. This virtual machine is an Ubuntu distribution of Linux that starts up with a Mozilla-based browser to allow for safer browsing. This appliance can also be used for learning Linux. If you close the browser, you can open a terminal window and have root access to the Linux operating system. This is a great way to start learning UNIX and Linux specifically.

Parallels

Web site: www.parallels.com/

OSes: Windows, UNIX, OS X

Parallels, Inc. offers virtualization software for Macintosh, Windows, and Linux systems running on Intel platforms. The latest version of Parallels for Mac fully supports OS X and Microsoft Vista. With support for USB 2.0, all your favorite peripherals will work with the guest operating system.

As part of Parallels for Mac comes Parallels Coherence. This tool allows Microsoft Windows applications to run as a native windowed application in OS X. This capability removes the limitation inherent to virtual machines that all applications on the guest operating system run in the same native window of the virtual machine.

Parallels Transporter is also included with Parallels for Mac. This tool allows you to convert existing virtual machines to a Parallels virtual machine. You can also migrate a native Microsoft Windows PC to a virtual machine.

Virtual PC

Web site: www.microsoft.com/

OSes: Windows

Virtual PC was originally written by Connectix Corporation. Microsoft bought Virtual PC in 2003, and it has been freely available from Microsoft since early 2006. Virtual PC runs only Microsoft operating systems along with OS/2.

Cygwin

Web site: www.cygwin.com/

OSes: Windows

Many of the tools here do not run natively under Microsoft Windows. Cygwin is a UNIX-like interface for Microsoft Windows. Cygwin has an excellent XWindows interface that also allows for remote X display.

Most tools that compile under Linux can be recompiled and run with Cygwin. This does require you to have access to the source code. The commercial UNIX applications do not normally support Cygwin.

Summary

As applications and networks become more complex, the ability to test security manually becomes tougher. The number of systems that administrators are responsible for grows also. Together, these conditions require information security professionals to rely on tools to do the job. Tools increase the consistency and repeatability of the tasks.

There are nine categories of tools. Which tool is correct for the job? You have to first figure out what type of tool is required and then choose the tool that best fits your work environment.

This chapter presented a list of common tools for an information security professional, but, of course, one chapter can't train you on their use. You must download and play with them, and as noted in the chapter's "Learning" section, virtualization tools provide a good way to play. If you mess up a virtual machine, the time required to restore it is negligible when compared to restoring your primary work machine.

All these tools have legitimate uses for information security professionals. They are also considered hacking tools. Do not install any of these tools on work machines unless you have written permission. Never use these tools against systems you are not legally authorized to target.

Interview Q&A

Q: How does a firewall (both host-based and network) affect the time required to run tools that perform network enumeration?

A: When a firewall is configured to reject unauthorized packets, the sending host receives a "connection refused" message. When a firewall drops the unauthorized packet without sending the connection refused message, the sending system must wait a minimum time before determining that the connection will not succeed. On many operating systems and in many applications, the number of retries and length of the timeout can be configured. The longer the timeout and the higher the retry count, the longer it takes to determine whether a service is responding.

Q: What are the common SNMP community strings? What other strings might you try?

A: Public and Private are the two most common community strings. Next try the company's name. Next are the corporate initials. Then, along with the corporate initials, try adding RO (read-only) and RW (read-write) to the front and back.

Q: For the following ports, what is the common service and why should you care about this?

1433

A: This is the port for Microsoft SQL Server. A number of worms have used MS-SQL as their attack vector. Many MS-SQL installations have configuration vulnerabilities. You should never be allowed to connect directly to a database server from the external untrusted network.

110

A: POP3 runs on 110. This is an unencrypted protocol for downloading e-mail. On many systems, the password for e-mail is the same as account sign-on. When you're network sniffing, both POP3 and IMAP are prime protocols to watch for to learn username/password pairs.

6667

A: Internet Relay Chat (IRC). Most botnets use IRC to communicate. All outbound connections to IRC should be blocked by default. If a business need exists, open connections only to individual IRC servers that are known to be safe.

5631

A: PC Anywhere is used by many organizations for remote administration. Many PC Anywhere installations are not configured with strong authentication. Most are not configured with encrypted connections, allowing for easy sniffing of all activity.

Q: When doing a security evaluation, how many automated tools should you use and why?

A: You should use at least one tool but preferably two or more. Using at least one automated tool increases the consistency and reliability of the work. No one tool can do it all. By using more than one tool, you lessen the number of false positives and false negatives.

Q: BiDiBLAH uses Google to gather information. Why use Google?

A: Many companies do not understand the completeness with which Google caches the Internet. Combine Google with the Wayback Machine (www.archive.org/web/web.php) and you can learn a lot about a company. By searching for e-mail addresses, you learn who key individuals are, along with, possibly, sub-domains. By searching Internet newsgroups, you may be able to determine what language and IDE the target is using to develop its primary application. Sometimes Google will even find code snippets from the application.

Q: How does ARP poisoning work?

A: Systems do not communicate directly with IP; they use the MAC address. When systemA is about to start a new connection to systemB, it must find systemB's MAC address. SystemA will broadcast an ARP request to the network. This request asks, "Who has IP Address B?" Normally, configured machines answer only when it is their IP address. In ARP poisoning, you respond to all ARP requests by saying that you are systemB when you are really systemH. Your machine will usually also constantly broadcast for all IP address on the network. This broadcast is normally picked up by all systems, and they fill their local ARP table with your MAC for all IPs.

Q: How accurate is banner grabbing for enumerating what application and version is running on a remote system?

A: You cannot rely on banner grabbing. Most applications can be configured to lie within their banner. Also, most applications can be configured to run on different ports than normal.

Q: Why will Port Security not stop ARP poisoning?

A: Port Security limits only the number of MAC addresses per port. When ARP poisoning, you are not sending multiple MAC addresses. You are sending multiple IP addresses and associating them with your one MAC address. If you can limit the number of IP addresses per port, you can severely limit the scope of ARP poisoning.

Recommended Reading

www.sectools.com/
www.iana.org/
Google Hacking for Penetration Testers (Syngress Publishing, ISBN 1931836361).
Google Hacks: Tips & Tools for Finding and Using the World's Information (O'Reilly Media, ISBN 0596527063).
Professional Pen Testing for Web Applications (Wiley, ISBN 978-0-471-78966-6).

Additional Resources

The following is a list of useful resources you should become familiar with:

http://ettercap.sourceforge.net/
http://kismac.de/
http://net-snmp.sourceforge.net/
http://nmap-scanner
    .sourceforge.net/
http://pbnj.sourceforge.net/
www.airmagnet.com/
www.appsecinc.com/
www.archive.org/
www.bastille-linux.org/
www.businessobjects.com/
www.cirt.net/
www.cisecurity.com/
www.coresecurity.com/
www.cygwin.com/
www.eeye.com/
www.foundstone.com/
www.iana.org/
www.immunitysec.com/

www.iss.net/
www.kismetwireless.net/
www.metasploit.com/
www.microsoft.com/
www.nextgenss.com/
www.nmap.org/
www.openwall.com/
www.oxid.it/
www.parallels.com/
www.saintcorporation.com/
www.sectools.com/
www.sensepost.com/
www.solarwinds.net/
www.spidynamics.com/
www.tcpdump.org/
www.tenablesecurity.com/
www.vmware.com/
www.winpcap.org/
www.wireshark.org/

Index